1812
NAPOLEON IN MOSCOW

'True historians aren't those who relate overall facts and limit themselves to general causes; but those who pursue facts down to their most detailed circumstances and reveal their particular causes.'

Giambattista Vico

'Human life is short and fleeting, and many millions of individuals share in it who are swallowed up by that monster of oblivion which is waiting for them with ever-open jaws. It is thus a very thankworthy task to try to rescue something of the memory of interesting and important events, or the leading features and personages of some episodes from the general shipwreck of the world.'

Schopenhauer

1812
NAPOLEON IN MOSCOW

PAUL BRITTEN AUSTIN

AUTHOR OF

1812: The March on Moscow

GREENHILL BOOKS, LONDON
STACKPOLE BOOKS, PENNSYLVANIA

Greenhill Books

This edition of *1812: Napoleon in Moscow*
first published 1995 by
Greenhill Books, Lionel Leventhal Limited, Park House,
1 Russell Gardens, London NW11 9NN
and
Stackpole Books, 5067 Ritter Road,
Mechanicsburg, PA 17055, USA.

British Library Cataloguing in Publication Data
Austin, Paul Britten
1812: Napoleon in Moscow
I. Title
940.27
ISBN 1-85367-195-9

Library of Congress Cataloging-in-Publication Data
Austin, Paul Britten
1812: Napoleon in Moscow / by Paul Britten Austin.
264 p. 24 cm.
Includes bibliographical references and index.
ISBN 1-85367-195-9
1. Napoleon I. Emperor of the French, 1769–1821 —
Military leadership. 2. Napoleonic Wars, 1800–1815 —
Campaigns — Russia — Moscow. I. Title.
II. Title: Napoleon in Moscow.
DC235.5.M8A87   1995
940.2'7—dc20

Designed and edited by DAG Publications Ltd.
Designed by David Gibbons; edited by Michael Boxall.
Printed and bound in Great Britain by Clays Ltd, St Ives plc.

Note:
First references to the eyewitnesses
whose accounts make up this 'documentary'
of Napoleon's invasion of Russia appear in
italic.

CONTENTS

To my son THOM
and my grandson BENNY
without whose patient encouragement
and computer expertise this work
would never have been possible.

PREFACE

This book is the successor to *1812: The March on Moscow*. A kind of word-film or drama documentary, it's edited, I hope not too inartistically, from the first-hand accounts of well over 100 of the participants, both French and 'allied', in the vast mass-drama of Napoleon's invasion of Russia.

I've resisted the temptation to comment on or evaluate their narratives. All strike me as authentic – if not necessarily accurate, and certainly not impartial. The events, after all, were extraordinary beyond imagining. And allowances must be made for hindsight. It's so easy to be wise after the event!

For reasons of space, I've seen it all from one side only – with a single co-opted witness from the Russian side in the highly critical, not to say caustic, person of General Sir Robert Wilson, the British representative at Kutusov's headquarters.

After the briefest of intermissions I resume in this volume exactly where its forerunner left off: at the gates of Moscow. At the head of his central army, originally some 350,000-strong and made up of Davout's I, Ney's III, Prince Eugène's IV, Poniatowski's V, and Junot's VIII Corps and the Imperial Guard, and spearheaded by Murat's four 'reserve' cavalry corps, Napoleon had crossed the Niemen on Midsummer's Day. But the Tsar's 1st and 2nd West Armies had refused him the pitched battle which, as twice before, would certainly have crushed them, and retreating separately eastwards, forcing him to follow in search of the resounding victory which was to force Russia back into his Continental System and – prime objective of the whole unprecedentedly vast and ever farther-flung campaign – compel Britain to make peace. Far away to the south, meanwhile, Schwarzenberg's Austrians and Reynier's Saxons (IX Corps) had quickly got bogged down manoeuvring against Tormassov's 3rd West Army which, if Russia and Turkey hadn't unexpectedly made peace, should have been fighting the hereditary foe in Moravia. To the northwest Macdonald's X Corps, mostly made up of Prussians, had invested Riga; while Oudinot's II and St-Cyr's VI Corps had pursued Wittgenstein through the blazing summer heats and, ravaged by sickness, also got bogged down at Polotsk.

On 28 July the main body, under Napoleon himself, had again been refused battle outside Witebsk; and after a ten-day pause there to recuperate, the advance had gone on. Napoleon had manoeuvred to circumvent Barclay de Tolly's 1st and Bagration's 2nd West Armies and snatch Smolensk, but failed. There, at last, on 17 August, the pitched battle he had been longing for was fought – indecisively. Smolensk, Russia's third largest city, had gone up in flames; and again the Russians had withdrawn in almost miraculously excellent order, leaving Napoleon no option (in view of the acute political hazards of staying where he was, so remote from his bases, and of the disastrous likelihoods if – after all this marching and fighting – he withdrew) but to push on eastwards and strike for Moscow. Once it had been occupied, he was sure, "his brother Alexander" would have to make peace. On 7 September the Russians had at long last stood and fought at Borodino, one of the bloodiest one-day battles of modern times and of which one could paradoxically say it had 'neither been won, lost nor drawn'. Again the Russian army had retired intact and certainly not beaten. And on 14 September a parley outside the gates of Moscow had led to a brief truce. Under it Murat's advance guard – at least two-thirds of whose horses were either dead of thirst, hunger, overwork or neglect, or had fallen at Borodino – was to follow on at the heels of the Cossacks' rearguard through the eerily deserted city.

It's at this – for all my protagonists – keenly anticipatory moment outside the gates of Moscow – a moment when Napoleon's 'face, normally so impassive, showed instantly and unmistakably the mark of his bitter disappointment [Caulaincourt]' – that they resume, exactly where they finished in the previous volume, their multifarious story.

For the sake of new readers, but I hope without becoming tedious to those who've so patiently read my first volume, I've tried to re-identify, in passing, at least the most important of my eyewitnesses by italicizing their names at their first reappearance. For bibliographical details of these and other sources, see the Bibliography (which, it should be noted, is supplementary to the fuller one in my first volume, which itemizes them all). As in *The March*, there is also an Index, by means of which the reader can, if he likes, follow our protagonists individually. At the same time I have of course tried to keep him informed as to the ongoing military situation.

In the interests of narrative pace, while always preserving my narrators' exact sense, I've sometimes taken liberties with the order of their words, phrases and even sentences. A little reflection will show why I've had to do this. A longish quotation may very well start where I, as 'film editor', want to cut it into my overall narrative; but very likely it will soon stray off into some other direction than the overall one it is necessary for us to follow. Hence my unorthodox use, made in good faith, of some of these translated passages which none the less form the essence of my tale.

Although on occasion I've used the present tense where the original is in the perfect, I've mainly retained the latter, in contrast with my own use of the present. If this – as one unusually militant critic observes – 'sets the pace for a racy tale with reduced regard for the details military history enthusiasts will demand', I can only beg their indulgence and hope my long-dead heroes too would have forgiven me these slight syntactic and grammatical deviations in the interests of the immediacy and vividness which characterizes their writings.

First and foremost my book is a kind of essay in the day-to-day, sometimes hour-by-hour reconstruction of six months of vanished time: a vast historical event which ended perhaps more terribly than any of its kind.

Paul Britten Austin
Dawlish, S. Devon, 1995

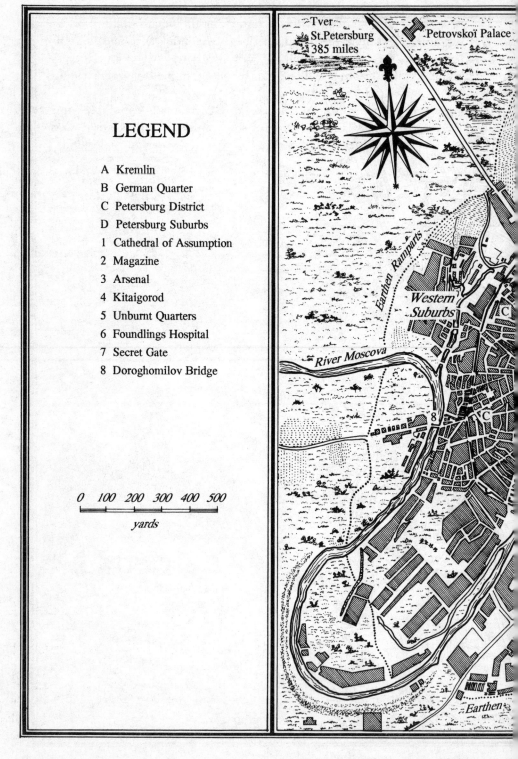

LEGEND

A Kremlin

B German Quarter

C Petersburg District

D Petersburg Suburbs

1 Cathedral of Assumption

2 Magazine

3 Arsenal

4 Kitaigorod

5 Unburnt Quarters

6 Foundlings Hospital

7 Secret Gate

8 Doroghomilov Bridge

0 100 200 300 400 500

yards

Tver
St.Petersburg
385 miles

Petrovskoï Palace

Earthen Ramparts

Western
Suburbs

C

River Moscova

8

C

Earthen

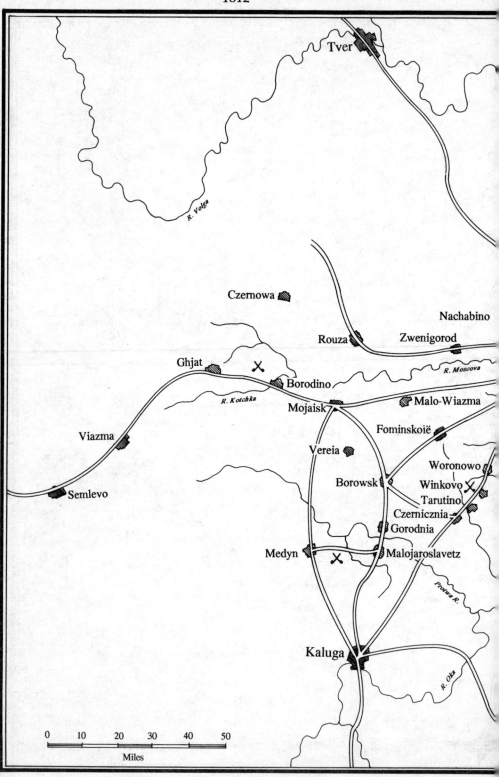

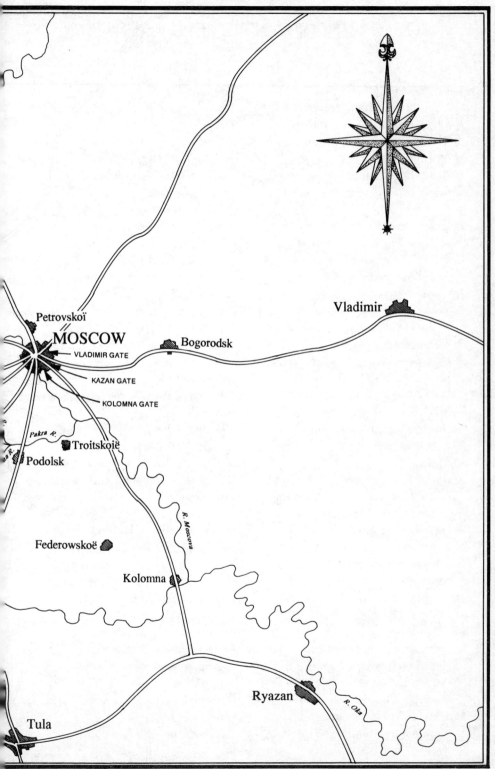

Vladimir

Petrovskoï

MOSCOW
Bogorodsk
VLADIMIR GATE
KAZAN GATE
KOLOMNA GATE

Pakra R.
Troitskoïe
Podolsk

R. Moscova

Federowskoë

Kolomna

Ryazan

R. Oka

Tula

SOME IMPORTANT EYEWITNESSES

L-A G. Bacler d'Albe, colonel, Napoleon's Topographer-in-Chief and closest collaborator.

A. D. Belliard, general, Murat's chief-of-staff.

V. Bertrand, carabinier sergeant in 7th Light Infantry (Davout's I Corps).

H-F. Biot, lieutenant, ADC to General Pajol, 2nd Cavalry Corps.

G. Bonnet, grenadier captain in the 18th Line, Ney's III Corps.

J-F. Boulart, major of Guard artillery.

A. J. B. F. Bourgogne, sergeant of the Fusiliers-Grenadiers of the Middle Guard.

P. C. A. Bourgoing, lieutenant, interpreter and ADC to General Delaborde, commander of a division of the Young Guard.

H. Brandt, lieutenant in the Vistula Legion, attached to the Young Guard.

A. de Caulaincourt, general, Master of the Horse, responsible for all headquarters transports and the courier service.

V. E. B Castellane, captain, orderly officer at Napoleon's headquarters.

D. Chlapowski, Colonel of the 1st (Polish) Guard Lancers.

J-R. Coignet, sous-lieutenant, formerly drill sergeant of the 2nd Guard Grenadiers, attached as orderly to Napoleon's 'little' or advance headquarters.

Dedem van der Gelder, Dutch ex-diplomat, general of brigade, commanding Dufour's [ex-Friant's] 2nd Infantry Brigade, I Corps.

P-P. Denniée, inspector of reviews, attached to IHQ. In 1842 he would publish Napoleon's day-to-day itinerary.

M. Dumas, general, the army's Intendant-General.

F. Dumonceau, captain commanding 6th Troop, 2nd Squadron of the 2nd ('Red') Lancers of the Guard, Colbert's lancer brigade.

V. Dupuy, major, then colonel of the 7th Hussars, 1st Cavalry Corps.

A. Dutheillet de Lamothe, lieutenant in the 57th Line infantry regiment, I Corps.

B-T. Duverger, Paymaster-captain to Davout's I corps.

G. de Faber du Faur, major commanding III Corps' reserve artillery, artist.

A-J-F. Fain, baron, Napoleon's Second Secretary.

Duc de Montesquiou-Fezensac, colonel commanding 4th Line infantry regiment, III Corps.

C. François, known as 'the Dromedary of Egypt', captain commanding one of the 30th Line infantry regiment's grenadier companies, Morand's division, I Corps.

L. Fusil, actress in the French troupe at Moscow.

G. de l'Ain, staff-captain, ADC to General Dessaix, general of division in I Corps.

G. Gourgaud 1st 'Officier d'Ordon-

14

nance' (senior staff officer) to Napoleon.

L. *Griois*, colonel of horse artillery, 3rd Cavalry Corps.

J. L. *Henckens*, adjutant-major, acting-lieutenant in the 6th Chasseurs à Cheval, 3rd Cavalry Corps.

D. *van Hogendorp*, Dutch general, governor of Vilna province.

H. *de Jomini*, baron, general, Swiss writer on strategy, temporarily governor of Vilna city, then of Smolensk.

B. *de Kergorre*, administrative officer attached to IHQ.

E. *Labaume*, captain on Prince Eugène's (IV Corps) staff, author of the first published account of the campaign (1814).

D. *Larrey*, Surgeon-General, head of the Guard's and the Grand Army's medical services.

C. *de Laugier*, adjutant-major of the Italian Guardia d'Onore, Prince Eugène's IV Corps.

L-F. *Lejeune*, baron, colonel, until Borodino one of Berthier's ADCs; thereafter chief-of-staff to Davout.

M. H. *Lignières*, count, captain in the 1st Foot Chasseurs of the Old Guard.

A. A. A. *de Mailly-Nesle*, count, lieutenant in the 2nd Carabiniers.

C-F. *Méneval*, baron, Napoleon's First Secretary.

A. *von Muraldt*, lieutenant in the 4th Bavarian chevaulegers, attached to Eugène's IV Corps.

A. A. A. *Montesquiou*, Quartermaster-General, attached to IHQ.

H-J. *de Paixhans*, inspector of artillery.

P. *des Loches*, captain, then major in the Guard artillery.

J. *Rapp*, general, Napoleon's most senior ADC.

Le *Roy*, major commanding a battalion of the 85th Line infantry regiment, Dessaix's division, I Corps.

P. *de la Faye*, lieutenant, secretary to General Lariboisière, commander of the Grand Army's artillery.

F. *Roeder*, captain in the Hessian Footguards, attached to the Young Guard.

H. *von Roos*, cavalry surgeon, 3rd Cavalry Corps.

M. J. T. *Rossetti*, colonel, ADC to Murat.

P. *de Ségur*, count, general, Assistant Prefect of the Palace, author of the famous but far from accurate *Napoléon et la Grande Armée en Russie 1812*.

T. J. F. *Séruzier*, baron, colonel commanding light artillery of 3rd Cavalry Corps.

R. *Soltyk*, count, Polish artillery officer attached to Topographical Department at IHQ.

K. *von Suckow*, captain, Württemberg infantry.

M. *Tascher*, lieutenant of 12th Chasseurs à Cheval, nephew of ex-Empress Josephine.

A. *Thirion*, regimental sergeant-major of the 2nd Cuirassiers, 1st Cavalry Corps.

C. *Wairy*, Napoleon's First Valet.

Sir *Robert Wilson*, the British government's representative at Kutusov's headquarters.

J. H. *Zalusky*, captain in the 1st (Polish) Guard Lancers.

CHAPTER 1

"FIRE! FIRE!"

Colonel Griois goes on a shopping spree – 'we take possession of Moscow as if it had been built for us' – a sinister silence – the Italian Royal Guard lodges itself military fashion – Napoleon enters Moscow – fire fuzes in the Kremlin – 'a lugubrious calm, broken only by horses' whinnying' – 'not exactly a spectacle to restore our spirits' – 'a signal like a firework' – 'the whole city was going up in flames'

For the first time since the Grand Army had crossed the Niemen at midsummer, 83 days ago, Colonel Lubin Griois, commanding 3rd Cavalry Corps' horse artillery, and his aristocratic friend Colonel Jumilhac, the corps' chief-of-staff, have slept in beds. It's the first time they've taken their clothes off since leaving Prussia in June. Last night they'd taken possession of a comfortable villa 'said to belong to a doctor' but abandoned by its owner, a couple of miles north-west of Moscow. Not far away Prince Eugène's mainly Italian IV Corps, to which 3rd Cavalry Corps has recently been attached, has bivouacked around the 'the miserable little town of Chorosewo'. Across the plain they can see the city's multicoloured onion spires, gleaming in the autumn sunshine. Since no orders have come, Griois decides to go on a shopping spree.

A keen observer of people and places, a lady's man of the most faithless nature but also a lover of Italian opera and paintings[1] and whose dominant passion is gambling, Griois, above all else in this world, loves Italy – i.e., northern Italy. In the south and Calabria he's had most unpleasant experiences, seen all sorts of horrors and been in the action at Maida in 1806 where Reynier's forces had been repulsed by unexpectedly steady British infantry fire. He's also been in the Tyrol, where he'd offered a pinch of snuff to Andreas Hofer and been desperately sad when that captured hero, at Napoleon's express order, had been shot by firing squad at Mantua. Leaving Verona – how he'd loved Verona! – in advance of his guns with his horses and equipment, 'about all I owned', he'd nevertheless been

> 'enchanted to do this campaign, whose immense preparations had announced its importance. I hadn't been able to leave Verona and the objects so dear to me without a contraction of my heart, augmented by a virtual certainty I'd never again see this town where at various times I'd spent about three years, where I'd lived so happily, and where I'd tasted every pleasure.'

Unlike Jumilhac, whose wit makes him delightful company for his fellow-officers but whom his friend regards as altogether too hard on the rank-and-file, Griois prides himself on knowing each of his gunners by name and on being so unembarrassed in Napoleon's presence as even to contradict him in technical matters.

Taking his orderly with him, he enters the city, hoping the rumour, which has been going the rounds ever since yesterday, of its being abandoned by its population, will prove to be much exaggerated. And in fact Griois finds there are

> 'still some inhabitants who'd stayed behind. But almost all were foreigners, Italians, Germans and Frenchmen, who seemed to be delighted to receive their compatriots. I saw a lot of them in the streets.'

That almost every shop is closed he ascribes to

> 'the merchants' excusable fear during the first moments of the occupation. The order and calm reigning in all the quarters I went through should soon dispel all fear and re-establish confidence.'

An Italian having indicated a 'rather ugly' café, Griois – presumably also the orderly – indulges in the delights of a *café crème*. But above all he craves wine; and an artillery captain of his acquaintance shows him where he can get some, in a Russian merchant's vast underground cellar. There he relishes a bottle of 'a sort of dry Madeira'. Finishing it off, his orderly is of the same opinion. And after loading him down with half-a-dozen more such bottles 'I left my merchant most content, to get in gold what he usually was paid for in paper roubles. Fully disposed to renew our provisions tomorrow and never more lack for any' Griois gets back to his gunners' bivouac outside the city and generously gives the rest of his bottles to his comrades.

Meanwhile, for the third time since entering Russia, Prince Eugène's troops – Italians, Dalmatians, Frenchmen, Spaniards and Croats – have been donning their parade uniforms. To enter Moscow, Europe's second largest and far and away most exotic capital, and march triumphantly down its streets with their bands playing is going to be a *journée* – a great imperial occasion. And IV Corps, headed by the Royal Guard, quits Chorosewo and sets off for the still distant city. At the head of the Royal Guard marches the Guardia d'Onore – a unit made up of 'sons of the best Italian families, each supported by his family with a Line lieutenant's pay'. Its adjutant-major, as Moscow step by step comes closer, sees that it's indeed an open city. Only an old earthwork, broken down in many places, surrounds it. But here, thinks *Césare de Laugier*, is an odd thing. And a very worrying one:

> 'Nowhere do we see a soldier, either Russian or French. At each step our anxiety grows, and rises to a climax when we make out in the distance a dense column of smoke rising from the centre of town.'

Almost more worrying – not a wisp is to be seen rising from any chimney.

Now the head of the column reaches the Zwenigorod barrier. But instead of passing through it, they're ordered to turn left and follow the city limits. Cross another approach road. And reach the Petersburg barrier. This time the Viceroy, followed by the Royal Guard, turns his horse's head to the right and rides between its two stone pillars topped with globes.

Not so IV Corps' other three divisions. To their intense chagrin they have to

'turn their backs on Moscow and go and camp in the plain outside. The 15th Division around the imperial château of Petrovskoï. The 13th at Auksecewskoï. And the 14th at Butyrki, with Ornano's [Bavarian] light cavalry deployed in front of them.'

As they ride in along the Petersburg suburbs' broad well-aligned streets, Eugène's glittering staff find its first houses tawdry and ill-built. But by and by, interspersed with these 'dreary wooden shacks which looked as wretched as the unfortunate people who'd lived in them', come 'others more beautiful ... superb and vast palaces'. Amazingly, not one of them seems to be occupied. And every shop is shut. Obviously the rumour is true. Moscow has been abandoned by its inhabitants!

Never has such a thing happened before.

Nor is there any sign of any other troops, whether Russian, French or allied. Césare de Laugier scribbles in his diary (in the present tense):

'Without uttering a word we're marching down the long solitary streets. The drums are resounding in dull echoes against the walls of the deserted houses. In vain we try to make our faces evince a serenity which is far from our hearts. Something altogether extraordinary, it seems to us, is about to happen. Moscow seems to us to be a huge corpse. It's the kingdom of silence, a fairy town, whose buildings and houses have been built by enchantment for us alone.'

The 'corpse' reminds him ('though here the impression is even more sepulchral) of the ruins of Pompeii and Herculaneum'. For his part Captain *Eugène Labaume*, on the Viceroy's staff, is struck by the extreme length of the streets,

'so long from end to end that the cavalry troopers can't even recognise each other. We saw them advancing slowly towards each other, not knowing whether they were friend or foe, though all were under the same flags.'

At last the order comes to halt. And the Royal Guard draws up in battle – that's to say parade – order on 'a beautiful spacious promenade'. This northern part of the city, they're told, with its 'magnificent and extraordinarily sumptuous timber houses', has been designated for IV Corps' cantonments. The Emperor has already entered Moscow. Unfortunately 'fires have been breaking out on all hands'. For lack of any civil authorities to issue billets,

> 'we're to lodge ourselves military fashion. The Viceroy gives the regiments the order, and the officers who're to implement it indicate the lodgings in charcoal, in capital letters, on each dwelling's front door. Likewise the new name of each street and square, each being known as "such or such company's street", or "such or such a battalion's quarter", "Fall-in Square, Parade Square, Review Square, the Guard's Square, etc."'

At first, in so vast an emptiness, everyone's expecting a trap. But then, insensibly,

> 'we take possession of Moscow as if it had been built expressly for us alone. This singular distribution allows each subaltern, for instance, to have a magnificent palace to himself, through whose sumptuously furnished apartments, no proprietor having put in an appearance to dispute its ownership with him, he strolls at his ease.'

Only in the superb Greek orthodox churches, where the altars are lit up by candles 'as on some religious feast day', are there any Muscovites. But even there the worshippers are mostly of the poorest kind, Russian wounded and stragglers.

No deputation having come out to implore his clemency and surrender the keys of the city, Napoleon has spent the night of 14/15 September in what the Master of the Horse, *Armand de Caulaincourt*, calls 'a mean tavern built of wood' standing to the right of the stone bridge that links the city with its western suburb, but which to baron *Joseph de Bausset*, the obese Prefect of the Palace, seems 'a fine timber house'. The night had passed quietly enough. True, a fire, attributed to the troops' carelessness, had broken out in the Stock Exchange – 'a superb building, larger than the Palais Royal in Paris and packed with exotic goods from all over Asia'; and only with great difficulty been put out – for lack of fire engines. More important, it seems, is that according to the King of Naples' reports from his headquarters in the Balashoff[2] family's palace in Yauza Street, not far from the Bridge of the Marshals and the Kazan Gate, the truce guaranteeing Moscow's peaceful evacuation is still holding. The Kazan Gate lies on the far eastern side of the city and beyond it his 10 to 15,000-strong advance guard is bivouacked. Murat says he's 'confidently expecting to seize part of the enemy convoys and break up the enemy rearguard, so completely disheartened does he believe the Russians to be.'

All these details, Caulaincourt goes on,

'together with the impression sure to be caused in Petersburg by the news of the occupation of Russia's second capital, which must certainly lead to peace proposals, delighted the Emperor and restored his cheerfulness.'

Likewise, albeit perhaps in lesser degree, his own. It's only a week since his brother Augustin was killed at Borodino at the head of the decisive – and unique – cavalry charge that had stormed the Great Redoubt. During the night Caulaincourt has had to interview a Russian policeman who, brought to headquarters, had

'prophesied there'd be many more fires still to come. The entire city was to be burnt down during the night. A simpleton who knew all that was afoot, he'd been very candid in all his avowals. But he was in such a state of terror he seemed a bit deranged. These details were incredible, and we paid no heed to them. We were far from thinking the governor and government had any ambition, as the Emperor said, to go down to posterity as a modern Erostratos.'[3]

At 6 a.m. Napoleon, mounting *Emir*, his favourite Arab grey, has made his triumphal entry, 'unembarrassed by any such tumult as normally goes with taking possession of a great city.' 'No sound', First Secretary Baron *C-F. Méneval* notices from his carriage as it slowly follows in his master's wake, 'disturbed the solitude of the town's streets. Moscow seemed to have fallen into a deep sleep, like the enchanted towns in *The Arabian Nights*.' Probably that intelligent man is as dismayed as Caulaincourt, riding a horse's length behind the conqueror who has already made triumphal entries into all the important capitals of Europe except London, by the 'gloomy silence reigning throughout the deserted city. During the whole of our long route we didn't meet a single soul.'

By and by 'on a hill in the middle of town' a large citadel comes into sight. Surrounded by a crenellated wall and flanked at intervals by towers armed with cannon, the Kremlin reminds Méneval's colleague, Second Secretary Baron *A-J-F. Fain*, of the Doge's Palace in Venice. Its three successive massive gates are 'made up of several vaults closed by barriers and topped by machicolations'. Entering its courtyards. Napoleon goes up the Strelitz Steps (where once Peter the Great massacred his rebellious guards) to the second storey and the great halls of state.

Antique in their splendour, the sparsely furnished State Apartments consist only of three halls and a bedchamber. No Tsar has lived here since the 16th century. But they'll suffice, at least for the time being, for Napoleon's personal headquarters; whether in tent or palace it never consists of more than three rooms.[4] In the Tsar's state bedroom the only other piece of furniture besides the bed, which stands to the left of the fireplace, screened off by an elaborate green tripartite fire screen, is a roll-top desk. And it's presumably at this that Napoleon by and by sits down and – in his own hardly legible handwriting – writes to his blonde young empress Marie-Louise in faraway Paris:[5]

> "Mon amie. – I have got your letter of the 31st, in which I read that you had received the letters from Smolensk. I've already written to you from Moscow, which I reached on the 14th. The city is as large as Paris, there are 1,600 steeples and more than a thousand fine palaces. This city is provided with everything. The nobility have left, the tradespeople have been compelled to leave too, the common people have stayed behind. My health is good, my cold has left me. The enemy is retreating, as far as can be judged towards Kazan. This fine conquest is the fruit of the battle of the Moscova [Borodino]. Tout à toi. NAP"

Meanwhile, down in the Kremlin's cellars, that fiery-tempered and – even by Grand Army standards – intensely ambitious staff officer, premier officier d'ordonnance *Gaspard Gourgaud*,[6] tall, brown-haired, thin and muscular and, on so triumphant an occasion, clad no doubt in full sky-blue uniform with silver aiguillettes, is making a startling, not to say alarming discovery. Some powder barrels. Although he'd been lightly wounded at Smolensk on 15 August, he'd been on his feet day and night throughout the campaign, and only yesterday was one of the first officers into Moscow. 'It was I who found the magazines, where there were three hundred kilograms of gunpowder.' An exploit for which he'll shortly be made a baron of the Empire. Other officers of the household are making other sinister discoveries. Hidden in the chimney of the imperial bedroom and elsewhere they're finding 'incendiary fuzes'. Made up of tow, bitumen and sulphur, all are constructed on exactly the same pattern. This causes Caulaincourt and his colleagues to take the 'half-crazed' policeman's nocturnal babblings more seriously. Fetched from the guardhouse, he repeats his story, which is immediately and frighteningly linked up with the disappearance, also allegedly at the orders of the temperamental Governor Rostopchin and his chief of police, Iwachkin,[7] of all the Stock Exchange's fire hoses:

> 'Search had been made for fire-engines since the previous day, but some of them had been taken away and the rest put out of action. Officers and soldiers were bringing in street constables and peasants who'd been taken in the act of flinging inflammable material into houses to burn them down. The Poles reported they'd already caught some incendiaries and shot them.'

Secretary Méneval, on the other hand, has been exploring the rest of the Kremlin:

'A second city in itself, it encloses the imperial palace, the Arsenal, the palace of the Senate, the archives, the principal public establishments, a great number of churches full of historical curiosities, objects used for the coronation of sovereigns and, finally, flags and trophies taken from the Turks. In one of the principal temples are the tombs of the Tsars. In this imposing basilica reigns a semi-barbarous magnificence, impressive and primitive. Its walls are faced with thick gold and silver plaques on which the principal figures of sacred history stand out in relief. Byzantine-style silver lamps hang from the vaultings and great many-branched candlesticks of similar materials stand on pedestals. In this sanctuary can still be seen a portrait of the Virgin attributed to St Luke. Its frame is enriched with pearls and precious stones. A great bell tower, known as the Ivan Tower, is surmounted by a gigantic cross, in the centre of which is encased a solid gold cross enclosing a fragment of the True Cross. This cross, together with several curious objects from the Kremlin capable of being transported, were to be sent to Paris.'

All this the army is finding very strange, very exotic, very oriental. No other European army has ever been so far east except the Poles a hundred years ago. And indeed very few travellers either.

Apart from its formidable artillery only the Imperial Guard, though it hasn't fired a shot since the campaign opened, is being allowed inside the city – it and the Italian Royal Guard. It's the invariable custom. All I, III, IV and V Corps' Line regiments, which have borne the burden and heat of so many a terrible day, have been ordered to bivouac in the vast 10,000-acre plain, largely covered with immense fields of cabbages and beetroot which 'round as bowls and fiery red throughout' are astonishing Ney's Württembergers, notably Private *Jakob Walter* of General Hugel's 25th Division. As for the cabbages, 'three or four times as big as cabbage heads we'd consider large', they rejoice the hearts of the men of the 57th Line. Evidently they're expecting their stay in Moscow to be a long one, for Sous-lieutenant *Aubin Dutheillet* sees them immediately get busy – at Napoleon's express orders – at making *sauerkraut*, which takes weeks to mature!

A strict order of the day has forbidden anyone to enter the city. But it doesn't apply, of course, to corps commanders or their staffs. One such officer, sent in to secure suitable lodgings for his superiors, is I Corps' paymaster, Captain *B. T. Duverger*. Entering by the Doroghomilov Gate, outside which Napoleon had yesterday vainly waited for his non-emergent delegation, Duverger, with such a plethora of empty palaces at his disposal, is in no hurry to choose; and makes for the Kremlin. Guard Grenadiers and Chasseurs are on duty at its gates, but no one hinders him – or anyone else – from going in. Mounting one of its towers, he looks out over

'the noble city in its whole extent. Far and wide there reigned only a
lugubrious calm, broken only by the whinnying of horses and the
tramp of troops down the streets.'

Coming down again, Duverger sees how many of the dregs of the populace
are venturing out from their hiding places and are already drunk. Near the
half-burnt Stock Exchange they're

'beginning to loot shops, and I joined with some soldiers of the Guard
to expel them. From time to time an isolated shot rang out, but more
as a result of surprise than animosity.'

Although all the magnificent and luxurious palaces have been deserted,
in some of them their fabulously wealthy owners have left servants and a
French-speaking superintendent behind with orders to make the intruders feel at home. 'On a very large square to the right of and not very far
from the town gate, in the great loop in the Moscova between the Kremlin and the entrance by the Mojaisk road,' Major *J-F. Boulart* of the Guard
Foot Artillery settles for the Petrovskoï family's great town house, and
finds it's an exception. It 'lacked any occupant to do us the honours.
Everything was silent around us. This silence had something terrifying
about it.' As for his guns, his gun-park and his bearskinned gunners –
whose dark blue turnout the Emperor himself on 5 June had found so
'handsome' – Boulart disposes them in the square and in the empty houses round about:

'On one side was a long straight promenade, planted with trees. On
the other a nunnery. I formed my park in square, the guns in battery
at the corners, the men and horses in the middle. I forbade the men
to absent themselves. Then, having dismounted, I sent my lieutenants
with a few gunners to the nearby streets to get some food. Everywhere
they found the doors closed and barricaded. So we had to force them.
In a trice everything was being pillaged, as it doubtless also was
throughout the city. Afraid of being taken by surprise, I ordered
everyone to come back at the sound of a musket shot.'

Everywhere 'in various private and public buildings' the invaders are
alarmed to find fire fuzes identical to the ones found in the Kremlin. General Laborde and a medical officer by name Jeanneau, for instance, have
just installed themselves in the Lubiana, Governor Rostopchin's own
palace, when to their horror they find some such fuzes in a stove pipe; and
hurry off to the Kremlin to tell de Bausset about it.

At 9.30 a.m. Napoleon is just leaving the fortress on foot, when two incendiaries are brought in. Both are wearing police uniforms and have been
caught torch in hand. Through interpreter Hyde d'Ideville they tell him

'how houses had been designated for this end, and how in the various quarters everything had been prepared for burning, so they'd heard, in accordance with Governor Rostopchin's orders. The police officers had scattered their men in small detachments and the order to implement their instructions, given yesterday evening, had been confirmed that same morning by one of their officers.'

Officer? Which officer? They're reluctant to name him; but in the end he turns out to be a humble police NCO. Where's he now? They've no idea:

'Their replies were translated to the Emperor in the presence of his entourage. The Emperor was deeply troubled. He couldn't persuade himself that the Russians would deliberately burn their houses down to prevent our sleeping in them, as he'd said at Viazma. He couldn't believe it was the result of a firm resolution and a great voluntary sacrifice. But the successive reports left no further doubt. Some of the arrested policemen were brought to judgement and eight or ten were executed.'

All over town it's the same frightening story. Already, Césare de Laugier goes on, confiding to his diary,

'it's fairly certain the fires aren't to be ascribed to accidental causes. Quite a few incendiaries have been taken red-handed, arrested, and brought before a military commission. It transpires from their admissions that these people have only been acting on orders received from Rostopchin and Iwachkin, the chief of police. Most of them are policemen, disguised Cossacks, employees, pupils at the theological school. Their statements have been collected, and memoranda have been drawn up to be publicized all over Europe. It's been decided to make an example of them by exposing their corpses hung from lamp-posts in the squares or from trees in the promenades, not exactly a spectacle conducive to giving us back our gaiety.'

Food is everywhere the prime consideration. After spending a chilly night beyond the Kazan Gate, the units of Murat's advance guard, too, are sending marauding parties back into town to find some, both for themselves and their half-starved nags. Meanwhile, in the plain beyond the city, the marauders' comrades are involved in amiable discussions with their Russian opposite numbers, 'both Cossacks and regulars'; how humiliated they're feeling after their endless retreat at the behest of Russian generals they never even see! How much they'd prefer to serve the Emperor of the French and King 'Mourad' of Naples, both of whom – in striking contrast – are always so near the scene of action! Strolling about in his fancy uniform of the day,[8] Murat, vainest of men and cynosure of every eye, is finding in such gratifying talk some small compensation for being in Russia at all, instead of with his adored family in faraway Naples.

The golden September morning turns into afternoon; and afternoon into evening. His men are happy to hear the armistice has been extended to 8 a.m. tomorrow. A couple of fires in the distance are ascribed, as usual, to the troops' negligence.

But then something extraordinary happens.

Darkness has fallen and it's getting on for 9 p.m. when Colonel *T-J-F. Séruzier,* whose horse artillery has led the advance all the way from the Niemen, sees

'a signal, like a firework. It went up from a château between Moscow and ourselves, to the right of the town, seen from where we were. And immediately we heard a loud detonation.'

Everyone else notices it too. M. l'Abbé *Surugué,* curé of the French parish of St-Louis-des-Français, is startled to see 'a ball of fire explode over the Yauza' (the tributary of the Moscova which flows into it in the eastern part of the city). And the Württemberger cavalry surgeon *Heinrich von Roos* is standing in his bivouac to the right of the Vladimir-Kazan road, not far from Russian rearguards' campfires which are 'burning admirably', and 2nd Cavalry Corps' gunners and cuirassiers are congratulating one another on the prospect of an imminent peace, when he and his comrades, too, both see and hear the

'terrible explosion.[9] Though hard to be sure of one's sense of direction at night, it seemed to come from the centre of town. So great was its violence, we first thought an ammunition dump or powder factory had blown up, i.e., if it wasn't an infernal machine. At first there was an enormous jet of flames from which balls of fire were coming out in a greater or lesser trajectory as if a mass of bombs and shells had been simultaneously thrown up. This explosion lasted about three or four minutes, and spread veritable stupefaction among ourselves.'

'The generals had just left us,' the Dutch general *Dedem van der Gelder,* commanding the 2nd infantry brigade in Dufour's division which all the way from Vilna has had the misery of being seconded from Davout's to Murat's command, writes,

'when a violent detonation was heard on the side of the Kaluga Gate. It was a powder magazine the enemy were blowing up. It seems to have been an agreed signal, for a moment afterwards I saw several rockets going up, and half an hour later fire broke out in various quarters of the town, notably in the Vladimir suburb where General Dufour and I had taken a house.'

Everyone, Dedem says, saw the explosion. It's Rostopchin's signal:

'It lasted three or four minutes, and put us all in a veritable stupor. As soon as I was sure they wanted to burn down the town for us I imme-

diately decided to join the division, which was bivouacked astride the
Vladimir road, underneath the town walls. I set up my headquarters in
a mill where I was sure of not being burnt. The wind was very strong
and it was very cold. One would have had to be blind not to see it was
the signal for a war to the death. Everything confirmed what I'd heard
in January at Rostock and Wismar about the Russians' intending to set
fire to everything and draw us into the depths of Russia.'

At first, Heinrich von Roos goes on,

   'the fire seemed restricted to the area where it had occurred; but
   after a few minutes we saw flames rising in various quarters of the
   town. Soon we could count 18 hearths of the fire, then more. We were
   all stricken dumb with amazement.'

Jerked out of their 'unusual gaiety', his Württemberger troopers are

   'all stricken dumb with amazement. We looked at each other, all with
   the same thought. Staff captain de Reinhardt gave voice to the general feeling: "Here's a bad sign! One that puts an end to our hope of
   peace, the peace we all need so!" Our camp dominated the town, and
   we watched this terrible scene without anything of it escaping us.
   Soon the flames reached the quarters closest to ourselves. The numbers of stragglers and refugees, too, had increased.'

In the extreme west of the city, still bivouacked in the square near the
Moscova bridge, Boulart's gunners are looking on from another angle.
They see

   'a fire, then a second one, then a third, closer and closer, a new one.
   Though these diverse fires, whose propagation nothing arrested,
   were in the part of the town furthest away from us, it was easy to read
   by their light.'

And in the Kremlin itself *Roustam Raza*, Napoleon's Armenian Mameluke
servant, asleep with drawn scimitar across the doorway to his bedroom,
wakes up to find the whole skyline on fire. Staff captain Labaume is watching from the northern district: 'By now the whole city was only an immense
bonfire.'

   Until this moment the wind has been blowing from the north-west. But
now it too seems to be obeying Rostopchin's order. Césare de Laugier, also
in the northern district, feels it 'suddenly veer to the south-west and reach
hurricane strength'. So that by 10 p.m. the Italians, too, realise the entire
city is going up in flames; and Paymaster Duverger and his comrades at I
Corps headquarters in the western district, abruptly awakened in their
'rather fine house by some lamentable cries', dress hurriedly and run out
into the street:

   '"Fire! Fire!", sinister voices were shouting. The horizon was red. The
   fire, moving in all directions, sounded like distant torrents. Inhab-

itants and soldiers were mingling in headlong flight. In the light of
the conflagration we read stupefaction and despair in their faces.'
Immediately opposite the Kremlin is the Kitai Gorod, or Chinese quarter.
Many of its exotic commodities, saved from last night's conflagration in the
Stock Exchange, had been laid out in the street and placed under guard.
But now the district's six or seven thousand little shops catch fire again.
Naturally the locals want to grab what they can, and the pickets have to
beat them off with blows of their musket butts. Caulaincourt, deeply asleep
in the Kremlin, is aroused by his valet,

'an energetic fellow who'd been in my service during my Petersburg
embassy.[10] He brought the news that for three-quarters of an hour
now the city had been in flames. I'd only to open my eyes to see it was
true. The fire was spreading with such ferocity that it was light enough
to read in the middle of my room. Jumping out of bed I send him to
awaken the Grand Marshal [Duroc], while I dress.'

From the Kremlin terraces it's possible to survey the whole city and its surroundings. And since the fire chiefly seems to be spreading in the districts
farthest away, Duroc and Caulaincourt, as the imperial household's two
most senior officers, decide

'to let the Emperor sleep a little longer, as he'd been so very tired
during the past few days,'

– largely no doubt because of the acute bladder trouble he's been suffering from ever since Borodino. Nevertheless they send word to Marshal
Mortier – commander of the Young Guard and military governor of
Moscow since General Durosnel has found the task of policing it too much
for him – suggesting he call the whole Imperial Guard to arms. Caulaincourt is himself responsible for all headquarters transport. Since his own
department is already scattered in various parts of the town, he mounts his
horse and rides out to see what's to be done:

'A stiff wind was blowing from the direction of the two points of conflagration visible to us, and it was driving the flames towards the centre. This made the blaze extraordinarily powerful. At about 12.30 a.m.
a third fire broke out, a little to the west; and shortly afterwards a
fourth, in another quarter. All lay in the direction of the wind, which
had veered slightly to the west,'

and is being aided and abetted by any number of incendiaries. At about
midnight Césare de Laugier sees

'incendiary bombs being thrown from the church towers, from the
tops of houses at every moment, and even in the streets. Anyone
caught red-handed is being shot out of hand. Many of these unfortunates are drunk and pass without transition from drunkenness to
death. We've even found several trying to pour out tar to revive the

28

fire at spots where it seemed to be dying out. Running like convicts, they were carrying incendiary materials hidden under their clothes and throwing them, almost under our very eyes, into the houses we've been occupying.'

By now the extent of the catastrophe is so obvious that Caulaincourt and Duroc can no longer take it upon themselves to let Napoleon sleep. According to Roustam's assistant 'Ali', Napoleon's 'second Mameluke', it's Constant who wakes Napoleon up to tell him Moscow is in flames; but comes out again, 'and since he didn't give us any orders each of us went back to bed'. Looking out of the window, Napoleon had exclaimed:
  '"This exceeds anything one could imagine! This is a war of exter-mination! Such terrible tactics are without precedent in the history of civilization. To burn down one's own cities! A demon inspires these people! What savage determination! What a people! what a people!"'

Up to now, according to Césare de Laugier, always concerned to defend the honour of the Italian Royal Guard, its rank and file have mainly been
  'carrying out their superiors' orders in the general interest, trying to master the fire and save pieces of cloth, jewellery, cottons, fine mate-rials and Europe's and Asia's most precious items of merchandise.'
But now at the incendiaries' heels
  'come the dregs of the populace who haven't fled, hoping to loot what they can. Locks are being forced, cellar doors bashed in, shops threatened by the fire are being sacked. Sugar, coffee, tea are the first things people are laying hands on; then it's the turn of leather, furs, cloths and all luxury merchandise.'
Whereupon the Italians,
  'excited by the example of this populace pillaging under their eyes, are letting themselves be carried away and putting everything to the sack. First and foremost the stores of flour, brandy and wine are rav-aged.'
And indeed why stay outside and starve when food to feed ten armies is being incinerated? One of Major Boulart's subordinates, the always critical, always querulous, Major *Pion des Loches*, a man who always knows best and is cleverer and more farsighted than anyone else, an incurable *Besserwisser*, sees masses of soldiers from the army corps bivouacked outside town on the plain, defying the ban on entering the city, come rushing in – no sen-tries can stop them. And in no time at all
  'the army was completely disbanded. Everywhere one saw drunken officers and soldiers loaded with booty and provisions taken from flaming houses. The streets were littered with pieces of faïence, with

furniture, with all kinds of clothing. The many women who'd been following the army, meaning to make us pay dearly for the fruits of their pillage during the retreat, were incredibly prompt to supply themselves.'

Everywhere are harrowing scenes, dreadful incidents. On his way to cross the river by a ford, Paymaster Duverger sees one such brawny harridan at work. Ousted from their burning palace, he and a friend are lingering in

'a main street where some poor women and children with hardly any clothes on were coming running from all directions, and already the fire was threatening to cut off their retreat on all sides. An old sutler- ess had placed herself athwart the road. I knew her. That very moment I saw her repulsing with her fist a grenadier who'd tried to stop her from coming into the town. There she stood, her savage green eye on the hurrying fugitives, stopping and searching them.'

So far he's paid no particular heed to her. But now, beside him, he sees another group,

'an old man, two or three children, a girl, beautiful despite her pal- lor, and a woman. Two working men were carrying her on a stretch- er. All were weeping so it broke your heart. The old cantinière flung herself at the sick woman, with a sacrilegious hand searching her clothes to see if they concealed anything of value. That day I was on the verge of fury – heaven forgive me for having struck a woman.'

Pion des Loches, too, sees the army's *vivandières* and *cantinières*

'laden with firkins of liqueurs, sugar, coffee and rich furs. The fire was raging in all quarters of the town and as it reached them the sol- diers were evacuating the places where they'd taken shelter and in turn seeking asylum in the next house.'

Fortunately there are men who act chivalrously. Griois is on his way back to his camp outside the city when he sees running towards him

'a young woman, her hair dishevelled, terror on her face. A nurse- maid was following her, carrying a child. She told me she was the wife of a French businessman whom the Russian army had taken away with it and she'd remained behind, alone with her child and this Russian servant.'

Now her house is on fire and she has nowhere to go. Forgetting to ask her name (can it be Marie-Louise Chalmé, she who'll soon be finding herself in Napoleon's presence?) Griois takes up all three refugees into his car- riage and out to Eugène's headquarters near Petrovskoï.

A man for whom his daily dinner is always of prime importance, the 85th Line's portly 2nd major *C. F. M. Le Roy*, is usually a great stickler for effi- ciency and discipline and always ready to set an example. But now even he, orders or no orders, isn't going to see a whole city roasted alive without res-

30

cuing some titbits for his ambulatory larder. Accompanied by his bosom friend Lieutenant Jacquet, 'the only man I ever wholly admitted to my confidence', he goes into town. Advancing down a fine street they find

'the flames so strong that their force was lifting the metal roofing of copper plates which covered most of the houses. Soon they fell back with a crash and, thrust sideways by the wind, were as dangerous to passers-by as the fire itself.'

For 5 francs the two officers relieve a ranker – he's anyway hugging many more bottles than he can carry – of a bottle of Bordeaux. After which, out of sheer curiosity, they enter a palace. Amazingly, all its apartments are unlocked, all the mahogany furnishings unscathed:

'The mirrors and pictures ornamenting it, the view out over a superb garden, would have made it an enchanting place to linger. I open a drawer. Inside are some sticks of sealing-wax, some playing cards, several embroidery patterns, a pretty toiletry set and many other things. In the next drawer are a pair of diamond buckles, a necklace of fine pearls, two rolls of turbans and two boxes. I'm just about to open them when I hear a man come into the room. I assume it's Jacquet, who'd stayed outside in the courtyard to try and get us some brandy or rum he was thinking he might find in the cellar. I call out to him to help me take something from the house. I open a bigger box. It contains a game of lotto with ivory markers. In the second I find the markers of a game of draughts. I'm just about to open a tallboy when I hear Jacquet's voice calling to me to come to his aid. Instantly I draw my sword, and rushing out into the corridor, which I find full of smoke, I make haste to rejoin my comrade who – the general conflagration being so distant – is as amazed as I am to find the house is on fire. From which I conclude that the person who'd come in could only have been a Russian incendiary. While we were still expressing our astonishment at such a singular fact, a well-dressed man came past us, greeting us politely. We returned his salute.'

Roving about the burning streets together with some fellow-Poles trying to find a way out of the holocaust or, alternatively, something to eat, is Count *Roman Soltyk*, an artillery officer who, because he speaks fluent French, has been attached to IHQ's Topographical Department. He tries calling up, in Russian, to the shuttered windows of houses where people are begging for protection:

'This succeeded several times. But our Polish uniform had already revealed us as enemies, and when we asked them what was causing the fire they only replied laconically, or else evasively. The principal of a college for young ladies who were still in their house pretended she knew no French – though to teach her aristocratic charges this, the second language of the rich, must have been one of her duties.'

And when Soltyk complains that he can't find any food,

'a twelve-year-old girl who'd been looking out of the window and following the conversation turned round quickly and said vehemently: "Food for the French! The putty of these windows is good enough to nourish them!" Though I turned it into a joke I admit I was much impressed. One could hardly hope to get a population to submit when children of twelve were so excited.'

The only Muscovites who seem to be beyond and above their city's trauma are some 'priests who, without distinction of rank or nation, were distributing alms and wine to all who passed in front of their holy retreat'. The scorching air is giving Soltyk and his fellow-Poles a monstrous thirst. 'One of them, as soon as he saw us approaching, offered me a cupful of wine,' which is gratefully accepted. The priests 'were making no distinction between rank or nation.

'Neutral in this great conflict, they were deploring the waywardness of men and had no other aim than to do what they could to assuage their evils.'

Napoleon's favourite ADC General *Jean Rapp*, a veteran who even in middle age walks 'with the jaunty gait of a hussar officer' but has been seriously wounded at Borodino, has already been awakened by his staff at midnight. But now the fire is beginning to eat into the district between the Kremlin and the Doroghomilov Gate; and at 4 a.m. they too are forced out of their palace. 'A few moments later it was turned to ashes.' After making their way to Marshal Mortier's house in the German quarter only for it too to go up in flames a few moments later, Rapp has to climb painfully back into his carriage and make for the Kremlin. Thanks to a shift in the wind it's still unthreatened. Only on his way there does he realize what's happening:

'Russian soldiers and craftsmen were slipping into houses and setting fire to them. Our patrols killed several of them in my presence and arrested an even greater number.'

En route, Rapp's party falls in with the Artillery Staff and its head, General Lariboisière 'and his son, who was sick' (since Lariboisière's elder son Ferdinand had died of his wound after Borodino, this can only be Henri); presumably therefore also with Henri's friend and fellow-ADC, Lariboisière's indefatigable 'man of letters', Lieutenant *Planat de la Faye*.[11] Together they all go and quarter themselves in a house on the river bank:

'My host was an honest hat maker who was sorry for my predicament and gave me all possible care and attention. Hardly was I installed in this kindly craftsman's house, however, than fire broke out in all the quarters around it. So I left in a hurry. If I'd delayed the least bit I could never have got away with my carriage, the street along the river bank being so narrow. We recrossed the river and stopped under the bare sky behind the walls of the Kremlin.'

But all the time the rising gale is bringing the fire ever closer. And finally Rapp's and Lariboisière's party, after again having to move on, settle in the neighbourhood of one of the customs gates, where houses are thinner on the ground and therefore less likely to catch fire. 'I occupied one belonging to a Prince Galitzin.'

Now it's the small hours of this unimaginably terrible night; and Soltyk and his fellow-Poles of IHQ's Topographical Department have finally lain down to rest outside a deserted church, also on the outskirts. By this time

'all the partial fires which were devouring Moscow in the night seemed to have joined together to form only one. The whole horizon was on fire. The church doors were open. As day broke, one of the orderlies chanced to go inside. A moment later he came back, pale, hardly able to get a word out. "Commandant", he said to me, "the church is filled with powder barrels and the windows are smashed." – "To horse, messieurs!" I shouted. "Our heads are lying on a powder magazine ..."

Five times the always amorously inclined General Kirgener, commander of the Engineers of the Imperial Guard, has had to change his lodgings before he and his staff finally ensconce themselves near the Petersburg gate in 'a kind of fortified château surrounded by water'. And there, fire or no fire,[12]

'hard though it is to understand in such circumstances, our dear general had leisure to engage in a love affair. A young slip of a girl found in our fortress was the cause of his little conflagration.'

Like Pion des Loches who, seeing the fire all the time coming closer to his artillery park is doing his best to keep his men from straying too far from it, many an anxious veteran has been asking himself:

'What if a few Russian cavalry regiments should come riding into Moscow tonight? They can easily cut us in pieces. For at the first glow of the flames the troops encamped outside the walls, instead of covering us, were leaving their units to take their part in the pillage.'

If the Russian high command has given no such orders it's because neither Kutusov nor anyone else except Rostopchin's police chief has had any inkling of that erratic personage's – wholly unauthorized – scheme: to evacuate the city and then burn it to the ground. Seeing the city burn

from afar, all Russian eyewitnesses are ascribing – and will long afterwards continue to ascribe – the inconceivable catastrophe to the 'atheis-
tic' Frenchmen's negligence, or wickedness. Many decades will pass
before it's clearly established that it's all been the work of 'the modern
Erostratos'.[13]

CHAPTER 2

NAPOLEON LEAVES THE KREMLIN

His dysuria passes over – 'This exceeds anything one could imagine' – 'the Emperor went to the spot' – Boulart goes to get orders – Napoleon quits the Kremlin – Petrovskoï palace – Sergeant Bourgogne's and Césare de Laugier's adventures amidst the flames – Murat's advance guard marches east

Moscow's in flames. But Napoleon's dysuria has gone over. At dawn, i.e., at about 7 a.m., he sends for his physician, Dr Mestivier: 'I'd just woken up. Showing me an almost full flask of urine, he told me he thought he was almost clear of the business, he'd urinated so abundantly and freely. But he showed some uneasiness about the sediment, which filled a third of the vessel. I replied that it was the result of a crisis which would quickly help him recover his health.' To be in the imperial presence is to be bombarded by questions.

'His bed was so placed that he couldn't see anything of the city. Whereupon he put his usual question:

"Anything new being said?"

I replied that a vast circle of fire was enveloping the Kremlin.

"Ah, bah!" Napoleon replied. "No doubt it's the result of some of the men's imprudence who've wanted to bake bread or bivouacked too close to timber houses."

Then, fixing his eyes on the ceiling, he remained silent for a few minutes. His features, which up to then had been so benevolent, assumed a terrifying expression. Summoning his valets [sic] Constant and Roustam, he suddenly jumped out of bed. Shaved himself. And quickly, without saying a word, had himself dressed, making movements expressive of his bad temper. The mameluke having by mistake presented him with the left boot instead of the right, Napoleon sent him flying backwards with his foot. As he hadn't made the head movement he usually dismissed me with, I remained there for almost an hour. Some other people came in, and Napoleon went into another room.'

Caulaincourt is certainly also in attendance at the levee. Looking out of the window he sees how the wind is

'fanning the flames to a terrifying extent, carrying enormous sparks so far that they were falling like a fiery deluge hundreds of yards away, setting fire to houses, so that even the most intrepid couldn't stay there. The air was so hot, and the pinewood sparks so numerous, that all the trusses supporting the iron plates forming the roof were catching fire.'

The Arsenal, a fine modern building whose courtyard, Griois will see, is 'ornamented with military trophies, guns and howitzers of colossal dimensions, most taken from the Turks in ancient wars', abuts the Tsars' ancient palace. Already it's being found to contain 18,000 British, Austrian and Russian muskets, 100 cannon with limbers, caissons and harness, as well as 'lances and sabres innumerable' and an immense amount of ammunition useful to the French. And prompt steps are of course taken to prevent the blaze from spreading:

> 'The roof of its kitchen was only saved by men who'd been stationed
> there with brooms and buckets to gather up the glowing fragments
> and moisten the trusses.'

Worse, even more perilous, down in the Kremlin's courtyards dozens of the Imperial Guard's artillery wagons, filled with highly explosive ammunition, are crammed together. And as the forenoon wears on and the fire in the city comes ever closer, the situation is swiftly becoming lethal. Watching from the Kremlin windows, Napoleon breaks out into exasperated ejaculations:

"What a monstrous sight! All those palaces! Extraordinary resolution! What men!"

By noon, despite everyone's efforts, the fire has begun to attack the Kremlin stables, containing 'some of the Emperor's horses and the Tsar's coronation coaches. Coachmen and grooms clambered on the roof and knocked off the fallen cinders.' Of the Kremlin's fire engines only two, put in working order during the night at Caulaincourt's behest, are intact. Everywhere the heat is swiftly becoming unbearable. Secretary Fain sees how the Kremlin windows are cracking as the flames attack the tower that links the palace with the Arsenal:

> 'Sparks were even falling in the Arsenal courtyard onto a heap of tow
> used in the Russian artillery wagons. The wagons of our own artillery
> were also standing there. The danger was immense, and the Emper-
> or was informed. He went to the spot.'

Méneval is alarmed to see such sparks, borne on the high wind,

> 'setting alight bits of oakum lying on the ground. Not that this dan-
> ger, which we were so fortunate as to baulk, worried Napoleon, whose
> soul never even knew what it was to be afraid.[1] As yet he didn't think
> it necessary to leave the Kremlin. On the contrary, the danger seemed
> to be keeping him there.'

Now the Master of the Horse, too, is himself in the thick of it:

> 'I may say without exaggeration we were working under a vault of fire.
> Everyone was doing his best, but it was impossible to stay more than
> a moment in any one spot. We were breathing nothing but smoke,
> and after a while even the strongest lungs felt the strain.'

Even the bridge over the river has become

'so hot from the sparks falling on it that it kept bursting into flames. But the men of the Guard and especially the Sappers made it a point of honour to preserve it. The fur on these half-roasted men's bearskins was singed.'

Guillaume Peyrusse is a young paymaster attached to IHQ who has an eye on and is forever scheming to occupy an as yet non-existent post as paymaster to the Emperor on his travels. He sees

'one of our outriders grab a Russian soldier at the moment when he was going to set fire to the bridge, break his jaw and throw him into the river.'

Yet still Napoleon persists in lingering in the Kremlin courtyards, among all those deadly ammunition wagons; and Fain is horrified to see how

'the Guard's gunners and infantrymen, apprehensive at seeing Napoleon expose himself to so great a danger, are only adding to it by their eagerness.'

In the end Lariboisière, whose responsibility all these caissons are, begs him to go away, 'pointing out that his presence is making his gunners lose their heads'. Aided by servants they're also helping Caulaincourt save Prince Galitzin's superb palace, occupied by Rapp and Lariboisière; likewise two other adjoining houses already in flames.

To Major Boulart, the danger to *his* ammunition wagons, parked in the square not far from the Doroghomilov Gate, seems to be becoming from moment to moment ever more imminent:

'While waiting for daybreak, I'd had all hay and straw cleared away from the neighbourhood of my wagons and had posted gunners to see the flaming sparks didn't fall on them, though with the wagons as firmly closed down as ours were and covered in canvas there'd been little to fear.'

But now the vast conflagration is taking gigantic strides toward him. Time's running out. And no one has sent him any orders. Realizing that he must do something before it's too late, he makes up his mind to go in person to the Kremlin, seek out General Curial, his immediate superior, and get his permission to quit 'this hell'. Some time after noon he gives his orders. 'In the event of the fire reaching the only street we could retreat by, they should leave the town in my absence.' Then he mounts his horse. And accompanied by an orderly sets off, hoping to find his way to the Kremlin. Soon, 'with a loud and sinister sound', palaces and iron roofs are crashing down all around them. The gale whistles in their ears. Holding their arms over their eyes, half-deafened by all this rumbling and roaring, they ride slowly onwards through the hot ash and debris falling on their heads. They've no guide, and the distance seems endless:

'Isolated in this desert, my heart shrinks. But soon I get to the region actually being devoured. To right and left flames are rising above my head. I'm being swathed in dense smoke. Further on, the heat is so great and the flames are coming at me so closely, I have to shut my eyes. Can hardly see my way ahead. Often my horse shudders and refuses to go on.'

But then, suddenly, the two men emerge out of this 'fiery zone' into quite another. Almost calm, it consists only of smouldering ashes. Surely they must have gone astray? No. There, rising in front of them, are the Kremlin's crenellated walls! Now it's about 3 p. m. Entering by the great vaulted gate, Boulart finds everyone

'dejected, in a remarkable state of consternation. Fear and anxiety stood painted on all faces. Without a word said everyone seemed to understand everyone else.'

Up in the state apartments he finds Prince Eugène, Marshals Bessières and Lefèbvre (commanding the Guard cavalry and infantry respectively) – Méneval says Mortier too – all vainly imploring Napoleon to leave. But since he seems to be 'afflicted by uncertainty' no one can do anything:

'However, the fire's intensity was growing as it came closer. The windows of the apartment occupied by the Emperor had caught alight and flames were whirling in all directions.'

Also present, certainly, is Berthier, Prince of Neuchâtel, most senior of all the marshals, Napoleon's chief-of-staff, the army's major-general. Now, if ever, he has reason to bite his fingernails to the quick! An orderly officer (Césare de Laugier will afterwards hear that it was Gourgaud)

'having come to tell him the fortress is surrounded by flames on all sides, is ordered to go up with the Prince of Neuchâtel to one of its highest terraces to confirm the fact.'

But so parched and unbreathable is the air up there, they're at once driven down again. And still Napoleon won't budge.

Now it's about 4 p.m. And Caulaincourt sees the Emperor is beginning to wonder whether the burning of the city isn't in some way co-ordinated with the Russians' military operations, 'though frequent reports from the King of Naples had assured His Majesty that they were pushing forward their retreat along the Kazan road'. Gourgaud, too, overhears Berthier point out that "if the enemy attacks the corps outside Moscow, Your Majesty has no means of communicating with them". Only this observation, Méneval sees, makes him decide to leave.

A couple of miles north of the city, not far from where the Army of Italy has its encampment on the plain by the Petersburg road, stands the Petrovskoï summer palace. A large 'Gothick' building, erected toward the end of the last century to celebrate Catherine the Great's victories over the Turks, it's a kind of imperial *pied-à-terre* for the Tsars to stay in on the eve of their coronations. Now one of Gourgaud's subordinates, Major Mortemart, is told to go and reconnoitre the safest way to get there. But he too, unable to get through the flames, soon comes back:

'It was impossible to get there by the direct road. To reach the outskirts we'd have to cross the western part of town as best we could, through ruins, cinders, flames even.'

So at last a decision is arrived at. IHQ will accompany His Majesty along the river bank. Only the 2nd Battalion of the 1st Foot Chasseurs of the Guard is to stay behind in the Kremlin and try to stave off the fire. Inspector of reviews, *P.-P. Denniée*, describes the imperial departure:

'He came slowly down the stairs of the Ivan Tower [from where he'd been watching the fire] followed by the Prince of Neuchâtel and other of his officers. Leaning on the arm of the Duke of Vicenza [Caulaincourt], he crossed a little wooden bridge which led to the Moscova Quay. And there found his horses.'[2]

At the stone bridge over the river Napoleon mounts *Tauris*, another of his Arab greys, and, followed by his entourage – Gourgaud of course among them (amidst all this heat, grime and ash his sky-blue uniform can hardly any longer be in the best of trims) – sets off,

'a Moscow policeman walking in front of him, serving as guide. For some time they followed the river and entered the districts where the wooden buildings had been completely destroyed.'

Thereafter 'avoiding streets where the fire was still at its height' the procession passes through 'quarters where the houses were already entirely burnt down. We were walking on hot ash.' Quartermaster-General *Anatole Montesquiou* and his colleagues are obliged 'to protect cheeks, hands and eyes with handkerchiefs and headgear and turn up the collars of our uniforms.' Méneval, Fain and the other secretaries ride slowly onwards in the headquarters carriages. Likewise the treasurers, Peyrusse among them:

'We had all the trouble in the world to get clear. The streets were encumbered with debris, with burning beams and trusses. In our carriages we were being grilled alive. The horses couldn't get on. I was extremely worried on account of the treasure,'

twelve strongly guarded wagons filled with perhaps some twenty millions in gold and silver coin.

But Major Boulart, braving the direct route, has got back to his regiment. He's just getting his guns and ammunition wagons under way and

'the head of my column was just about to recross the Moscova when the Emperor, his march retarded by my long column, appeared with his staff and went on ahead of me'.

A most dangerous moment, says General Count *Philippe de Ségur,* the Assistant Prefect of the Palace and responsible for its pack mules. Some men of I Corps, he says, have guided IHQ out of narrow burning streets; and Marshal Davout

> 'wounded at Borodino, was having himself brought back into the flames to get Napoleon out of their clutches or else perish with him. Transported with joy he threw himself into his arms; the Emperor received him well but with that calm which never abandoned him in peril.'

Did the Iron Marshal really do that? It's hard to imagine Davout transported with joy in any circumstances. (Nor had be been 'wounded', only badly bruised when his horse had fallen on top of him.) Ségur's dramatic prose must always be taken with a largish pinch of salt. On the other hand he's on the spot, and Davout is certainly devoted to Napoleon's interests. What is true is that 'to escape from this vast region of evils, Napoleon still had to overtake a long powder convoy which was passing through it' – i.e., Boulart's. A single unheeded firebrand or flaming roof-shingle settling on one of his powder wagons and quickly burning a hole, first through its the canvas cover then the lid, is enough to blow the entire Imperial and General Staffs – and indeed the whole Napoleonic régime – sky-high. The sober-minded Boulart confesses to having felt 'gentle satisfaction' at his Emperor's providential escape.

After which the whole procession, Guard artillery and all, winds its way in drenching rain – now it's falling in bucketsful – round the north-western suburbs.

At the Petersburg Gate the ever-prescient Pion des Loches, who since 6 a.m. has had his Guard battery limbered up and ready to leave the city, finds the officer in charge of the picket half-seas under:

> 'Unable to go a-pillaging, he was levying a tax on all soldiers coming out with booty. He thought he was doing himself an honour in showing me his guardhouse filled with bottles of wine and baskets of eggs. All his men were dead drunk and he himself couldn't stand up.'

If the Kremlin has impressed everyone by its oriental splendours, the Petrovskoï summer palace seems merely odd. To Colonel Griois, who yesterday had had an opportunity to look at it before going on his shopping spree, its

> 'very antique construction, surrounded by high brick walls and its heavy and severe overall appearance made it seem more like a state prison than a sovereign's palace'.

Reminding Roman Soltyk of Hampton Court, to Captain Count *V. E. B. Castellane,* another of Napoleon's orderlies, its style seems 'Greek, truly romantic'. Just now it's surrounded by an ocean of mud, through which camp stools and beds have to be fetched from Eugène's headquarters near-by. For if the Kremlin's furniture had been sparse, here there is none at all! Even tables have to be improvised. Nor does the Petrovskoï summer palace have any outbuildings; so in no time the entire Imperial and General Headquarters staffs[3] and the Administration, altogether some 700 persons, are trying to squeeze inside out of the rain. The entire artillery staff – Lariboisière, his son Henri, his 'man of letters' and his six 'ill-educated' staff captains who run Planat's errands – all have to cram themselves inside one small downstairs room. At its window Planat reads

'two letters to Lariboisière by the light of the distant fire. We were only some six miles from Moscow, and from there we saw the whole town perfectly. From this vantage point we could assess, better than hitherto, the full extent of the conflagration. The fire seemed to be burning everywhere. The town was no more than a single blaze.'

Is it as fascinating as Smolensk? Somewhere out on the plain with the baggage train a certain dragoon captain Henri Beyle, alias the future great novelist *Stendhal*, thinks not, but is wittily finding it

'the most beautiful fire in the world. Forming an immense pyramid, like the prayers of the faithful it had its base on the ground and its summit in heaven.'

Abbé Surugué, like everyone else, is noticing how the flames' undulations 'whipped up by the wind, are exactly emulating the waves raised by a storm at sea'. After supper Montesquiou and his colleagues at Petrovskoï can't resist going to take another look 'at this fiery spectacle that was doing us so much harm, and to which we nevertheless kept returning'.

But Caulaincourt, who's been on his feet for 21 hours, is too exhausted for any reflections, whether humorous or aesthetic. Just scribbles in his notebook: 'Arrived at 7.30 p.m. To bed.'

Some ten or fifteen miles away to the south-west General Colbert's crack Lancer Brigade, made up of the famous 1st (Polish) and 2nd (Dutch) Lancers of the Imperial Guard, is advancing eastwards. Two thousand men strong, its horses are heavily laden with saddle furniture, including such extras as scythes to cut standing crops and axes to fell trees. The brigade, without news or orders for a week now, has been scouring the countryside in the direction of Borowsk but has found no signs of an enemy. Captain *François Dumonceau*'s 6th troop of the Red Lancers' 2nd squadron has probed particularly far afield; but seen 'only a few rare Cossacks'. Now he's on his way back to brigade headquarters, apprehensive that he'll be repri-manded – not for the first time – by his disciplinarian chief for being away too long. Instead he's surprised to be congratulated.

A somewhat cold-blooded young man, the Belgian captain has a keen eye for facts, events and details which he promptly notes down in his diary. Always it's been his ambition to see the Aurora Borealis. And that evening, seeing an immense glow in the sky as the column advances along the Moscow road, he takes it for granted that his ambition is being fulfilled. But his Polish colleague, Captain *Josef Zalusky* of the 1st Guard Lancers, places quite a different interpretation on this glow in the night sky; assumes 'the two armies to be in presence again, preparing for another major battle in front of Moscow. We felt bitterly frustrated at not taking part in it.'

That night the brigade reaches the Sparrow Hill, from which the cheering army had first seen the city, two days ago:

'We found it surrounded, occupied and guarded by our comrades the
Horse Chasseurs of the Guard. Together with some other officers I
galloped over to our friends, asked them at once: "And Moscow?"
"There isn't any Moscow any more." "What d'you mean?" "It's burnt
down – look!"'

Poles and Dutchmen gaze out through the darkness over an immense smoking mass:

'Only a little fragment, such as the Kremlin, dominating the town from its height, had been saved. Imagine our terror, from the military, political and personal points of view! We were exhausted by marching all the way from Kovno. Our clothes were in rags, we'd no clean linen, and we were counting on the capital's resources! The Chasseurs interrupted our reflections by offering us Don wine, fizzy like champagne. We drank to the Emperor's health, to the expedition's happy outcome, and, somewhat consoled, resumed our march. We were making for the Kaluga road, to pass the night there. Having immediately supplied ourselves with various things we'd so long desired, above all Turkish tobacco, we spent our first night oblivious of torments. *Jucunda sollicitae oblivia vitae.*' – Happily oblivious of life's cares.

Marshal *Louis-Nicolas Davout*, Prince d'Eckmühl, an even stricter disciplinarian than Colbert, is disliked and feared by almost everybody. Though only some 15–18,000 of his brilliantly disciplined I Corps, originally 69,500 strong, are still under his command, it's not – as is the case with Murat's cavalry – for any lack of care for them on Davout's part. Now he has set up his headquarters in a convent near the Doroghomilov Gate.

There, 26 Muscovites, arrested as incendiaries, have been brought in. Though most of their identities turn out to be fictitious, it's obvious they're men of many civil occupations – farriers, stonemasons, house painters, policemen, a sexton ... and only one, a lieutenant of the Moscow Regiment, is a military man. The first session of the court-martial, presided over by the commanding officer of the 1st Guard Grenadiers, is rather thorough. Though it orders ten of these unfortunates to be shot, the guilt of the sixteen others is found 'insufficiently proven'. And they're sent to prison. But elsewhere many others aren't even being given the benefit of any doubt. Fezensac takes an obviously innocent civilian under his protection but has to hand him over to another officer, to whom he 'recommends' him. The other, mistaking it for a sinister innuendo, has him shot. No wonder Lieutenant *von Kalckreuth*, riding across Moscow with the 2nd Prussian Hussars – a regiment reduced by its long marches from four squadrons to only two – finds

> 'in the streets many dead Russians, to a great extent old people who, caught red-handed setting fire [to buildings] had been shot on the spot.'

Moscow has two great military hospitals, one of which Napoleon will afterwards declare on St Helena to have been the finest and most commodious he'd ever seen. Both have immediately been occupied by Surgeon-General Baron *Dominique Larrey*'s medical service. Nobly devoted as always to his humanitarian task – overwhelming because Napoleon has repeatedly refused 'the noblest man he has ever met' adequate means for carrying it out – Larrey, together with 'a very small number of my comrades', has remained behind in the burning city in 'a stone house, isolated on the summit of a free-standing quarter near the Kremlin, whence I could observe at my ease all the phenomena of the terrible conflagration'. He and his assistants are doing what they can for their wretched patients, and Larrey himself, as usual, is carrying out many of the amputations and other operations. But as the fire approaches, some 1,000 of them, allied, French and Russian, fall into a panic. Jump out of upstairs windows. And for lack of any means of transport, lie on the pavements with shattered bones and re-opened bleeding wounds, beyond all medical help, and being roasted alive.

But virtually all the other generals have fled. And it's their fault, Labaume thinks, that the pillage is rapidly growing worse. Their absence has unleashed the Furies:[4]

> 'No retreat was safe enough, no place holy enough, to preserve the Muscovites from the soldiers' greed. They, the vivandières, the convicts and prostitutes, running about the streets, broke into the abandoned palaces and seized from them everything that appealed to their cupidity. Some covered themselves in gold and silver cloths. Others, without the least discrimination, put the most highly esteemed furs on their shoulders. Many covered themselves in

women's and children's fur capes and even the galley-slaves hid their rags under fine coats. The rest, going in a mob to the cellars, forced in the doors, grabbed the most precious wines, and staggered off carrying away their immense booty.'

Griois, venturing back to buy some more wine and provisions, witnesses a scene that would be comic if it weren't so horrible. Amid the burning buildings he sees some soldiers emerging from a ladder that leads down to a cellar, where there's a terrible

'dispute, or rather fight, going on among looters who're cutting each others' throats in the dark! Soon emerges from the stairway a dragoon, pale, covered in blood and wine. He took a few steps and, hardly out into the street, fell, expired amidst the bottles he was clutching and only let go of as he died. In the scrimmage he'd had a sabre run through his body.'

At that moment Griois recognizes the army's Quartermaster-General, Count Mathieu Dumas, one of the Emperor's closest collaborators:

'He draws his sword, strikes out to right and left, reaches the stairway and seizing by its hair the first head to present itself he recognizes ... his own cook, who was coming up again laden with bottles, half-drunk, his white waistcoat spattered with wine and blood. It would be hard to imagine anything more comical than the general's astonishment, anger and vexation at seeing his servant emerge among the soldiers' burst of laughter. He gave him not blows of his sword, but kicks, and went away in despair at seeing that the disorder couldn't be mastered and that everyone was mingling in it.'

As they make for the Kazan Gate, Kalckreuth's Prussian hussars are 'often having to trot so as not to be hurt by the debris of collapsing houses or the heat, and braving all dangers and entering blazing houses' to get some food or wine. Kalckreuth and his servant and his friend Lieutenant Manteuffel dismount and can hardly get in through the mob of French soldiers of all arms:

'The first cellar had already been emptied of the wine it had contained, and in the second, several chasseurs were handing bottles to each other. It was impossible to get down there.'

Though other soldiers are shouting loud warnings that the house is about to collapse,

'no one heeded their advice. Fortunately, I mingled with the chasseurs and in this way got a few bottles they handed to me and which they thought they were giving to their comrades. Afraid lest the floor of the first cellar, where we were, was going to collapse under the weight of the mob and that then no one would escape, we contented ourselves with our sparse booty and, not without difficulty, got out of it.'

The gatehouse of the courtyard is already in flames. Only their horses' fleetness can save them. Leaving through the Kazan Gate, Kalckreuth and his comrades rejoin their unit about two miles beyond Moscow.

Even the Kremlin is being pillaged. Rummaging about in its vaults under the church of St Michael and busy rifling the tombs of dead Tsars, some Guard grenadiers are disappointed to find nothing more valuable than the coffins' silver name-plaques. Their only booty is a beautiful young girl who's fled there from her wedding day. Only yesterday she was to have married a Russian officer. Now the grenadiers take her, quivering with terror and praying to the souls of long-dead Tsars to protect her, to their general, 'who immediately forms designs on her virtue'.

Now it's the morning of 16 September. Though the rain's still pouring down, the whole city's one vast blazing pandemonium. Larrey is horrified to see the common people being chased

'howling from house to house. Determined to save their most precious belongings, they'd loaded themselves with bundles they could hardly carry and which one often saw them abandoning to escape the flames. Women with children on their shoulders and dragging others by the hand, were running with their skirts tucked up to take refuge in the corners of streets and squares. Old men, their long beards caught by the flames, were being dragged along on little carts by their children.'

From the 4th Line regiment's camp, about three miles west of the city, its newly appointed Colonel *Montesquiou-Fezensac* – an aristocrat who until Borodino was one of Berthier's ADCs – making a vain attempt to go to the Kremlin, is 'keenly afflicted by this spectacle' and determined to do all he can 'to distract my regiment's gaze from miseries I couldn't alleviate.'

When at about midday yesterday (15 September) the fire had first begun to pose a serious threat to the Kremlin, *François Bourgogne*, a sergeant in the Fusiliers-Grenadiers of the Middle Guard, had been sitting with a comrade with their 'backs against the enormous guns which guard each side of the Arsenal', breakfasting with some friends in the 1st Foot Chasseurs.

'These, I ought to say, had some silver bullion, ingots the size and shape of a brick, taken from the Mint. They were promising to do business with a rabbi whose synagogue had burnt down, and with whom they were amusing themselves by forcing him to partake of a succulent ham.'

Suddenly there'd come a shout 'To Arms!'. Loading a package containing 'three bottles of wine, five of liqueurs and some preserved fruits' on to the poor rabbi, Bourgogne and his friend had immediately gone back into the town to try and find their own regiment and 'staggered through the streets with no worse mishap than getting our feet scorched'. Again and again they'd lost their way. When they'd left the regiment it had been in the main square. But where has it gone? Reaching the Jewish quarter, their beast of burden utters a cry of despair and faints:

'We hastened to disburden him and, opening a bottle of liqueur, we made him swallow a few drops, and then poured a little over his face. By and by he opened his eyes. When we asked him why he'd fainted, he told us his house had been burnt down and that probably his family had perished. With these words he swooned again.'

And there they'd left him. But then one of their own party too had collapsed and had to be left to his fate. Another being half-blinded by flying sparks, they decide to turn back:

'The idea struck us of each taking a piece of iron sheeting to cover our heads, holding it to windward. After bending the iron into the shape of shields we set out, one man leading, then myself, leading the half-blinded man by the hand, the others following.'

There follow endless peregrinations through the burning streets:

'It's 11 p.m. when we at last reach the place we'd left the previous evening. Since I'd had no rest since arriving in Moscow I lay down on some beautiful furs our men had taken, and slept till 7 o'clock next morning.'

While Bourgogne and his comrades had been wandering about in the inferno, a vélite battalion of the Italian Royal Guard had also been called to arms with orders to hunt down incendiaries. Ordering his battalion to fall in, its adjutant-major is horrified at the chaos all round him,

'where the only law is the law of the strongest – soldiers wandering aimlessly about, covered in sweat, smoke-blackened, laden with loot – Russian wounded dragging themselves along as they try to flee from the fire – raving inhabitants, groaning, screaming, yelling, not knowing where to find a refuge.'

All round are only burning and collapsing buildings through which Césare de Laugier and his white-and-green uniformed grenadiers have the greatest difficulty in making their way:

'After innumerable detours we find the road ahead is barred by flames. But we push on. Crossing the ruins of a burning palace at the double, we emerge on the other side into another alleyway, where we again find ourselves blocked by a sea of fire.'

"Go on, go on!" shout the men who're bringing up the rear. "No, no!" cry those at its head, at all costs they must turn back! The one course is as impossible as the other. Stunned by the noise of the madly whirling flames in the roaring hurricane which seems to be blowing from all quarters at once, their situation is becoming untenable:

'Blinded by sparks, by burning cinders, by fiery embers, suffocated by this rarified burning air, streaming with sweat, we don't even dare look about us because the wind's blowing a fiery dust into our eyes, forcing us to close them. We're overcome by impatience, almost by madness. Our cartridge pouches, filled with cartridges, our loaded muskets, only increase our peril.'

Another building comes tumbling down just as they emerge from it, injuring several grenadiers. Whereupon the whole battalion panics:

'The earth's burning, the sky's on fire, we're drowning in a sea of flame. Our uniforms are scorched and smoke- blackened, we're having to extinguish the falling cinders with our bare hands. At last the battalion gets moving again. The sappers, by great efforts, cut us a passage leading into a little square where, jammed tightly together, we momentarily recover our breath and our courage.'

They've long ago lost all sense of direction. But what's this? Breaking into the courtyard of a burning palace, they see 'a carriage with its back to the opposite wall' and, inside it, 'a Russian drummer, asleep amidst his loot and dead drunk. Rudely awakened, terrified, he tries to run off.' Though they don't know a word of Russian they try to get him to realise they're only trying to find a way out; and 'he, realizing his fate is tied up with ours, understands. Escorted by sappers and under the adjutant-major's vigilant eye' – Laugier, like Caesar, here writes of himself in the third person – 'he leads the battalion through a little wooden cabin and out into a

'narrow tortuous alley, most of it already in ashes. Under falling tiles, the ground burning the soles of our shoes, the drummers beat the charge with one hand while clinging to each others' jackets with the other, not to lose touch.'

Again the sappers use their axes, this time to demolish a little wall. And lo and behold, after five hours of this 'fiery hell', the vélites of the Guardia d'Onore suddenly find they're

'in a vast field, on the banks of the Moscova! With what joy we gulp in lungfuls of fresh pure air! By now it's 2 a.m. The weather is rainy.'

But where are all those beautiful palaces they'd occupied only yesterday? They've vanished. Instead, ordered out to Petrovskoï, they bivouac there under lashing rain. 'A novel spectacle,' the adjutant-major confides to his diary,

'to see a victorious army encamped around a city in flames, having lost at a single blow the fruits of its triumph and the resources which could have restored its physical strength.'

Neither that day nor the next does the fire abate, or the rain give over. Nor does the looting abate. While his battery had still been parked in the as yet unburned western district it had seemed to Major Boulart there'd been 'a continual procession of our soldiers,' above all from I Corps, 'carrying wine, sugar, tea, furniture, furs, etc., to their camp, and no one opposing it'. But now he reflects that it's just as well something is being saved from the flames, 'and most of what was saved was profitable'. Césare de Laugier:

> 'Wednesday morning: There's no shop in the town centre which isn't the prey of the flames except a book shop, and another, also in Lupra-va-Blayontence. Resin, brandy, vitriol, the most precious merchandise, all are on fire at once. Torrents of flames, escaping from this immense brazier, are crowned by thick clouds of smoke. The boldest still risk their lives by going into this furnace, then come out again all burnt, but laden with jewels and riches. Seeing this, others try to follow their example; but, less fortunate, don't re-appear.'

Bivouacked out there in the mud near Petrovskoï where they're 'established in English-style gardens and lodged under grottoes, Chinese pavilions, kiosks or greenhouses around the châteaux where their generals were', even staff officers can find no shelter.

> 'Our horses are tied up under acacias or linden trees, separated from each other by borders and flower beds. A truly picturesque camp, enhanced by the men's novel costumes! Most, to shelter from the weather's insults, had donned garments of the same kind as those we'd just seen in Moscow. Soldiers dressed like Tartars, like Cossacks, like Chinese, were walking about our camp. Here was one wearing a Polish toque; others tall Persian, Bashkir or Kalmuck bonnets. Another, wearing women's clothes, is standing beside one who's dressed up like a pope. And all the while hands, expert or novice, are practising on pianos, flutes, violins, guitars, from which they mostly extort discordant noises. In a word, our army presented the appearance of a carnival.'

Albrecht von Muraldt is a 21-year-old lieutenant in the 4th Bavarian Chevaulegers who, ever since leaving Vilna, where they'd been detached from St-Cyr's VI Corps in July, have been part of the Army of Italy. After Borodino he's been recommended for the cross of the Legion of Honour. To him IV Corps' camp looks like

> 'a market place. A lot of carriages had been driven out to behind our lines. Somehow or other every officer had got hold of one. Carpets, covers, satin cushions, porcelain dinner services lay scattered everywhere, either offered for sale or used for barter. The ground was so littered with empty or broken bottles one could hardly stand to arms without endangering oneself or one's horse.'

As for the Italians' campfires, they're

> 'veritable bonfires of paintings and luxurious furniture. All around, officers and men, filthy and blackened by the smoke, are seated on

elegant chairs or silken settees. Spread out on the ground here and there in the mud are cashmere shawls, precious Siberian furs, Persian cloth of gold. Over there men are eating around cooking pots off silver plates and cups. What an uproarious carnival!'

Out at the Kazan Gate Sous-lieutenant *Pierre Auvray*'s 23rd Dragoons are sending '40 men to go and pillage the town' while waiting for orders. Auvray himself confesses to have taken 'from an individual a casket of gold, table silver and jewellery, whose value I didn't know'. Also, more excusably, some linen and cloth to clothe himself with. Not many yards away another lieutenant, *Heinrich von Brandt* of the Vistula Legion, sees

'in our bivouac alone a considerable amount of silver, enamelled goldsmith's work, table linen, precious cloths and furs being brought for the men to lie down on. Thereto a mass of such chattels as chairs, torches, etc., which the pillagers were forcing Russians to carry for them. Famine was being followed by excess. All our huts were stuffed with victuals and every kind of liquid, meats fresh and salted, smoked fish, wine, rum, brandy, etc. Around all the campfires people were cooking, eating and, above all, drinking to excess. Each new arrival of pillaged objects was greeted with joyous vivats!'

He's thinking that all this unrestricted looting by both officers and men is 'the logical consequence of the first order to lodge troops in the town military fashion and of the disappearance of the authorities who could have regulated it. It had begun with shops that sold food, wines and spirits, and with lightning swiftness had spread to private dwellings, public buildings and churches.'

The whole flaming city is being rummaged and turned inside out:

'Such unfortunate inhabitants as had remained behind were being illtreated, shops and cellars forced open. The city rabble, taking advantage of this disorder, shared in the pillage and led the troops to cellars and vaults and anywhere else they thought might have been used to conceal property in the hope of sharing in the pillage.'

By now even Fezensac has been obliged to let the men of his 4th Line Regiment go into town and take whatever they like. For is this really pillage? Gourgaud, at least, doesn't think so. In these extraordinary circumstances to call it 'looting is an abuse of language and an unspeakable harshness'. And one day in a future neither of them can conceive he'll take Ségur physically to task for calling it by that ugly name.

Only Murat's 25,000-strong advance guard, slowly following the 'defeated' and 'demoralized' Russian rearguard eastwards through the steadily falling rain, is having to leave this feast of plunder further and further behind it. Five miles beyond the city, on 15 September, chasseur lieutenant *Maurice*

Tascher – a nephew of the ex-Empress Josephine and like his two brothers who are also in the army a cousin, therefore, of Prince Eugène – has bivouacked 'about five miles beyond the city' amidst 'a dangerous abundance. In Moscow, fire and pillage,' he writes in his lapidary but useful diary.

Made up of some 12,000 infantry and 8,000 cavalry, not all mounted, Murat's force is a small army in itself. Besides the dwindled remains of Nansouty's 1st and Sébastiani's 2nd 'Reserve' Cavalry Corps, it also includes what had been Friant's, but since that general's wounding at Borodino is now Dufour's 1st infantry division, made up mainly of Frenchmen but with a sprinkling of recalcitrant Spaniards. Also the two battle-hardened Polish foot regiments of Claparède's Vistula Legion. In liaison, out on its right wing, is Prince Poniatowski's – also much-reduced – Polish V Corps.

Marching stolidly along the Kazan road, Sébastiani's light cavalry is 'driving before it' the usual swarms of Cossacks who, once again, are up to all the wearisome tricks they'd played on it all the long way from Vilna to Moscow: pretending to mount attacks, then, when the light cavalry has formed up in battle order, vanishing into the woods where they either let their pursuers exhaust their horses or else fall into an ambush. But who is driving whom? Next day (16 September), Sébastiani's leading (2nd) light cavalry division is

'driving them before him for twelve miles through beautiful, well-
aligned villages which they're no longer burning',

when it falls into just such a well-planned artillery ambush. Even Murat's life, Tascher sees, is momentarily in danger. And he also catches a glimpse of someone else whose imminent death will also play a certain part in the campaign: General Platov, the Cossacks' supreme hetman's son.

A more feckless, if gallant, light cavalry general than Sébastiani could hardly have been chosen to lead the advance guard. Already, since leaving Vilna, he has twice let himself be surprised – 'I don't know how it is,' his mother-in-law is wittily saying in the Paris salons, 'but my son-in-law goes from one surprise to another.' And in the army he has already earned himself the sobriquet 'General Surprise'. A Corsican relative of the Bonapartes and Napoleon's former ambassador in Constantinople who, among other things, had been the driving force behind the defeat of Admiral Duckworth's squadron in the Dardanelles, Sébastiani is a little man with a dull complexion but a pair of lively black eyes and long curly black hair, who according to Griois 'supplied the want of any education with an astounding self-assurance' – much the same assessment, that is, as Captain Zalusky of the 1st Polish Guard Lancers has already made of him.[5] Coupled with Murat's total insouciance when it comes to his troopers' well-being, or even their horses' survival on the march,[6] it's not surprising if Tascher and his comrades are often going to be in parlous straits.

Also on the march, of course, is Dedem van der Gelder. No one is more critical of Murat's handling of his troops than he; and ex-diplomat though he is,[7] he has been far from diplomatic on that point. Ever since Smolensk he's been suffering from a badly bruised chest – the effect of a spent musket ball that had hit him at Smolensk as he'd led his infantry into action against the city gate. But now, as the blazing city recedes into the distance, the pain's becoming so acute that Dedem finds he no longer can sit his horse. During the night of 16/17 September he feels he's had enough, at least for the time being. And gets Murat's permission – permission doubtless only too readily granted – to hand over his command of Dufour's 2nd infantry brigade and go back to Moscow:

'At a distance of more than six miles the light of the flames lit up the road. Coming nearer, all I saw was a sea of fire, and since the wind was very strong the flames were lashing about like a furious sea. I was happy to find my mill again [near the Vladimir gate], and all night I enjoyed from it this unique spectacle, horrible but majestic and imposing.'

Even if not quite so 'poetical', 'grandiose' or 'sublime' as the burning of Smolensk, Dedem fancies he has before him the spectacle of 'Samarkand taken by Tamerlane'.

CHAPTER 3

THE FAIR OF MOSCOW

The fire abates – Napoleon returns to the Kremlin – horses in churches – the Yellow Palace goes up in flames – rumours in the Kremlin – 'If Your Majesty still retains any of your former feelings for me' – 'famine was followed by excess' – food and furs – Coignet's bad stroke of business – growing shortage of necessities

Not until the third day does the fire begin to die away, for lack of fuel:

'At last, on 18 September, the fire having noticeably died down and the horizon beyond Moscow having cleared, the Emperor re-entered the town. At 9 a.m. he mounted *Moscow* and crossed the town. Our return was no less gloomy than our departure. I can't say how much I'd suffered since my brother's death. The horror of all that was going on around us added to my grief at his loss. Seeing all these recent events broke me down completely. Although one cannot exclusively be affected by one's own personal troubles in the midst of so many public disasters, one is none the less grieved by them. I was over-whelmed. Happy are they who never saw such a grim spectacle!'

Reaching the Kremlin, Caulaincourt helps Napoleon change to *Warsaw*, another of his five Arab greys. And on it he rides

'about that part of the city to the right of the theatre. Came to the stone bridge. Went out through the Kolomna Gate. Followed the city moat. Passed in front of the two military hospitals, the Yellow Palace. Returned to the Kremlin at 4 p.m.'

Its antique, not to say uncomfortable, milieu is little to Napoleon's neo-classical taste. Even before the fire had forced him out to Petrovskoï he'd had the town searched for something more up to date, and the luxuriously furnished Yellow Palace of Sloboda, also built for Catherine the Great, had been pointed out. Now his 50-year-old but already white-haired ADC Count *Louis de Narbonne*[1] is ordered to go there with Berthier and see if it'll do. They find all the doors locked, have to climb in through a window. Méneval, who's also one of the party, finds the lamps still have candles in them. Otherwise 'this royal dwelling seemed to be deserted'. Narbonne reports back to Napoleon just as he's reviewing the Fusiliers-Grenadiers in one of the Kremlin courtyards. Whereupon their Sergeant Bourgogne is ordered

'to join a detachment of Fusiliers-Chasseurs and Grenadiers and a squadron of Polish Lancers, altogether 200 men, commanded by a general whom I took to be General Kellermann. We left at 8 p.m., and it was 9.30 before we came to a spacious building at the far side of Moscow. Built of timber and covered with stucco to resemble marble, it seemed to be much the same size as the Tuileries. Our object was to secure it against fire. Guards were immediately posted outside, and, to make assurance doubly sure, patrols were sent out. I was detailed off with several men to inspect the interior, to see if anyone was hidden there.'

Bourgogne searches through its apartments for incendiaries but doesn't find any. Considers himself

'fortunate in having a chance to see this immense building, furnished with all the splendour and brilliance of Europe and Asia. Everything seemed to have been lavished on its decoration.'

But though he and his men take every possible precaution against its being fired,

'a quarter of an hour afterwards it broke out behind us, in front of us, to right, to left, and we couldn't see who'd set it alight. There it was, in a dozen places at once, and flaring from every attic window! The general immediately called for sappers to try to cut it off, but it was impossible. We had no pumps, not even any water. Half an hour after the blaze had broken out, a furious wind had got up, and in less than ten minutes we were hemmed in by the fire, unable either to advance or retreat. Several of us were hurt by falling timbers.'

But they nab the incendiaries!

'Directly afterwards we saw several men, some with torches still burning, coming out from under the grand staircase by some subterranean passage and trying to slip away. We ran after them and stopped them. There were 21 of them, and eleven others were arrested on the other side. These weren't actually seen coming out of the palace, and nothing about them showed they were incendiaries. More than half, however, were obviously convicts. Within an hour the palace was entirely consumed. The utmost we could do was to save some pictures and a few other valuables.'

The blaze has also set fire to the whole surrounding district,

'built of wood and very beautiful. It was 2 a.m. before we could get out of this hell. We set out again for the Kremlin, taking with us our prisoners, 32 in number. I was put in command of the rearguard and of the prisoners' escort, with orders to bayonet any who tried to run away or refused to follow.'

Bourgogne tries to save the lives of an obviously innocent Swiss resident whose home and family have perished in the fire and of a tailor and his son – amidst all the soot and filth only washerwomen are in more acute demand than tailors!

But when Narbonne, next day, gets back 'to take possession of this palace, it had been utterly consumed'.

The Italian Royal Guard, too, has moved back into town. But what a difference in the Petersburg district!

'Only the stone palaces retained some traces of what they'd been. Isolated on this heap of charcoal and ashes, blackened by smoke, these debris of a new town looked like the relics of antiquity.'

Since the churches are built of stone or brick and stand somewhat apart from the dwellings, it's mostly they that have survived. Now they're being used to lodge both men and horses:

'The neighing of the horses and the soldiers' horrible blasphemies are replacing the sacred and harmonious hymns which used to resound under these sacred vaultings,'

the sententious Labaume records in his 'little notebook, no bigger than my hand' in which he's daily jotting down his impressions and experiences.

'All the churches except four or five were turned into stables. They have big iron doors and locks and the French felt safer there at nights. Their horses were covered in cloths made from priestly vestments. In Tchoudov Cathedral we found a dead horse. In another church they were melting down gold and silver and using the images of our saints for firewood. In the church of the Petrovka convent was the big public slaughterhouse.'[2]

What kind of effect such behaviour might be expected to have on pious Russians could have been learnt from experiences in Spain. But evidently hasn't been. Rather the contrary. Everyone is indignant at the Russians for having burnt down their sacred city. Even the usually calm and thoughtful Méneval is so furious at Rostopchin's 'infernal idea of removing the pumps' that he thinks the army should 'march on Petersburg and burn it down. What possible advantage could this monstrous sacrifice be to Russia?'

Naturally all sorts of rumours are going the rounds. At IHQ, back in the Kremlin, 'it's most positively believed', paymaster Peyrusse writes in one of his letters to his friend André in Paris,

'that it's all been a plan proposed by the English to attract us to Moscow and in the midst of the fire and the disorder of a town delivered over to pillage fall on the Emperor's headquarters and the garrison. The General Bacler Tolli [Barclay de Tolly], minister of war, had shared this opinion; but the Emperor Alexander, to whom one can do the justice of believing him a stranger to this terrible attentat, had taken the command of the corps covering Moscow from General Tolli. General Kutusov had disapproved of this ferocious act, and replied that it would be better to defend the town to the last extremity. But nothing stopped the governor. Pressed by the Grand Duke Constantine[3] and incited by some inconsiderable lords, it was he who ordered the town's ruin.'

All of which, if Peyrusse and his colleagues only knew it, is less than half true – Rostopchin's scheme had in fact been quite unknown to the Tsar, to Barclay or to Kutusov, none of whom would ever have acceded to it. IHQ has a few spies who are reporting on the confused brawling relationships at Kutusov's headquarters. One of them is a Captain La Fontaine. Born and brought up in Moscow, he is riding to and fro through the Russian lines, even, when necessary, requisitioning fresh horses in the Tsar's name. Schulmeister[4] isn't here, and wouldn't be any use if he were – Russian isn't one of the languages Napoleon's chief spy commands. One wonders how IHQ has even come by such a mixture of fact and fiction? Can it be thanks to a certain Marie-Louise Chalmé, thirty-year-old wife of the French manager of a large hotel? Herself owner of a milliner's shop on the fashionable Bridge of the Marshals, she'd lost everything except her children and the clothes she stood up in and taken refuge at Eugène's headquarters. Eugène had sent her in a hackney coach to the Petrovskoï summer palace where Mortier had received her and taken her to Napoleon, waiting in a window recess of a large, sumptuously decorated – but otherwise empty – hall. Their interview had lasted an hour, and had evidently touched on political topics, for Napoleon had asked her what she thought of the idea, already dismissed by him at Witebsk in August, of freeing the Russian peasants:

"One-third, Your Majesty," she'd replied, "would perhaps appreciate it. The other two-thirds would have no idea of what you were trying to do for them."

After which she'd been conducted back to IV Corps' headquarters.

Far from wishing to liberate the Russians peasants or anything of that sort,[5] Napoleon's most pressing concern, Caulaincourt sees, is to exculpate both the army and himself of 'the odium of having caused the fire it had in fact done its utmost to put out, and from which self-interest was enough to exonerate it'. And in the streets Pion des Loches reads an order of the day

> 'in which he accused the Russians of having burnt down their own capital. Any inhabitant who didn't go to register with one of the twelve military commandants was to be killed. For individuals caught torch in hand the punishment was the same. As a result, twelve Russians were hanged in the square where I'd originally stationed myself. Several generals, setting themselves up as judges, had others hanged at the doors of their houses.'

Drastic measures indeed; but not likely to convince the Tsar of the Grand Army's innocence, still less the panic-stricken but furious Petersburg populace. Something more diplomatic is needed. So Lelorgne d'Ideville, head of the Statistical Department, who has lived in Moscow and is acting as Napoleon's interpreter, is ordered 'to find some Russian to whom all the details of the affair could be confided and who'd repeat what he was told in the proper quarters'.

This, it seems, is easier said than done.

Virtually every Muscovite of any social standing has fled. Of the few who've lingered, one is the intrepid if somewhat obsequious governor of the Foundlings Hospital, one of the few large municipal buildings to have survived the fire. Ivan Akinfievitch Tutolmin is also a councillor of state. On the eve of the Grand Army's arrival he'd evacuated all his charges over the age of 15, but himself stayed behind with his 500 younger ones and sent a message to Napoleon, pointing out that his institution was under special protection of the Dowager Empress. Whereupon, at 9 p.m. on 14 September, a picket had been sent to guard it.

Introduced into Napoleon's study, he effusively – doubtless prompted by d'Ideville – expresses his gratitude to the man whom, so he says, he's teaching his charges to call 'their father'. More to the point, he requests permission to write to Petersburg and tell his patroness of her foundation's miraculous escape.

Protected by the etiquette which forbids anyone to speak first when addressing a sovereign, Napoleon, as usual, bombards his interlocutor with peremptory questions. How is Tutolmin's hospital organized? Administered? He wants to know every detail – but just then a new outbreak of the fire distracts, or seems to distract, his attention. Going over to the window, he bursts out into a lacerating indictment of Rostopchin:

"The scoundrel! Fancy daring to add this monstrous, man-made, cold-blooded fire to the calamities of war, which are already so vast! He fancies he's a Roman, but is nothing but a stupid savage!"

Then, interrupting his own peroration, he suggests that Tutolmin – why yes, of course he may write to the Dowager Empress – shall add a few lines. And himself dictates them on the spot:

"*Madame. The Emperor Napoleon groans to see your capital almost wholly destroyed by means which, he says, are not those used in regular warfare. He seems convinced that if no one comes between him and our august Emperor Alexander, their former friendship will soon reassert its rights and all our misfortunes cease.*"

One of Tutolmin's assistants is 'allowed' to take the letter under a flag of truce to the outposts. But will it reach the Tsar, its real addressee?

By next morning d'Ideville has unearthed another putative emissary. This one is received in the vast Throne Room, bisected by a great roof beam supported by two marble pillars and 'gilded and blackened with age', whose only use has been for state banquets.

Ivan Yakovlev, brother of the Tsar's minister to King Jérôme Bonaparte's court at Cassel, is a chronic, almost pathological procrastinator.[6] Although urged by his household to leave town when everyone else had been doing so, he – for quite other reasons than Tutolmin – had dallied too long. His palace burnt down, and with a three or four days' growth of beard, this aged courtier of Catherine the Great appears before the all-powerful Emperor of the French, portent and symbol of the new century, wigless, half in rags, in an old riding-coat, a grubby shirt and two odd and muddy shoes. Flying into one of his theatrical rages which everyone finds so terrifying,[7] Napoleon fulminates again at the 'vandal' Rostopchin:

"This war is fostering a relentlessness stemming neither from Alexander nor from myself. It's the British who're dealing Russia a blow she'll bleed from for a long time to come. Peter the Great himself would have called you barbarians!"

Suddenly he comes to the point. Why does Yakovlev want a passport? Aren't the city's markets being reopened by imperial order? Isn't everything being set to rights? And when Yakovlev replies diplomatically that Moscow just now isn't the most pleasant place for a gentleman and his family to be in, asks him whether in that case, if he's granted a passport, he'll deliver a letter to the Tsar?

But of course.

At 4 a.m. next day the elderly emissary, roused from the temporary lodgings Mortier has found for him, is taken to the Kremlin. This time he finds Napoleon snuff-box in hand, pacing his study in his dressing-gown, looking gloomy.[8] Picking up his letter off the table, he hands it to Yakovlev. Addressed "To my brother, the Emperor Alexander," it's very long; and reads:

"Having been informed that the brother of Your Imperial Majesty's Minister in Cassel was in Moscow, I have sent for him and talked to him for some time. I have charged him to go to Your Majesty and make my sentiments known to you. The beautiful and superb town of Moscow no longer exists. Rostopchin has had it burnt. Four hundred incendiaries have been arrested in the act. All declared they were lighting fires at the orders of the Governor and Chief of Police. They have been shot. The fire seems at last to have ceased. Three-quarters of the houses are burnt down, a quarter remains. This conduct is atrocious and senseless. Is it intended to deprive me of a few supplies? These were in the cellars which the fire could not reach."

And why, Napoleon's letter goes on

"destroy one of the world's most beautiful cities, the work of centuries, to achieve so feeble a purpose? This is the conduct that has been followed since Smolensk, reducing 600,000 families to beggary. The fire-engines of the town of Moscow had been wrecked or removed, and some of the arms in the arsenal handed over to malefactors, who obliged us to fire a few roundshot at the Kremlin to dislodge them. Humanity, Your Majesty's and this great town's interests required that

it be put into my hands on trust, since the Russian army had left it exposed. The administrations, magistrates and civil guards should have been left behind. That was what was done twice in Vienna, in Berlin, and in Madrid. That was how we ourselves acted at the time of Suvarov's incursion.[9] The fires are authorizing pillage, in which the soldier indulges, disputing the debris with the flames. If I supposed such things to have been done at Your Majesty's orders, I should not be writing this letter; but I find it inconceivable that you, with your principles, your good heart and your sense of justice, should have authorized such excesses, unworthy of a great sovereign and a great nation. While having the fire-engines removed from Moscow, Rostopchin abandoned 150 field-guns, 60,000 new muskets, 1,600,000 infantry cartridges, over 400,000 pounds of gunpowder, 300,000 of saltpetre, the same amount of sulphur, etc."

At last he comes to the point:

"I have waged war on Your Majesty, without animosity. A letter from you before or after the last battle would have halted my advance, and in return it would have pleased me to be in a position to sacrifice the advantage of entering Moscow. If Your Majesty still retains some remnant of your former feelings for me, you will take this letter in good part. In any case, you cannot be other than grateful for my having informed you about what is going on in Moscow. Napoleon."

But Yakovlev's mission, too, comes immediately unstuck. The Russian outposts to the north of the city send him sent straight to Winzingerode, a German general in the Russian service, commanding in that sector. As he comes in, Winzingerode is himself sealing a letter of his own to the Tsar. Reads Napoleon's. Is Yakovlev insane? He must be, he tells him, to have made so bold as to undertake such a mission! Sends him under arrest to the Russian Minister of Police.

How unpsychological can one be? As if only too well aware of the inherent absurdity of blending arrogance with humble pleading and that every line of his letter betrays the anxiety over Russian intransigence he's trying to hide, Napoleon only tells Berthier and Lelorgne d'Ideville, 'with whom he discussed it freely', about his letter.

No reply, of course, will ever be received – no more than to his two earlier letters to 'his brother Alexander' from Vilna and Smolensk.[10]

Only about four-fifths of the city is in ashes. Seeking new quarters for Prince Eugène, Labaume hears that 'according to the count of the Engineer-Geographers a tenth of the houses were still standing'. Some 5,000 of its original 30,000 dwellings are in fact found to be still habitable. Already the army corps' staffs and the Imperial and Royal Guards have been ordered to return; and now everyone is installing himself according to rank and dignity. Pion des Loches, for instance, is settling back into Prince Bargatinski's palace and all the time, in view of small fires which keep breaking out here and there, taking great pains to preserve it,

'because of the provisions it contained. Its cellar alone was worth great sacrifices. I was on foot day and night for a week. As the fire had approached, my gunners had pulled down all the palings in the neighbourhood, so effectively that their dwelling – and mine – was among the very few houses of the quarter that had been spared. I'd seen twenty others in its neighbourhood go up in flames together. If M. le Prince Bargatinski found his Moscow palace again it's thanks to me.'

Newly arrived from Spain is Colonel Serran of the Guard Engineers. Since works have been put in hand to update the Kremlin's defences against a *coup de main* – Césare de Laugier hears that the Emperor himself has designed them – they're passed to Lariboisière's department and given to Serran to execute. To be near the works Serran chooses,

'five hundred yards away, the Palace of Prince Kutaisov, barber to the Grand Duke Paul, who by a stroke of good luck rather common in Russia, had acquired immense properties and had his son made a prince. The Prince [Emil] of Hesse [– Darmstadt] was lodged beside us.'

Serran is constantly in touch with Berthier and Duroc, 'whom the Emperor sometimes came and visited'.

As yet – for the first time since crossing the Niemen – there's plenty of food. Moscow, like other cities, is surrounded by windmills; and Caulaincourt, requisitioning one of them, arranges for IHQ's supply of wheat flour – 'which was already beginning to be scarce'. Returning to the city at 6 a.m. on 19 September, Major Le Roy, guided by a soldier of the 85th Line, marches his men along the quay 'where there were some boats laden with grain', and after passing through 'a long suburb, ending at the stream which flows into the Moskova' bivouacks at the foot of a windmill:

'On the other side were two rows of houses flanking the road. The weather having taken a turn for the worse and looking like rain, which in fact fell as night came down, I put my two companies into them and barricaded the bridge. I also managed to put a battalion into shelter in some nearby houses. Next day I visited my sentries. The sergeant placed near the river had found a grange filled with sacks of grain, made of bulrushes, sewn with string, and heaped up to the necks. I told the staff about it, and towards evening the food administration came and took charge of it for the army's benefit.'

Immediately on IHQ's return to the Kremlin a cookhouse service has been organized 'and great activity deployed on building ovens' – whose bread, to judge from earlier instances, will mostly go to the Guard. One of its *can-*

tinières has installed her kitchen behind the high altar of its cathedral. All round the city the immense fields of the huge beets and cabbages, so delightful to the hearts of Private Jakob Walter and Lieutenant Dutheillet, are being carefully cut.

'Numerous stacks of hay were also brought into town, and the potato fields within a radius of six miles were cleared. The transport wagons were in constant use.'

As for potatoes, Regimental Sergeant-Major *Auguste Thirion* and his steel-clad brothers-in-arms of the 2nd Cuirassiers are busy harvesting these 'precious tubers, a piece of gastronomic good luck'. Stendhal, unable even in the most desperate circumstances to restrain his flippant witticisms, writes home that they've become almost sacred: 'We're on our knees in front of some potatoes.'

All this is well and good. In the town's cellars there's no shortage of jams, liqueurs, tea and coffee and other luxuries. Much of the Kitai Gorod has survived:

'It was here that one found products from China. It consisted mainly of a long road, each of whose houses, regularly built in a severe and uniform style, turned out to be a vast shop. I was struck, I'd almost say saddened, by the silent calm which reigned in this quarter whose shops were full of tea.'

But though Paymaster-Captain Duverger is 'rich in furs and pictures, in boxes of figs, coffee, liqueurs, macaroni, salted fish and salted meat' when he entertains his general and ten other officers to a banquet on a leg of beef and they all drink to 'entering Petersburg', he has neither *vin ordinaire* nor – more ominous – any white bread to offer them. After a few days even Caulaincourt is already finding 'wheat beginning to be scarce, so I had a large supply of biscuits baked.'

For once in a very long while the army's horses have plenty of forage, at least for the first week or so:

'The grain and fodder warehouses along the quays had escaped the fire; and between Smolensk and Mojaisk, and since the battle until we'd reached Moscow, the army's horses had been so short of provender that everyone hastened to go foraging to get them some. During the two days of the 15th and 16th they'd got in enough hay to last for several months.'

So it seems. The army's Quartermaster-General, Count Mathieu Dumas (a man with a 'perfect knowledge of facts, an always captivating way of talking and a perfect distinction of manners') estimates there's enough food in the ruined city to feed the army for six months. And Surgeon-General Larrey agrees. Larrey has set up a kind of medical pool where French and Russian surgeons, in a unique collaboration, are working side by side.

Some 5,000 of their patients are either Frenchmen or allies. Himself he's working day and night in 'Moscow's most beautiful hospital' – a building which Boulart, looking out of the windows of 'quite a fine house said to belong to a doctor' out at Petrovskoï (perhaps the very one Griois and Jumilhac had occupied) sees standing up among the smouldering ruins. 'A fine monument of modern construction and grandiose, it was full of Russian wounded, whom it had saved'.

Struggling with overall and indeed overwhelming administrative problems, meanwhile, is the former French consul-general at Petersburg, de Lesseps.[11] Since having to beg a bit of bread for himself from the 20-year-old Breton War Commissary *Bellot de Kergorre*[12] at the Mojaisk hospitals, this 'honest man' whom Napoleon had dismissed for sending in reports that didn't agree with his preconceptions, has covered the 70 miles to Moscow, and immediately on arrival, 'despite his urgent request to be excused all duties,' has been appointed Intendant, i.e., civil governor. De Lesseps hasn't 'forgotten the thirty years of hospitality he'd been met with in Russia'; and his manner of carrying out the task so arbitrarily imposed on him stirs both Caulaincourt's and Méneval's admiration:

> 'This excellent man was doing all he could to put a stop to many evils, among them the issue of false paper money,[13] the theft of many small sums, as well as the destruction of such archives as had been saved from the fire. He collected, sheltered, nourished and in fact saved quite a number of unfortunate men, women and children whose houses had burned down and who were straying about like ghosts amidst the ruins.'

Many are members of the French colony – for instance the French troupe of actors who, after the Peace of Tilsit in 1807, had settled in Moscow under the Tsar's protection. Its director is one of the notable foreigners who'd been forcibly evacuated by Rostopchin. But most of the troupe had stayed behind. Thanks to Caulaincourt's protection one of them, *Louise de Fusil*, a most resourceful woman of 32, has found shelter in an outbuilding of Prince Galitzin's palace, near the Kremlin. Meanwhile Lieutenant *Paul de Bourgoing*'s kindly and drily humorous General Delaborde, whose division of the Young Guard hadn't been at Borodino and only arrived at Moscow on 14 September, is providing board and lodging for two others, Mesdames Anthony and André, who have also lost everything.

Among Russian 'ghosts' is Count Zagriasski, the Tsar's former Grand Equerry. Like Yakovlev, he'd lingered in Moscow, unable to tear himself away from his palace 'on which he'd lavished a lifetime of care' – only to see it go up in flames. Together with many other homeless and ruined individuals, Caulaincourt kindly takes his ex-opposite number under his wing.

A few – but very few – Russians are allowing themselves to be co-opted into de Lesseps' civil administration.[14] Césare de Laugier hears how

'the town has been divided up into twenty districts, and 50,000 roubles in copper have been placed at the disposition of the syndics to provide speedy help for the indigent. There's only one snag. The difficulty of carrying so much small change about, heavy as it is, renders the execution of this generous action almost impossible.'

While ever fresh fires are breaking out, now here, now there, what's left of the city is being looted, but now not so much for personal consumption as for sale or barter. Even the Kremlin isn't being spared. Though there are Grenadier and Chasseur sentries stationed in its triple vaulted gateway,

'infantrymen were going in, looking for the provisions of every kind it contained in such abundance. But on coming out from the interior courtyard each has to pay 5 frs. to the grenadiers or else abandon his booty – in which case he's treated as scum, stripped, and driven away. They may deny it, these grenadiers who were held up to us as models of courage and honour, but the whole army will certify it for a fact. Marshal Lefèbvre issued an order on the subject and covered the footguards with the most sanguinary reproaches.'

Everywhere markets have sprung up. Not the city's regular ones – no Muscovite is allowing himself to be enticed back into the city by Napoleon's decree. But purely military ones. Of these the great square outside the Kremlin is the scene of only one among many. Thirion accuses the men of the Guard, above all, of this mercantile behaviour, 'so that the army thereafter called them the merchants or Jews of Moscow'. True, old Marshal Lefèbvre, commander of the Guard infantry, has issued the strictest orders. No Russian is to be allowed into the Kremlin. Any found trying to get in is to be shot out of hand. Patrols shall be on the alert day and night at all points, from one end of the Kremlin to the other. And no guardsman is to be allowed to go out without his captain's permission, 'such leave only to be given very rarely.' The Guard, however, always unruly, pays little heed. Newly fledged Sous-lieutenant *Jean-Roch Coignet* sees its rank and file 'roving through the town like wild beasts in a charnel house, seeing to do some stroke of business'.

Who should know better? Coignet's one of them himself. But then, alas, just as he's 'found' a gorgeous Siberian sable fur, he has the misfortune to be detailed off from the Emperor's 'smaller' staff – the only one that's always in attendance – to assist a staff colonel, 'a hard man with a nasty face', who's been entrusted with evacuating corpses from Larrey's two hospitals; but is far more interested in enriching himself:

'We were lodged with an old princess, all four of us with our horses and servants. The colonel alone had three to himself, and he knew how to use them. He sent us into the hospitals to get the sick evacuated. Himself never! He stayed behind to do business. In the evenings he left with his servants, equipped with candles. He knew that the pictures in the churches are relief-work on a silver plate. He had them taken off their hooks to take their silver leaf, put all the saints – male and female – into the melting pot and made ingots of them. He sold his thefts to Jews for bank notes.'

One evening the odious staff colonel shows Lieutenant Coignet his *emplettes* ('little purchases'), and Coignet's so

'imprudent as to show him mine. He insisted I exchange it for a Siberian fox. Mine was sable, but I had to give way. I was afraid of his vengeance. He was so barbarous as to strip me of it to sell it for 3,000 frs to Prince [sic] Murat. This looter of churches dishonoured the name of Frenchman.'

Coignet claims that he and his comrades protected women and children against looters.

Everyone knows that winter's coming daily closer. And anyone who, like Coignet, had been in Poland in 1807 has some inkling of what that will mean. Among the officers, notably, who can afford to pay to get themselves good furs. Russia's famous furs are in high demand. Peyrusse of the Imperial Treasury, however – whether because he's working so very hard or spending so much time worming himself into Grand Marshal Duroc's and Secretary Méneval's good books with a view to his imagined promotion – is finding it singularly hard to find one that's to his taste. Though coffee, tea and sugar abound, he writes home to his friend André ('the men have all taken to drinking sugared water') 'few furs have been found. One sees an immense quantity of ordinary fox. Every ranker has one. But nothing really pretty or rare.'

Well, not quite. In the end he buys himself 'a black astrakhan, which doesn't leave hairs on coats' and three cashmere shawls:

'Two of them are pretty, the man who'd taken them didn't want to sell. The third had been cut in two and shared between two soldiers to wrap stockfish and had cost 40 frs. I bought it off Roustam, the Emperor's valet [sic] for 250 frs.'

If the officers are concerned to get themselves furs, the rankers, who, knowing themselves to be mere cannon fodder, usually live fecklessly *au jour le jour* and jettison or destroy anything they haven't any immediate use for, seem mainly to be dreaming of instant wealth:

'Whilst only few of us thought of providing ourselves with warm clothes and furs against the coming winter, many laded themselves down with a mass of useless things.'

Not so *J. L. Henckens*, NCO and acting lieutenant in the 6th Chasseurs à Cheval, a regiment which has lost *all* its commissioned officers, either killed, wounded or unhorsed at Borodino. Born at Eygelshoven, a few miles from Aix-la-Chapelle, Henckens regards himself as 'almost a Fleming' and besides his native German and French has taught himself to speak Italian – his regiment had long been stationed in northern Italy – and also has a smattering of Polish and Russian. Completely indispensable to Squadron Commander de Feuillebois, commanding the 6th Chasseurs ever since its well-liked Colonel Ledard had died in Henckens' arms of three mortal wounds in the Great Redoubt,[15] Henckens is obviously extremely competent and experienced. When the fire had forced Napoleon out of the Kremlin, each of Grouchy's light cavalry regiments out at Petrovskoï had been ordered to send a party of fifty men and NCOs into town, as an escort for Murat. Instead, Henckens' party, when they'd got there, had been detailed off to protect what he calls 'the Great Theatre', where they'd made the acquaintance of some actors of the French troupe. Saving the surrounding quarter from the flames and sending any soldiers they found straying about in town back to their units, some of Henckens' chasseurs had brought him various useful or valuable objects, saved from the flames –

'one, for instance, a sackful of gold watches. Another had brought me a load of shawls in very striking colours he'd taken off an infantryman who was sent back to his regiment outside the town and asked me to be allowed to carry off his booty to make a shelter for himself at his bivouac. I'd deposited the shawls in the theatre, where the actors told me they were cashmeres of great value.'

One of his patrols, Henckens goes on, had come across a store of furs, and one of his chasseurs had asked him:

"Lieutenant, I've a lot of little packets of furs I've put in a forage bag. What am I to do with those things?"

Feeling the packets, Henckens had decided the furs would come in very handy against the cold, which cannot be very far off. Stuffing as many as he reasonably could into his pistol holsters and coat, he'd taken them back to the regiment to show to Feuillebois and ask his advice. Feuillebois, promotes him acting adjutant-major. Feels the furs. And tells him:

"As far as I can tell, it's the finest petit gris, the rarest and most precious I've ever seen."

One of the chasseurs, a tailor by profession, is set to work to turn them into waistcoats; 'according to his calculations he could make each of us at least two'. And those that are left over he can keep for himself. Henckens and his acting CO themselves sit down and help him: 'though our talents as tailors were limited to sewing on a button or making small repairs, everything went swimmingly.'

Petits-gris are in specially high demand. Engineer-Colonel Serran's travelling companion on his long journey from Spain, a Captain Cornault, also provisions himself 'like a Tartar' with fifty of them. And General Delaborde's ADC and interpreter, Paul de Bourgoing, 'with youthful light-headedness and lack of foresight', provides himself

> 'not with the amplest and warmest fur, but the one which seemed to me most elegant in shape and colour. Instead of one of the excellent black bear pelts, or wild or white wolfskins, I bought a very pretty Polish-style coat in dark blue cloth, richly adorned with silken fringes and lined with black astrakhan. At that moment I thought much more of my own pleasure, walking about in my general's suite with an elegant garment in the presence of Mesdames Anthony and André than of arming myself against icy winds.'

But when it comes to choosing a fur for his little servant Victor, the Parisian guttersnipe and would-be drummer boy whom he 'out of kindness' has brought with him on the campaign, he wisely buys him a *witchoura* – a heavy Russian wolfskin overcoat. Also a horse. To replace his own worn-out mare, Paul de Bourgoing buys from his brother, one of Ney's ADC's, a mount which had belonged to a Captain du Breuil, killed by a roundshot at Borodino while galloping after his marshal along the flank of the Württemberg columns. No one but the most feckless is unaware of the threat posed by the Russian winter. Napoleon himself orders Lefèbvre to get fur waistcoats for the Guard to wear under their greatcoats; and Ney is collecting sheepskins. One of his regimental officers, *Guillaume Bonnet*, newly promoted major in the 18th Line – still bivouacked out on the plain – buys himself a fox fur of more modest value than – but equal use to Peyrusse's astrakhan. Only 'by dint of much effort and repeated threats' does von Muraldt, out at the Petrovskoï camp, get *his* servant, 'who was going into town every day, to get me a good fur-lined overcoat'.

For there are much more fascinating objects freely to be had but of much more dubious value. One day, von Muraldt goes on:

> 'some of our people forced their way into a vault where they found a mass of stamped lead plates – what they were intended for I don't know – which they dragged out to our bivouac in the belief that they were silver.'

Colonel Griois' gunners too, still encamped like Muraldt's Bavarian light horse out at Petrovskoï, discover,

> 'a considerable mass of metal plates, some of them weighing up to 10 pounds. As far as I could see they were nothing but an alloy of tin and zinc. But they had the colour and brilliance of silver, and had been taken, so it was said, from the stores of the Mint. Everyone was loading himself down with them, by preference over everything else.'[16]

Since these plates bear an official stamp, Muraldt finds it's

'almost impossible to convince the men they're not silver. They filled
their kit bags with them and, heavy though they were, loaded them on
their emaciated horses. Only by the strictest measures could we pre-
vail on them to let them be or throw them away.'

Everywhere objects of luxury make a strange contrast with the general lack,
steadily becoming more noticeable, of the most indispensable foodstuffs:

'It wasn't rare to see soldiers who had no shoes, in tatters, seated amidst
bales of rich merchandise, or covered in the most expensive shawls,
precious furs and vestments embroidered with gold or pearls. Or else
neglecting the masses of tea, coffee and sugar, preferring to them a bit
of black bread, a slice of horsemeat and some drops of muddy water.'

Everywhere the precious and semi-precious objects Lieutenant Brandt had
seen dragged out to his bivouac outside the Kazan Gate are being 'bought
back for a song by those ignoble junk merchants, mostly Jews, who on such
occasions seem to rise up out of the ground'. Although as far as Peyrusse
can see there's not a single shop open in the whole town, in the markets,
'where most of the rag-and-bone men are guardsmen or the army's
employees', Le Roy and his friend Jacquet find

'gold, silver, diamonds, in a word all kinds of expensive luxury items.
One gold coin was being bought at twice its value. As for the pearls,
diamonds and brilliants, we were all much more on our guard. We
knew from experience that Russians love false diamonds. Beside us I
saw five silver ingots weighing about 10 pounds sell for 300 frs. A few
days later these ingots had fallen to twelve francs apiece, only to be
abandoned later on on the highway like petty cash.'

Can it be they're only zinc and tin alloy? Le Roy buys what appear to be
packets of Turkish tobacco, only to find they actually contain tea, admittedly 'enough for the rest of the campaign'. And on the three or four occasions when Griois comes back into town to 'lay in a stock of victuals of every
kind', though he nowhere sees

'a single inhabitant, the streets which the fire still hadn't reached
looked like a veritable fair, all of whose participants, merchants and
purchasers, were military men. They'd turned merchant. It was to
them officers of every rank came to provision themselves.'

All of which is very bad indeed for discipline. The 26-year-old violin-play-
ing Captain Count *M-H. de Lignières*[17] of the lst Battalion of the Foot Chasseurs of the Old Guard, disapproves intensely; but converts his 'savings', he
too, into Treasury bonds and stuffs them 'inside the lining of my waistcoat,
the gold cash in my belt'.[18]

At the Niemen the Grand Army had started out with a host of officers' carriages unprecedented in any previous campaign. Coming across 'some shops

which contained a great number of carriages which were at the disposal of anyone who fancied them', it has seemed to Griois that the moment has come to replace the light travelling carriage that's brought him all the way from his beloved Verona and which by now is in rather poor shape:

'Several generals and some of my own comrades had helped themselves to these carriages, to replace their own, rendered more or less unserviceable by the road. I went where I was told to, and merely had to choose from among some one hundred new carriages, of the greatest elegance. I took one of the lightest calèches, and as it was already getting late I had it taken to the town house occupied by General d'Anthouard [commander of IV Corps' artillery]. Next day I came back to get it and have it driven to my cantonment. But during the night the fire had made enormous progress and forced d'Anthouard to quit his lodging. My carriage wasn't there any longer. It had been taken away or burnt. I was happy to find my own again, which I'd abandoned the day before.'

Although M. l'Abbé Surugué of the French colony's church of St Louis is astounded and shocked to discover that his post-revolutionary compatriots haven't a single padre in their ranks,[18] he's sure the Frenchmen aren't the worst robbers. And another elderly Muscovite of German extraction, who'd imbibed a hatred for the French with his mother's milk at the time of the Seven Years War, agrees that the damage the Frenchmen are doing isn't usually of the senseless kind:

'Even in the midst of their excesses their courtesy showed through, though not always. While Württembergers and Poles behave like vandals, the French only rob to satisfy life's necessities. The Bavarians leave nothing behind them.'

Unfortunately another French resident, the Chevalier d'Ysarn, gives the lie to these patriotic generalizations. He'd been riding in his carriage toward the Kazan Gate when some French cavalry troopers had forced him to dismount, exchanged his elegant boots for their own route-worn ones, and told him to count himself lucky, as an *émigré*, not to have fared still worse.

Not all the looting is private. Napoleon has plans of his own. 'Guard sappers were being used to demolish the cross of the church of the Kremlin, which was in silver and gold. All was melted down into ingots, a prodigious quantity of silverware, silver and gold.' The cross itself, which orthodox Russians regard as particularly sacred, is to be taken back to Paris to embellish the dome of the Invalides.

'Many generals, officers of all ranks, were buying silver ingots or silverware, jewels and precious stones for a song from the soldiers and putting them in their trunks, the generals in their wagons.'

But at IHQ, where Peyrusse is always hard at work under his chief, General Count Daru,

'all this has given us a very wide berth. I'm clinging to M. Daru who welcomes me very well and whom I, in a moment of famine, have made accept twelve bottles of very good quality Burgundy. He and I paid all the wounded on the battlefield, etc. He's been able to see how active I am. But he has no places at his disposition.'

All Peyrusse is concerned with is to get hold of a few luxuries for the wife of his friend André, with whom he has plans to set up a nice little apartment in Paris.

Bread may be becoming scarce. But wines are abundant. In the house of his aged princess, Coignet and his colleagues have access to

'thousands of bottles of Bordeaux, Champagne wines and Demerara sugar. Every evening the old princess made us take away four bottles of good wine and sugar (the cellars were full of barrels). She often came to visit us. So her house was respected. She spoke good French.'

'We're not dying of hunger, as one might expect,' Césare de Laugier writes in his diary amidst the blackened ruins of the Petersburg district, on 29 September. 'We're swimming, so to speak in abundance, though – let me say in passing – without owing it to the Administration, but to our own lucky discoveries.' And von Muraldt agrees:

'Though there was wine, sugar, coffee, etc., in superfluity, we were still suffering from a lack of bread, meat and fodder for our horses.'

And already the Guardia d'Onore's adjutant-major is seeing 'detachments made up of various arms' having to be sent out to bring back foodstuffs and forage 'even to a distance of twelve miles.'

Meanwhile many officers, as well no doubt as inarticulate rankers, are all too aware that, peace or no peace (and as yet there's no sign of any), they've a very long way to go to get back to the Niemen; still further to Germany, France, Italy or Spain.

CHAPTER 4

A DISCONSOLATE ADVANCE GUARD

Kutusov fools Murat – 'we're beginning to suffer from the cold' – disastrous affair at Malo-Wiazma – redispositions – the Red Lancers lose a troop – 'they buy prisoners from the Cossacks to put them to death' – Lahoussaye's grotesque incompetence – Griois' billet at Winkovo

Meanwhile, day after day, Murat's cavalry, sometimes held up by Cossacks, sometimes not, has been pushing on eastwards down the Ryazan road through
'magnificent countryside, covered in châteaux and villages. Châteaux of remarkable elegance. We come across a few peasants, but many have armed themselves and joined the Russians.'
All the blithe talk of Russian war-weariness is turning out to have been illusory. The Cossacks dodging about ahead of Maurice Tascher's chasseur regiment seem to be anything but demoralized. And on 21 September he notes in his diary: 'It seems the Russian army has taken another route.'
So it has.
That day, leaving two regiments of Cossacks as a cavalry screen to lure the French on as far as possible down the Ryazan road, Kutusov has suddenly switched his main force southwards toward the charming little town of Pakra – situated athwart the River Pakra, its name means 'red', but also 'beautiful'. Justly assessing the strategic situation, Kutusov – in a movement which would have been impossible if Murat had done as Napoleon had recommended when approaching Moscow and skirted the city to the south – has decided to place the Russian army between Napoleon and Russia's two greatest arms factories, at Kaluga and Tula. He'll not only have the rich plains of the Ukraine at his rear but from the whole of southern and eastern Russia also be able to absorb and train the recruits who will soon be pouring in.
A whole day passes in futile pursuits before Sébastiani tumbles to the enemy's manoeuvre; and Murat, crossing the River Moscova on the Kolomna road, again enters into a brief truce. All this means that next day (23 September) Tascher's chasseurs have to make a flank movement towards Podolsk to catch up.

Meanwhile, 30 miles to the west of Moscow, something utterly shocking has occurred.
Napoleon had spent the last night before reaching Moscow in Prince Galitzin's sumptuous country palace at Malo-Wiazma. On the Smolensk

highway, it had been 'the first château really worth the name we'd seen in Russia' – though all its furnishings, Captain Count V. E. B Castellane had been distressed to see, had as usual been smashed up by the advance guard. Since then Malo-Wiazma has been occupied by a squadron of the prestigious Dragoons of the Guard, an élite regiment if ever there were one. Since they're 'daily being bothered by numerous pulks of Cossacks', on 22 September Lieutenant-Colonel Schuurmann, commanding a battalion of the 33rd Line, a regiment largely consisting of Dutchmen whose other battalion had remained in and around Minsk, hundreds of miles to the rear, is

> 'ordered with some fractions of his battalion and those [sailors] of the Danube and Hesse-Darmstadt, together some 300 men strong, and with 200 dragoons, to make a reconnaissance in the enemy's direction. The detachment as a whole, however, was commanded by Colonel Marthod of the Guard. The dragoons formed the advance guard, and the infantry followed in column.'

After a couple of hours this flying column is just reaching a vast forest when pistol shots are heard in the distance. And the column debouches against the enemy:

> 'The latter was disposed in a semicircle in a plain, its two wings supported by the forest. It consisted wholly of cavalry – as far as could be assessed at a distance, a force of some 4,000 men. Reaching the plain, our troops took up their positions. The cavalry drew up in line of battle on the highest point in the terrain. Our lieutenant-colonel received orders to place himself with the infantry about 100 paces to its rear. Meanwhile our skirmishers opened fire in order to make themselves masters of the village situated in front of them. Realizing that the happy outcome of the affair depended on capturing this village, Schuurmann marched for this point at the pas de charge [180 paces a minute] and drove out the enemy that was there.'

While all this is happening, Colonel Marthod and his dragoons have

> 'made a movement to the front and charged the Russians' left wing. Seeing it, their centre and left wing flung themselves forward at a prolonged gallop, cut off the dragoons' retreat, and in a twinkling of an eye overthrew everything in their path. Meanwhile our infantry had re-emerged from the village, if possible to support the dragoons. But at that moment it was no longer feasible. Within a few instants all [but a few of] the dragoons were sabred. When Lieutenant-Colonel Schuurmann was again more or less in the middle of the plain, all the enemy cavalry, which had finished off the dragoons, made a charge against his men. But the latter, having formed square, were calmly awaiting it.'

No fewer than six charges are made against the square, but each is driven off. In the intervals between them Schuurmann marches his square off the plain to master the wood he must retreat through. Some of the Russian horsemen have dismounted and are firing their carbines at the square, killing or wounding a number of Schuurmann's men. At the same time the Russians have

'placed two of their squadrons in front of the wood to prevent our infantry from getting into it, and furthermore brought up into the gap some artillery, which immediately began firing at the square. The lieutenant-colonel, knowing all too well he was irremediably lost if didn't make himself master of the wood, decided to attack the two squadrons at bayonet point. This movement was carried out so energetically that our men completely routed the Russians and seized the wood, after which they were able to operate their retreat to Galitzin's château.'

The day, Schuurmann will tell the Dutch major *Henri-Pierre Everts* when the 33rd's two battalions are reunited later on, had cost him 120 of his 300 men, and two officers:

'The Dragoons of the Guard were even worse treated. Very few came back, and they only owed their safety to their horses' swiftness. Colonel Marthod, too, was gravely wounded and fell into the enemy's hands.'[1]

In the Kremlin the episode comes as a terrible shock. Kutusov had sent out all his cavalry, and with odds of 20 to one it had celebrated its biggest success. Caulaincourt sees how

'this slight reverse irritated the Emperor as much as the loss of a battle. It made more impression than the loss of 50 generals made hors de combat at Borodino.'

As for the 33rd, it's the regiment which has already been so outraged by Davout's atrocious treatment of it at Minsk in August, when in a fit of fury he'd forced it to march past with inverted muskets for having left behind so many stragglers.[2] And though General Verdun, the commandant at Malo-Wiazma, 'paid warm homage to our troops' conduct', the wretched Schuurmann is so gravely demoralized when he sends in his report on the affair to Berthier that he doesn't even 'dare ask for anything to the profit of anyone in the regiment, no matter how well it had behaved'.

Perhaps they wouldn't have got anything anyway?

The Malo-Wiazma episode, it seems, strikes the whole army as in some way symptomatic.

Immediately orders are given for all the cavalry and other outposts around Moscow to be reinforced. Broussier's division of IV Corps and the

three Bavarian chevauleger regiments leave Petrovskoï and move back to a
position on the Smolensk highway, some three hours from the city. Ney too
has to send units to reinforce the Malo-Wiazma position, among them the
18th Line.

Troops are also sent south of the city to block the Kaluga road which
Napoleon had wanted Murat to occupy the day before they'd got to
Moscow, but which for some reason he hadn't. In steadily falling rain two
of Davout's infantry divisions are sent to contain the enemy and bivouac
beyond the forest. One of these is Friedrichs', comprising the 85th Line.
On 21 September Major Le Roy had commanded a marauding excursion
to the west of the city.[3] That day the regiment, marching south along the
Kaluga road, had had a serious brush with Cossack regulars, who'd stabbed
twelve of Le Roy's men with their lances. It might have turned into a large-
scale affray if the Russians, 'several cavalry regiments and Cossacks, supported by two guns', hadn't retired. Obviously it had only been a
reconnaissance in force. Next day, after he has rejoined the regiment in its
bivouac behind a wood, his men occupy

'a big, rich abbey, shaped like a citadel. We stayed there. The abbey
was pillaged and several of our rankers carried off rare and curious
objects.'

On 26/27 September they go on to occupy a château where Le Roy sees
'for the first time, boxed apple and pear trees already shut up in the
orangerie, for fear of the winter'. On the 29th they occupy a large village
further along the Kaluga road: 'Never in my life have I seen a muddier
place, nor wetter mud. We were in it up to the middle of our legs, in the
middle of the road, impossible to walk along the roadsides.' And there they
stay for four days, until it pleases someone to extricate them from the mud.
Then they'd marched hither and thither, to left, to right, to close up on the
advance guard, but without seeing any enemy. 'Food was becoming more
and more rare.'

The Red Lancers, too, had had to leave their comfortable quarters in
'the large village of Troïlskoïe-Galantschiwo' where they'd confidently
been supposing peace must soon follow, 'as on the morrow of Austerlitz,
Friedland and Wagram'. On 23 September, joining up with their Polish colleagues, cantoned in a nearby village and 'circumventing the many veg-
etable gardens the town was fringed with on its south side,' they'd made for
Podolsk, which they'd also found abandoned by its inhabitants. 'Thus
ended, for us, our stay at Moscow, of which everyone had expected so
much.'

Such postings, as Le Roy has already found out, are no sinecure. Two
days later the imprudent Lieutenant Doyen lets Colbert's leading troop be
inveigled into an ambush by 'too ardently pursuing a few enemy scouts' at

the entry to a village. A second troop, sent to its assistance, is also within an ace of being overwhelmed. Surrounded on all sides, it doesn't lose its head. In the nick of time, just as the second rank faces about – a critical moment – Dumonceau's troop turns up on the scene:

'Our unexpected appearance made the enemy relinquish his grip and he withdrew without waiting for our charge, yet continued to harass us to the point where the whole regiment had to be engaged in incessant skirmishes lasting more than an hour, without any ground being gained or lost.'

Suddenly the Russians draw off. Tyskiewicz's brigade of Polish chasseurs, sent by Murat to meet the Guard Lancers, has come up in their rear. But the Red Lancers' entire advance troop has been lost. It's the second such loss during the campaign.[4] Even so, Colbert is 'pleased he'd had a chance to appreciate his regiment's valour and was so good as loudly to express the justice due to it'. Not that General Colbert is a man easily pleased. Next day Dumonceau, too, is reprimanded – not for the first time during the campaign. This time it's for too eagerly following up yet another Cossack force, also withdrawing in front of them.

In a cold rain which will continue falling for eleven days and nights, Murat's force advances slowly south-westwards, with Poniatowski's I Corps marching in parallel a few miles away to the west. Tascher's notebook:

'27 *September:* beyond Podolsk, snow. We're beginning to suffer from the cold. *28 September:* famine. Lack of bread and forage. *29 September:* approaching the village of Winkovo.'

There Tascher's chasseurs run into Russian infantry and have to retire behind a ravine, while Poniatowski's guns, still somewhere to the right, seem also to be heavily engaged.

By now, also out on Murat's right flank, Griois and the horse batteries of (Grouchy's) 3rd Cavalry Corps are here too. While still attached to the Army of Italy in the plain north of Moscow, he'd 'changed cantonments almost daily, but always on the Petersburg road and about twelve miles from Moscow,' the last one being in a superb château. But then, in the evening of 21 September, he'd been ordered to move south 'several leagues along the Kaluga road'. Leaving his rather worn-out carriage and his effects – 'almost all I owned' – with his servant in Moscow, he and his friend Jumilhac, 3rd Cavalry Corps' chief-of-staff, hadn't omitted to pay their respects to Grouchy 'who still hadn't entirely recovered from his wound'. The popular cavalry commander had entertained them to

'a very good dinner. At about 10 p.m. we'd got on our horses again, crossed the town by the light of the fire which was still going on, albeit less violently for lack of nourishment, and having marched for several hours halted in an abandoned hamlet until the morrow, when we rejoined our corps, which I didn't leave again.'

Grouchy's good dinner had been the last either Griois or Jumilhac will enjoy for some time; for they're in for a period of 'long and harsh abstinence' they'll not soon forget. Now, in that unusually fierce fight of 29 September,[5] the Russians have occupied a very strong position, and Griois is aiming all his guns at the same point and they're firing as fast and hard as they can when

'Murat came and placed himself in the middle of my batteries and from there examined the Russians' movements. At that moment someone brought him a dispatch. He read it and, without getting off his horse, wrote a reply on one of his tablets, with the same sangfroid as if he'd been inside his tent. Yet at that moment a rain of roundshot, shells and grape was falling on us and causing his horse to swerve and make leaps and jumps which he didn't even notice. I forgot the peril to admire the King's perfect impassiveness and martial bearing, brought out even more by his opulent and bizarre accoutrements.'

Murat may fail utterly to look after his cavalry on the march, but Griois, like everyone else, is full of admiration for him on the battlefield:

'Never did ADCs or orderly officers bringing him orders or information in battle have any difficulty in finding him. They made for the point where the fighting was going on and on the side where the attack seemed liveliest. They were sure to find him there. It was the *beau idéal* of courage.'

At Russian headquarters, hardly five miles away to the south, there's an Englishman of a very different stamp. Nursing a profound scorn and hatred for 'Bonaparte' and all his works, he desires nothing more or less than his and the Grand Army's total annihilation. General *Sir Robert Wilson* is the British government's special envoy and ever-critical liaison officer at Kutusov's headquarters. Passing through Petersburg with his aide, the young Lord Tyrconnel, he – as the sly and aged Kutusov very well knows – has made good personal contacts with the Tsar, whom he doesn't hesitate to inform of what's gong on at the front. Wilson heartily dislikes the one-eyed, slothful, cunning and aged Kutusov almost as much as the Tsar does. He suspects him, rightly, of having only Russian, not British, interests at heart.[6] Like the Tsar, 'the English general' (as he always calls himself – like Caesar, Wilson always refers to himself in the third person) is determined to scotch any dealings with the enemy – the more so as he clearly sees Murat's troops are in an ever more parlous condition. 'Every day since I've been here,' he writes at the end of September, 'prisoners in parties of 50, and even of 100, have been brought in, chiefly wounded. During the five days we remained at Krasnoi Pakra, 1,342 were delivered to the commandant at headquarters. Of course many more are killed, for such is the inveteracy [implacability] of the peasants that they buy prisoners off the Cossacks for several roubles to put them to death. Two guns have been taken by the peasants; vast quantities of baggage, etc., both going to and from Moscow; much melted silver, which I myself have seen:'

Evidently he's met some dragoons of the Guard, captured at Malo-Wiazma, whom he calls simply

'the guards – of whom two [sic] squadrons were taken. [They] told me that they had been obliged to blow up a convoy of 60 powder wagons, rather than suffer them to be made a prize. In brief, the Spanish guerrilla warfare never was more successful, and certainly was not so formidable to the enemy. The prisoners, not French, but foreigners, all hold one language: they all describe themselves as victims to an insatiable ambition and say that privations of every kind have been the prelude to their loss of liberty.'

On 28 September Wilson, who seems to take such Russian reports at face-value, rides out

'to the advanced posts, which remained on the river Pakra. The enemy had lodged themselves opposite, but without any disposition to inconvenience our parties. Five hundred Frenchmen have been taken by the Cossacks as the enemy's column retrograded from the Kolomna road; and yesterday 14 carts, two of which contained gold and silver to the amount of 15,000 ducats, were taken on the Podolsk road.'

Among the Cossacks' captives is a General Ferrier and his two ADCs. Murat tries to get them exchanged; but the offer is turned down. 'The position of the mutual outposts,' Wilson continues, on 1 October, a day when Tascher writes in his diary 'the Cossacks are carrying off a lot of foragers, servants and baggage,'

'was the most extraordinary I had ever seen in war, for they were so interwoven as to present fronts on all points of the compass, and I do not think I ever got so close to an enemy's corps for the purpose of reconnoitring it as I did to Prince Poniatowski's. It was almost the same thing as being in his camp. At night the Cossacks attacked and killed 200 Cuirassiers on a foraging party, and made 85 prisoners.'

By now Tascher's chasseur regiment is reduced to only four troops, his own company to fourteen men. And the cold is becoming 'rigorous'.

Grouchy, one of Napoleon's best cavalry leaders, is still in Moscow, recuperating from his wound. At Borodino both he and Griois, commanding his artillery, had suffered severe contusions from bits of spent grape – Griois, less severely, in the small of his back. Though this had been very painful – his belt had deadened the shock – Griois hadn't been disabled. But the bit that had hit Grouchy – his 23rd wound – had hit him in the chest, wounding him so severely that he'd had to hand over 3rd Cavalry Corps to his senior divisional commander, General Lahoussaye.

While Grouchy is generally seen as 'brave, prudent, enjoying the confidence of his troops', Lahoussaye is one of those brave but bumbling military men who have the trick of infallibly doing the wrong thing in all circumstances. New to the corps, he's certainly anything but prudent. Indeed the reputation has preceded him of being a complete ass. Some of his officers regard him as a fraud. And no one has any confidence in him. Just now 3rd Cavalry Corps, out there on Murat's right, 'for the ten or twelve days when we were acting in isolation, often without any communication with Murat', is floundering about under its new commander's grotesquely incompetent leadership.

'We did nothing but make marches and counter-marches with no reasonable goal to them and no other result than to put the horses 'on their teeth' and often expose ourselves to shameful scuffles.'

One day, Griois goes on, waxing more and more indignant,

'after we'd been pushed back from position to position, some Cossack pulks which had some guns and were trying to hold up our march, General Lahoussaye, more over-excited than usual, gallops ahead of the tirailleurs and orders the cavalry riding in column on either side of the road and my artillery to follow his movement. Hardly have we reached the top of a hill which dominates the road than we see, a hundred yards or so away, considerable lines of cavalry which, supported by infantry and artillery, seemed to be waiting for us.'

Now the only remedy for such an unreconnoitred advance lies in putting a good face on it:

'Unfortunately the general had lost his feeble head and at the sight of these forces he hadn't expected to run into, he turned tail as quickly as he'd come: "Retreat, at the gallop!" he shouted, giving the example; and ordered my artillery to do the same. In vain I pointed out to him it was the infallible way to lose it, and that it would be much better to retire by echelons, successively taking up position. He wouldn't listen, and went on yelling "At the gallop!" I took care not to carry out his order, and General of Brigade Watier, who was in command of the advance guard's light cavalry, didn't do so either. The dragoon division's good countenance, in line behind us, the fire opened by my guns as we retired from position to position, brought the Russians to a halt and put an end to the combat. We lost quite a lot of hussars and chasseurs in the advance guard platoons, which fell at the first shock, and we were fortunate to get off so cheaply from a scuffle where we could have been crushed.'

Other instances of Lahoussaye's incompetence follow. Having ordered a precipitate retirement down a hill and across a stream, he loses a lot of his baggage train, which promptly takes to flight across the fields. Meanwhile 'without giving any orders, he went from one regiment to another, anxiously asking whether anyone had seen his cook and canteens'. Griois himself is within an ace of being taken prisoner, together with two of his guns, which Lahoussaye has imprudently mingled with his skirmishers and which are suddenly surrounded by a swarm of cavalry:

'On 1 or 2 October we were advancing towards the King of Naples, who was fighting not far away from us. From the liveliness of the firing and the musketry we estimated it to be a hot affair, and our corps' arrival might well decide it to our advantage.'

Everyone urges him to make haste. But Lahousssaye

'remained drawn up in battle order for several hours, close enough to the scene of action for us distinctly to hear the soldiers' shouts and our Poles' hurrahs. Towards evening, however, he decided to plunge into a forest which formed a long defile in front of us. We marched in column along the paved road which passes through the forest, but our movement was becoming pointless. The firing had ceased, we didn't know the outcome, and if it hadn't turned out well for us it had been most dangerous, without infantry, to get ourselves into a defile where the cavalry couldn't act. Night was falling and everyone was feeling amazed that Lahoussaye didn't make us retire, when to our great surprise he ordered us to halt and bivouac for the night. Generals and colonels represented to him that his order was absurd. But he replied drily that his orders must be carried out. General Chastel again insisted on the danger of passing the night in this defile. Then, seeing his observations were useless with such a man, he declared that he took it upon himself not to obey.'

Retiring with his light cavalry division, Chastel leaves Lahoussaye to his 'hardly describable rage, at once risible and insane, at seeing his authority flouted. He became agitated, he lamented, saying since he was taken for an imbecile he didn't wish either to command any more or even be on his horse. Dismounting, he threw away his hat, swearing he'd deal with these mutineers. Meanwhile General Chastel and his troops were on the move. Lahoussaye stayed with the dragoon regiments whose colonels were preparing to follow Chastel. He opted to follow the movement that was flouting his orders and we bivouacked near a little village. The event finally discredited him.'

Another incompetent high-up, strangely enough, both in Castellane's and Griois' opinion, is no lesser a personage than Marshal Bessières, commander of the Guard cavalry.[7] After the Malo-Wiazma affair he'd been ordered to push forward a column in the direction of Podolsk. And for a few days he remains personally on the scene, Griois meanwhile noticing how

'his orders at each moment contradicted each other, I not being able to refrain from pointing it out to him. Most fortunately he left us next day, for there's no doubt I'd have been very much in his bad books, and being the weaker, would infallibly have become his victim.'

Though the two Guard lancer regiments feel Bessières' eye upon them and redouble their discipline, they're shocked to be told to

'suppress all trumpet calls and observe a deep silence in the mornings, so as not to disturb the marshal's sleep. These precautions seemed strange to us. We couldn't conceive that such a chief as the Duke [of Istria], so famous for his military exigencies, could need to be so mollycoddled, while we were still subjected to the dawn regime before daybreak. So we were inclined to ascribe it to an act of courtesy on our general's part.'

Colbert's Lancer Brigade[8] hadn't taken part in the fights of 27 and 29 September near Pakra, near though it had been to 3rd Cavalry Corps, which had. To Dumonceau's regret,

'our brigade didn't budge and from 26 to 30 September we profited from this to form a convoy of wounded and crippled men, who were sent back to Moscow by the direct route we'd just reached.'

Pakra, when the Russians' withdrawal and the reconstruction of bridges over its two rivers enable the Lancer Brigade to reach it at Murat's heels, turns out to justify its name:

'The river flowed gracefully through a verdant valley, at the foot of steep and wooded heights, crowned by a redoubt of considerable appearance. This valley's picturesque aspect and the banks running along the other side were further embellished by the village of Gorki, flanking the river and forming, for once, a group of pretty dwellings, made to look like English cottages, surrounded by greenery and flowers.'

Advancing again, Dumonceau realizes how inadequate Murat's force really is to stand up to the entire Russian army:

'The 1st, 2nd and 4th Cavalry Corps were all no little enfeebled in comparison with their original strength. There was all too little infantry to oppose the entire Russian army.'

But Kutusov has his plan. Dictated neither by demoralization nor enfeeblement, it's to fall back on to an entrenched position in front of the village of Tarutino.[9] On 4 October, pushing on through woods, the light cavalry of Murat's advance guard are 'totally routed', for lack of infantry to support them, and lose about 100 men. Later that day they run into a long line of Russian artillery, supported by Cossacks and any amount of regular cavalry. Wilson:

'The cannonade recommenced about noon, and the French cavalry fell into a Cossack ambuscade – 500 were killed and 180 made prisoners. It was a very gallant affair, most ably conducted.'

And Tascher: 'Our guns retire for lack of ammunition; the lines of cuirassiers advance. All the regiments reduced to 4, 3 or 2 troops; my company has 5 chasseurs. The Russians are burning [villages and crops] again.'

It must be in the midst of this affair that Captain *Victor Dupuy* of the 7th Hussars returns delighted to his own regiment. For many weeks now he's been serving as ADC to his brigade general Jacquinot. But only yesterday he'd been summoned to the 7th Hussars' regimental headquarters, to receive his commission as chef d'escadron. It's under appropriate but utterly exceptional circumstances he's confirmed in his command:

'We were advancing. The enemy soon put in an appearance and put up a more serious resistance than usual. He was supported by a numerous artillery, which inflicted some losses on us. At the moment when it was playing most strongly, Colonel Eulner had me formally recognized in my new rank in front of the regiment, drawn up in line of battle. Never was a reception accompanied by such noisy music! The colonel could hardly make himself heard! For the rest, I was glad to see the end of the ceremony. It would have been cruel to get a cannonball in one's back while it was going on.'

But Bruyères' once magnificent light cavalry division – which had fought at Borodino with barely 1,000 troopers, and which the 7th Hussars belong to – is now down to a mere 400 horses. Yet it has to chase the Russians off the plain beyond a deep ravine. That night it's Dupuy's business to place the outposts and liaise to his left with Sébastiani's light cavalry division – it too, once 3,500 strong, but down to a 'few hundred'. The night's so dark he doesn't manage it.

On a slope down to a lake lies the village of Winkovo. That night Griois and Jumilhac settle in among its ruined timber cottages, 'the first we found vacant', in the lower part of the village, near the lake. Among the miseries of Griois' situation is a minor yet extraordinary one. Earlier, arriving at one of his bivouacs, he's dropped a glove,

'and neither I nor my orderly had been able to get it back out of the mud my horse's foot had trampled it into. This loss, so light in any other circumstance, was for me a very cruel one. I would have no chance to make it good, and throughout the retreat I'd only have one glove. I remember, too, that by a sort of superstitious presentiment I regarded being unable to find this object I'd just seen fall at my horse's feet as a nasty augury of what was to come.'

Though their cottage, like all the others, has only 'one room with a chimney-less stove and several sheds open to all the winds' it does have 'rather a vast courtyard, with shelter for our horses'. Unfortunately, hardly have Jumilhac and Griois lain down to sleep than the building goes up in flames. So do four or five of its neighbours. After vain attempts to put the fire out, the two artillery colonels – the one so culture loving, the other such witty company among his fellow-officers but, in Griois' view, too hard on the rank and file – have no option but to gather up their 'few effects and, laden with saddles, portmanteaux, etc., evacuate our terrified horses'. Outside, in an ocean of mud, they hold a 'sort of council of war' while their orderly officers try to find them some other dwelling. At last one is found in the higher part of the village, and they, 'with a loaf or two of munition bread, already items of luxury', bribe some soldiers to evacuate it. But when this habitation too goes up in flames, they finally settle, most uncomfortably, in a cottage at some distance from the village.

And there, in the wide plain between Winkovo and Kutusov's entrenched camp at Tarutino, the ever-dwindling regiments of Murat's once magnificent cavalry command are going to stay – and starve – until the Russians choose to turn them out of it.

But Colbert's lancers have remained in the rear, at the Woronowo ravine, together with General Friedrichs' infantry division, 'facing a fine big farm of red brick, with two storeys, occupied by the Duke of Istria's staff'.

CHAPTER 5

SETTLING IN FOR THE WINTER?

The pleasures of Moscow – 'a foetid stench impregnates our clothes' – stealing one's enemy's mustard pot – a masquerade – why doesn't the Tsar make peace? – Murat brought to a standstill – Lauriston's baffling mission – 'they'll light bonfires in Petersburg'

'The fire having died down,' writes Boulart, 'we began to enjoy the pleasures of Moscow, i.e., its palaces and what they had to offer.' Does he sometimes play his flute to while away the hours? Or Captain *H. F. Biot*, ADC to the wounded General Pajol, his violin? If so they say nothing about it. 'We had no linen and very little crockery,' Boulart goes on,

'but at the servant's suggestion I had a hole made in a freshly plastered wall and behind it we found prodigious quantities of china, glasses, kitchen utensils, vinegar and mustard, the best China tea and some table linen. In another corner, also walled up, I found a fine library. I shared my riches with my comrades and even some generals. My house became the meeting place for those less fortunate than ourselves who loved good meat and wine. Yet the days passed drearily. We had no other sources of distraction than our libraries, and no one is really tempted to read books who has such reasons for disquietude as we had.'

The shattered city offers other consolations than cultural or culinary ones. Its blackened ruins swarm with prostitutes, by no means all of whom, alas, are professionals. 'Nearly dying of hunger', other wretched women are being

'obliged to surrender themselves at discretion to the first comers. In every house still standing one saw nobody but these creatures, who'd installed themselves as if they owned them. They took possession of ladies' ornaments and in payment for their own favours – often very bitter ones – accepted as presents rich dresses the army had pillaged, and silver bullion.'

It's the wreckage of a world. Walking through the smouldering streets, Major *L-J. Vionnet* of the Fusiliers-Grenadiers of the Middle Guard – Bourgogne's regiment – keeps on coming across 'old men in tears at this appalling disorder'. Everywhere there are great open spaces. But visibility is poor and everything is veiled by a blue haze from the smoke of bivouac fires. Sent from Mojaisk to fetch supplies for Junot's VIII Corps, which is supposed to be looking after the Borodino wounded, a Westphalian bandmaster finds 'all the streets full of French soldiers, who'd lit huge fires beside their pyramids of stacked muskets. A regular camp life had developed. The Frenchmen greeted us in a very friendly way, often calling out to me "Long live the good army of Westphalia! Long live King Jérôme Napoleon!"'

Never has Friedrich Klinkhardt, in a lifetime devoted to teaching his musicians to play the Napoleonic armies' (to our ears) rather dumpy march tunes, even imagined such chaos:

'Here a soldier was holding forth to a circle of attentive listeners. There an affair of honour was being fought out. Now a band played tunes. Now one saw senior officers strolling arm in arm down the streets. Beaming faces looked out from windows of palaces, and some pretty women even nodded to us. Everything was full of life and bustle.'

This in the western, unburned district. But as Klinkhardt comes nearer to the Kremlin and the devastation around it, he and his comrades see 'smoking ruins in which every gust of wind was fanning a bright red flame. Choking smoke was blowing in from all directions.' 'The whole time we were in Moscow,' writes the cavalry surgeon Dr. *Réné Bourgeois*,

'the ashes never ceased smoking and were forever lighting up again from time to time in various places. Truly terrifying phosphoric flames came from amidst these vast ruins. We seemed surrounded by the lava of a scarcely extinct volcano which at every moment threatened to erupt again.'

'So here we are,' Césare de Laugier has written in his diary on 25 September,

'amidst smoking ruins, walls that at each moment threaten to collapse, half-burnt trees. The numerous sign-posts marking the limits of the various districts produce the effect of isolated columns or cenotaphs in a vast cemetery. The mass of ashes exhales a foetid stench that impregnates our clothes. No one knows where the Russian army is, or what it's up to; only that Murat and Bessières, with the Guard cavalry, have been sent to look for it. The most varied rumours are going the rounds.'

Amidst Moscow's blackened skeleton of log-paved streets, its huge but mostly gutted palaces, its great gardens, its vast parks, its churches and its cathedral with nine gilded towers, one pleasure which costs nothing is to go sightseeing. A visit to the ancient palace of the tsars and old patriarchs, standing up starkly on its high ground and within its deep ditch and behind high crenellated walls set with cannon, with its arsenal and six churches, is *de rigueur*, a 'must'. To many who, like Boulart, can only relish the neo-classical style, its architecture which 'has nothing regular about it, says nothing. The Ivan Tower, built beside the cathedral, is remarkable for its dome and the immense silver [sic] cross which surmounts it. At its foot and quite close to this tower, we see, deep in the ground, the biggest bell ever cast, weighing, so we're told, 160,000 kilos.'

Twenty-eight inches thick, it has fallen when the beams supporting it caught fire. The Kremlin's superb crypt 'where one sees the tombs of the tsars', though pillaged, also appeals to sightseers.

The Poles, particularly, are relishing the sweets of revenge. For them it's an important bicentenary – in 1611, after brilliant victories, their ancestors had occupied the Kremlin, but been forced to retreat, leaving their garrison to be massacred. Hasn't Russia within living memory always intervened in the affairs of Poland, and always disastrously? Hasn't she, by inflaming their own internal conflicts, scotched every attempt to update and modernize their grotesquely feudal system, where any landowner can veto any reform? And in the end, though defeated in several pitched battles, participated in the country's successive partitionings and, in 1794, massacred part of the population of Warsaw?[1] One Pole who's taking a special delight in Moscow's occupation – even its destruction – is Captain *Josef Zalusky* of the 1st Guard Lancers. While the Lancer Brigade had been stationed out on the Kaluga road he'd

'as soon as possible got permission from General Krasinski, who was in Moscow in attendance on the Emperor, and gone into this capital where, with pain, it's true, but with even more animosity, I walked about the burnt streets, recognizing there this people who have spread so many fires on our land, from the Baltic to the Tatra Mountains, from the Black Sea to beyond the Vistula, even into Pomerania! Reaching the Moscova bridge beneath the Kremlin, I halted at this point whence the eye embraces so wide a view, and thought how my compatriots, Dmitri's companions, had been executed, and that it was the [bi]centenary of 1612. Thinking also of the Prague Massacres, I told myself "the shade of Jasinski is avenged! From the victims' tomb we can expunge the inscription Exoriare aliquis nostris ex ossibus ultor."'[2]

In the Kremlin the immensely wealthy Polish aristocrat Dominique Radziwill, 'who was, or was soon going to be, a major in our regiment',[3] has found his ancestor's sword. 'Glass in hand' Zalusky and Krasinski examine it 'with emotion'. And more than by the Kremlin's granite hall, its arsenal or ancient churches, Zalusky's impressed by the 'rows of Polish culverins and cannon, stamped with the coats of arms of the Polish kingdom and of various Polish families'.[4] Being a count and a Guards officer, he's given lodgings, 'not in a palace, but in a very comfortable house belonging to a certain Soltykow. Not merely had it not been pillaged, but nothing was lacking and I was treated perfectly by the dvorecki [major-domo]. Despite a courteous reception, I told him I was going to pillage his master's house, and was going to take the mustard pot to make myself a drinking glass out of it, and that I was also going to put the horn tobacco spoon into my pocket to serve me as a camp spoon; and that for his master's sake I hoped no one would pillage his house worse than that.'

Two appeals are made, in de Lesseps' name, on 1 and 6 October, to the legitimate inhabitants, promising them protection if only they'll return to their homes and occupations; and to the peasants to come and sell their produce at market. Both fall on stone-deaf ears. Not one shop is open. And above all there's a desperate shortage, above all, of tailors.

Not quite so desperate, however, in this grim realm of soot and ashes, as the lack of washerwomen. 'Of all the hardships of this campaign,' one officer had written during the long march from the Niemen, 'having to do our own laundry was one of the most humiliating.' Sergeant Bourgogne is therefore particularly delighted when, in an unexplored wing of the provisional guardhouse to which he's been committed for having saved his two tailors from the firing squad, he finds two women sitting on a sofa. With them, dead drunk, is one of the convicts Rostopchin had released with orders to burn down the city and who'd promptly been booted downstairs. The washerwomen – as they're immediately promoted to be – turn out to be no less fond of Danzig gin than Bourgogne himself:

'I stayed for some time with these two sisters, and then returned to my room. I found there an NCO of my company, who'd been waiting for me a long time. When I told him of my adventures he seemed delighted, as he could find no one to wash his clothes.'

Keeping it a secret until 10 p.m., an hour by which everyone else is asleep, Bourgogne and the NCO, who 'seemed to think the two Muscovite ladies would be only too honoured by being asked to wash and mend for French soldiers', together with their sergeant-major, go and fetch them:

'At first, not quite knowing where we were taking them, they made a lot of difficulties, but made me understand I was to go with them. I went to our quarters, where they followed us willingly, laughing as they went. We found a small room free, which we made over to them, furnishing it with whatever we could find – all kinds of pretty things the noble ladies of Moscow hadn't been able to carry away. In this way our friends, though they seemed to be common servants, were transformed into elegant ladies – ladies, however, who had to wash and mend for us.'

Bourgogne hears a 'loud report of firearms' – several convicts and members of the police have just been shot. But his two Swiss tailors, father and son, have been released, and he finds them busy at work

'making some capes out of the cloth off the billiard tables we'd taken to pieces. I went into the room where we'd left our women, and found them at the wash tub and – not surprisingly, being dressed up as baronesses – making a very poor job of it. For want of anything better we had to make do with them.

Dancing is another, if exceptional pleasure. The NCOs of the Fusiliers-Grenadiers organize a ball –

'a real carnival, as we were all disguised. First of all we dressed up the women as French marquises. As they knew nothing of such matters, Flament and I superintended their toilette. Our two Russian tailors were dressed out as Chinese, I as a Russian boyar, Flament as a marquis. Even our *cantinière*, Mother Dubois, wore a beautiful Russian national dress. As we had no wigs for our marquises, the regimental wigmaker dressed their hair. For grease he used suet, and flour for powder. They looked splendid, and when everyone was ready we began to dance.'

They've all been imbibing a lot of punch.

'For music we had a flute played by a sergeant-major, accompanied by the drum to keep time. As the music struck up and Mother Dubois advanced with our quartermaster, our marquises, excited no doubt by the music, began jumping about like Tartars, flying from right to left, swinging their arms and legs about, falling over backwards, getting up, only to fall over again. They seemed to be possessed by the devil. If they'd been wearing their Russian clothes there wouldn't have been anything very extraordinary about it. But to see two French marquises jumping about like lunatics made us nearly die with laughter, and the flautist was obliged to stop playing, the drum filling up the pauses by sounding the attack.'

After the ball is over, Mother Dubois, in her lavish costume – she's perfectly well aware of its value – fails to be recognized by a sergeant of the guard on police duty:

'Seeing a strange lady in the street so early, and thinking he'd found a prize, he went up to her, and tried to take her by the arm and lead her to his room. But Mother Dubois, who had a husband, and moreover had drunk a good deal of punch, dealt the sergeant such a vigorous blow on the face that she knocked him right over. The sergeant was so furious we had our work cut out to din into his head that he mustn't arrest such a woman as Mother Dubois.'

All this is only part of a still vaster masquerade. Though soon in the ninth month of pregnancy, Mother Dubois never walks abroad except in a dress of silver lamé. Another of Bourgogne's comrades appears in the costume of a gentleman from the days of Louis XV.[5] Rummaging in aristocratic cupboards, thousands of men, both veterans and conscripts, many of whom had 'never heard of coffee or white bread except by report' until they'd been conscripted, are decking themselves out fantastically in the contents of the city's surviving palaces.

The rest of the day that Sergeant Bourgogne had set his 'marquises' to work at the washtub he'd been 'busy arranging our quarters and getting in provisions, as it seemed we were to be staying here for some time.' If Major Boulart, too, like Caulaincourt, like everyone else, is

'collecting furniture and all sorts of things abandoned in the city
which might come in handy for our domestic arrangements,'

and in general acting as if sure he'll 'have to pass the eight months in Moscow that must elapse before spring,' it's because that's exactly the intended impression Napoleon is giving at the dinners he's inviting his generals to after the daily 1 o'clock Kremlin parades. All his talk is of his glowing prospects; and of the "60,000 Polish Cossacks" which Abbé *D-G.F. Pradt*, his plenipotentiary ambassador in Warsaw, will shortly be sending him:

'He attributed all his difficulties simply to the trouble caused by the
Cossacks, for, he insisted, he had more than enough troops to fight
off Kutusov and go wherever he wanted to. The rigours of winter, the
total lack of precautions against cold, etc., didn't enter into his calculations.'

To stay the winter in Moscow, Berthier and Duroc are now convinced, 'was his favourite idea'. Even Caulaincourt, though sceptical at first and rather sure that all this table talk about wintering in Moscow is

'affected, and merely due to his wish to give a turn to public opinion,
to ensure the collection of provisions, and, above all, to support the
overture he'd made,'

for a week and more has been listening to

'the Emperor in his intimate circle conversing, acting and issuing
orders, all on the presumption that he was going to stay in Moscow.'

Now he's beginning to wonder whether the Emperor doesn't mean what he says,

'and for some time even those most closely in his confidence entertained no doubts on that score. Seeing the season so far advanced
without any preparations made for our departure, I too ended by
doubting whether we'd evacuate Moscow voluntarily. It seemed to me
impossible the Emperor would even think of a retreat when the frost
set in, especially as no measures had been taken to protect the men
nor any steps taken to enable the horses to cross the ice.'

Even Count Daru, the most experienced, the most loyal and the most indefatigable of all Napoleon's administrators – a man who'd once promised to
obey his orders providing he'd always be allowed to speak his mind freely
– though at first he'd supported Napoleon's idea of marching northwards
'beyond the 55th parallel' and attacking Petersburg, is now advising him to
settle in. Or, alternatively, leave only a strong garrison in Moscow and
establish himself at Kaluga, key to the Ukraine, with its milder climate and
its vast grain resources. But all the time Napoleon is discussing his plan

> 'in such positive terms that the most incredulous among us ended by
> believing he intended to carry it out. Even the Grand Marshal and the
> Prince of Neuchâtel seemed convinced we'd be staying in Moscow.
> Everyone was laying plans accordingly.'

And the message is really getting through. Even Césare de Laugier, though
on 25 September he'd been struck by 'an outbreak of general rejoicing just
caused by orders to leave on 28 September,' is noting that

> 'the instructions we keep getting seem to indicate that the Emperor
> intends to spend the winter here, or in the surroundings. The heads
> of the units have been ordered to provide them with food for six
> months.'

But why, above all, isn't the Tsar ready to make peace? At Petersburg, to
judge by news that's come in, the burning of Russia's 'old' capital has
unleashed panic. Even the crown jewels have been put aboard a ship, ready
to sail for London. 'On 22 or 23 September,' Napoleon sends for Caulaincourt:

> 'The Emperor, who for a long time hadn't discussed affairs with me,
> asked me whether I thought the Tsar would be disposed to make
> peace if overtures were made to him. I replied frankly that it seemed
> to me the sacrifice of Moscow argued a far from pacific disposition. It
> was scarcely probable he'd have set fire to his capital with the inten-
> tion of signing a peace among the ruins.'

This, while he'd been out at Petrovskoï watching the holocaust, had in fact
been Napoleon's own spontaneous reaction. How then has he come to
convince himself of the opposite?

Now Napoleon wants to send Caulaincourt to the Tsar, with whom he'd
been on such friendly terms, during the four years when he'd been French
ambassador to Russia.[6]

'"Will you go to Petersburg?" the Emperor asked me. "You'd see the
Tsar. I'd entrust you with a letter, and you'd make peace."'

But Caulaincourt's a man (according to Ségur and others) 'more capable of obstinacy than flattery, endured rather than listened to, and sincere
to the point of giving offence'. And he declines:

"It'd be useless to send me on such a mission. I shouldn't even be received." Assuming a jocular and kindly air, the Emperor told me I didn't know what I was talking about: "That fire was the sort of folly a madman might boast of when he kindled the flame, but repent of next day.'"

The Tsar will be all the keener to seize this chance, he goes on, reverting to a notion he'd already entertained even before leaving Paris because his nobles, "ruined by this war and the fire, desire peace. The Emperor Alexander is stubborn. He'll regret it. Never again will he obtain such easy terms from me as I'd have made now. He's done himself so much harm by burning his towns and his capital that there's nothing more I'd have asked of him." All he'll have to do is to impound British shipping. Or if there's a misunderstanding on that point, and the Tsar thinks he, Napoleon, wants to retain Lithuania, he's wrong. He doesn't.

At this Caulaincourt, no doubt remembering the Tsar's words to himself and to Narbonne,[7] says that Alexander won't make peace until the soil of Russia has been evacuated. Even to go and see Kutusov at Tarutino will be useless.

Whereat Napoleon, 'turning abruptly on his heel':

"Very well, I'll send Lauriston. He shall have the honour of making peace and saving your friend Alexander's crown for him."

But what if he won't make peace? Then, Napoleon confides uneasily to Fain in the privacy of his cabinet, the Grand Army will be like "a ship frozen in by the ice. Anyway, Alexander won't let me go so far. We'll come to an understanding, and he'll sign a peace treaty."

Will he? Caulaincourt's scepticism, if better informed than most people's, is by no means unique. Even Paymaster Peyrusse, ingratiating himself with Daru in the Kremlin, is writing home to a friend: 'How can we count on a peace with a people who've nothing to lose, who've chosen to lose everything to save everything?'

A certain Major Fribler of the 85th Line, also has no such illusions. One day before they'd moved to the Kaluga road, he and Le Roy had sat together discussing peace prospects:

"'*Ma foi*," said Fribler, "you who frequent the staffs[8] ought to know more about what's going on than I do. But from the system the enemy has adopted since the campaign opened and which he's persevered in of destroying everything in passing, I think we'll never be able to negotiate with him, not after such a sacrifice, which I regard as a national effort and an act of patriotic virtue. You've too much common sense, my dear major, not to see the trap we've fallen into. He's trying to lure us as far as he can from our reserves, while waiting for the winter. If we're forced to retire by the same road as we've come by, what will it offer us? What to do with an army weakened to less than half its strength, its cavalry exhausted and soon on foot? From all of which I conclude we should retire as quickly as ever we can, having extracted from this town everything we can carry.'"

The portly major had replied uneasily that the Emperor doubtless knows what he's about; but agreed that eight more days in Moscow would suffice. This has been Berthier's opinion from the outset. And Narbonne, at Napoleon's behest daily visiting his wounded fellow-ADC Rapp to inquire after his health, is of the same opinion – and repeats it to his young secretary *A. F. Villemain* – that the Russians, so far from wanting to make peace, are 'entertaining us with pretty talk, so as more easily to prepare the revenge and make it so much the more certain'. Lariboisière, too, goes so far as to tell Planat de la Faye 'during the first fortnight of our stay in Moscow: "If we stay here another fortnight our return to France is really at risk."' Hadn't that been Napoleon's own spontaneous opinion? Hadn't Fain, that first morning out at Petrovskoï, heard him talk of letting the army rest up for a few days and then marching on Petersburg?

Despite the valuable fortnight which has gone by, the option still seems open to him. And around the turn of the month he tells Duroc, who's more of a yes-man than the all-too candid Caulaincourt: 'Moscow's a bad position. We should only stay here long enough to reorganize.'

On October 3, after a sleepless night, he presents the Petersburg scheme to Eugène, Berthier, Bessières and Davout:

"We must burn what's left of Moscow, march via Tver on Petersburg, where Macdonald[9] will come to reinforce us, while the Viceroy and the Prince of Eckmühl secure the vanguard."

Only Eugène, Fain notes, approves of this idea, of which Daru had earlier approved, of marching northwards 'beyond the 55th parallel, attacking Petersburg and so ending the war'. Davout and Berthier, for their part, stress the dangers of such a long march. The intervening country is difficult, often swampy. And they'll have Kutusov and the main Russian army at their heels; all just as winter – the dreaded Russian winter – comes on. That winter which will soon be here.

So the scheme's dropped. Perhaps he hasn't seriously entertained it anyway?

Next day he sends for another of his ADCs, General Lauriston.

Like Caulaincourt, whose successor he'd been at the Petersburg embassy, Lauriston is an aristocrat, of Scottish extraction. A marquis of the *ancien régime*, at the Brienne military school before the Revolution he'd got to know a certain pale-faced lanky-haired Corsican cadet with the uncouth name of Napoleone Buonaparte. Though Lauriston and Caulaincourt don't like each other they're agreed on the futility of making approaches to the Tsar. And Lauriston, too, says he has no taste for such a mission. In his view the army ought to retreat forthwith, via Mojaisk.

"I like simple plans," Napoleon replies. "And the less tortuous a path is the better I like it. But there's one path I won't set foot on again unless peace is signed. And that's the one I've come by."

With these words, without further discussion, he hands Lauriston a letter to the Tsar, and orders him to go to Murat's headquarters, see Kutusov, and obtain a safe conduct:

"I want peace. I must have it. I want it at all costs, providing only our honour is saved."

Already an order has been sent off to Murat, to write to Kutusov as follows:
    'It being the Emperor's intention to send one of his ADCs to General-in-Chief Kutusov, he wishes to know the day and hour when, and the place at which, the general is willing to receive him.'
And next morning (5 October) Lauriston's carriage 'accompanied by a numerous suite' rolls out through the Kremlin's vaulted gateway, bound for Winkovo. *En route* it passes through the neighbourhood of the village of Woronowo, where the Guard Lancer Brigade, after various manoeuvrings on Murat's right flank and rear in the Podolsk region, has just arrived. Captain Zalusky and his fellow Poles of the 1st Guard Lancers
    'with surprise and regret see him pass through on his way to Kutusov. In our eyes Napoleon was compromising himself by showing a wish, and thereby his need, for peace, and by extending his stay in Moscow ever longer, hoping for a treaty.'
(But Napoleon can't care less what the Poles think. He's quite prepared to sacrifice them anyway; and has been, since the campaign opened.)[10]

Lauriston's carriage and its entourage rolls splashing down Winkovo's single muddy street. He alights, presents his credentials to Murat and explains his errand – which is certainly very much to Murat's liking. He's never wanted any part of this war anyway; his sole desire is to get back to Naples and his family as quickly as possible. Then Lauriston orders his coachman to drive him to the Russian outposts, and there, under a flag of truce, requests permission for one of his ADCs to present himself at Kutusov's headquarters.

To Wilson's fury, Kutusov, despite his orders from the Tsar – the strictest possible – to have no parleying whatever with the enemy, promptly agrees to meet Lauriston. Not at his headquarters, admittedly. But between the outposts. Wilson, not trusting Kutusov an inch, protests vehemently. And Kutusov, aware that the British general is in personal contact with the Tsar, hastily changes his tune and sends Prince Volkonsky, one of Alexander's own ADCs, instead. This, from Lauriston's point of view, isn't good enough. Refusing even to speak to Volkonsky, he orders his coachman to turn around and drive back to Murat's headquarters.

But Kutusov has other critics and enemies besides Wilson – his head-quarters is a hotbed of intrigue and dissension. One such critic and dissenter to the Field Marshal's policies is General Bennigsen, his own chief-of-staff. And that day, Bennigsen, hearing that the King of Naples is at the outposts, has come out to meet him:

'The conversation was very insignificant, Murat's principal remark being "This is no climate for a King of Naples."; but the appearance was pernicious and any unnecessary address of these invaders as a sovereign a wilful piece of base behaviour,'

thinks Wilson. Finally it's agreed that Lauriston shall be received this evening at Kutusov's headquarters, three miles behind the Russian lines. Strictest etiquette is to be observed. And in fact Lauriston gets a firm but most ambiguous reception. At first, Wilson's British uniform doubtless stressing the political aspect, both Volkonsky and Wilson are ostentatiously present 'in council'. After which they both withdraw to the next room, where they wait while Kutusov – devious as can be – and Lauriston – brisk and businesslike – have a private but 'very animated' conversation.

First Lauriston (according to what Kutusov will tell them as soon as it's over) complains of the barbarities being committed by the Russians towards the invaders.

'"Must this strange war," he asks, "this unique war, last for ever? My master has a sincere desire to end this dispute between two great and generous nations and to end it for ever." To this the Marshal answered, that he had no instruction on that point, nor did he wish to communicate any of this to the Tsar, and that he'd be "cursed by posterity if I were to be thought the prime mover of any kind of settlement, such is my nation's present frame of mind."'

As for acts of barbarity, he can't "civilize a nation in three months who regarded the enemy as a marauding force of Tartars under a Genghis Khan."

"But at least there's some difference!"

Lauriston comes back, much upset by the comparison:

"In fact there may be, but none in the eyes of the people: I can only answer for my own troops."

'General Lauriston,' Wilson goes on, 'had no complaint to make against them. He then adverted to an armistice, saying that "Nature herself would, in a short time, oblige it." The Marshal said he had no authority on that head.'

To this Lauriston again ripostes: "You must not think it's because our affairs are desperate. Our two armies are about equal. You are nearer your supplies and reinforcements than we are, but we also have reinforce-ments.'"

He admits that Napoleon's Spanish affairs are just now going badly – as a result of Marmont's stupidities at Salamanca Madrid is temporarily in British hands,[11]

"Doubtless Sir Robert Wilson has his reasons for exaggerating things." Kutusov denies it. But Lauriston persists:

"But numerous corps which are on the march to those countries will soon change the state of affairs. Do not think, Sir, that we're reduced to extremity. Our armies are equally strong. True, you're closer to your reinforcements. But we too are receiving them."

As for the burning of Moscow, it had been "so inconsistent with the French character, that if we take London we shan't set fire to that city".

With these optimistic words Lauriston hands Kutusov Napoleon's letter. Hardly even glancing at it with his one good eye, Kutusov lays it aside on the table. Only at Lauriston's urging does he pick it up again and skim through its contents. Being addressed to the Tsar, he consents to forward it to Petersburg, while pointing out that some time – indeed quite a lot of time – must necessarily go by before an answer can arrive. After half an hour more of talk Lauriston, speaking 'in such a manner that every person was satisfied he'd been disappointed,' takes his leave.

From Wilson's point of view it's Bennigsen's intervention in Lauriston's mission that has spoilt the outcome. According to Murat's 38-year-old Neapolitan ADC Colonel *M-J-T. Rossetti*, too, it had been Bennigsen who'd

'asked for a negotiation and proposed an armistice, which was accept-ed, the only condition being to give each other twelve hours' warning before resuming hostilities.'

Although Kutusov swears to Wilson on his honour that there's no 'con-vention' between him and Murat, all firing suddenly and mysteriously ceas-es. And discussions – what Tascher calls in his diary 'a battle of politenesses between the French and Russian generals, Bennigsen, Kutusov, Mineval-ovitsch [*sic*]' – follow and continue into the next day.

Naturally all ranks have been eagerly discussing the mission's purpose, which is quickly assumed to be identical with its outcome. As Lauriston sets off for Moscow, Griois, like everyone else, hears that

'a sort of armistice has been agreed, not to be broken without giving each other several hours' warning. For the rest, it was purely local, and didn't extend either on the flanks or the rear of our position. The news spread in our bivouacs and there was general rejoicing. Together Jumilhac and I drained the last bottle of wine we still pos-sessed and had been keeping for some great occasion.'

Among the Lancer Brigade, guarding the Kaluga road twelve miles to Murat's rear, the armistice gives rise to

'various comments, among others to a renewed supposition that peace was near. At all events the immediate consequences were a kind of tacit suspension of hostilities. Each side avoided the other and seemed no longer to wish to get into a fight – '

precisely the result desired, of course, by Kutusov. When one's enemy is gravely short of food and desperate for forage, what's the point of fighting?

But back at the Kremlin Lauriston gives a much more glowing report on his mission than its outcome warrants. And a delighted Emperor exclaims:

"When they get my letter in Petersburg they'll light bonfires."

As for his letter, Kutusov forwards a copy of it to the Tsar, with a recommendation that it shall not be answered.

CHAPTER 6

MARAUDING PARTIES

No hay or straw – Le Roy commands a marauding party – 'every day the circle's being drawn tighter' – Césare de Laugier meets the locals – 'I asked him politely in Latin' – Paul de Bourgoing fights his way out – Ney's reconnaissance in force

Nor is it only Murat's men who are short of essentials. In a Moscow stuffed with tea and coffee, jams and liqueurs, bread and – above all – hay have quickly become rarities. Writing home around the turn of the month (but his letter will be captured by Cossacks) a French NCO tells his sister that 'the horses are gnawing at their mangers for lack of it'. Even a general of brigade like Dedem, nursing his bruised chest in his mill on the outskirts, can't

'get a sack of oats without a permit from the Quartermaster-General, and that was hard to obtain. Only hay and straw were lacking. The Prince of Neuchâtel himself was sending out to the villages to get some.'

Where has it all gone to? Evidently Daru is doing his job of getting in stocks for the winter only too well. By no means all the villagers have fled,

'probably because flight had presented greater difficulties, there being so many of them and the environs of Moscow being so densely populated. Perhaps also because some who'd meant to flee hadn't been able to because the French army, as soon as it had taken possession of Moscow, had spread out in all directions. Finally, it's possible that, being more affluent, they'd found it hard to abandon home and hearth.'

Whether the analysis of the artillery officer, the Marquis *de Chambray*, is right or not, when Dedem sends a sergeant and some men to get him some eggs, chickens, etc., with strict orders to pay for them, 'taking' only some hay, the peasants beg the soldiers to make haste, for fear of the Cossacks; who treat them as an inferior species.

These are everywhere in the town's environs. The very first day after settling at Petrovskoï, Laugier had seen them hovering only a few hundred yards away, waiting to pounce on anyone who strayed from the Italian camp. At dawn on 21 September, notwithstanding Le Roy's well-posted sentries,

'the Guard Chasseurs who'd gone reconnoitring were driven back at the double by enemy cavalry as far as the houses where I'd stationed my two companies. Being under arms, they opened fire and shot down three Cossack regulars. But that didn't mean a dozen of our men weren't stabbed by these gentlemen's lances.'[1]

Dedem makes a pact with the local priest, allowing him to go on ringing his church bell provided his parishioners supply him with necessaries, but the men of the 4th Line, bivouacked with the rest of Ney's III Corps to the west of the city, have all this time been

'so short of almost everything, and only with difficulty managing to get hold of black bread and beer, that strong detachments were having to be sent out to seize cattle in the woods where the peasants had taken refuge, and yet often returning empty-handed. Such was the supposed abundance from the looting. Though the men were covering themselves with furs, they soon no longer had clothes or shoes. In short, with diamonds, precious stones and every imaginable luxury, we were on the verge of starving to death.'

This being the state of affairs, marauding parties are the only solution, not always a very successful one. Simple at first, they've soon become exceedingly problematic:

'Our outposts extended hardly two days' march beyond the town. The Emperor could get no certain information on the Russian army's position. The Russians, on the contrary, were informed about every movement we made; and few days passed without our hearing painful news of their having carried off such or such a battalion, such or such a squadron, sent out to protect our marauders searching for food,'

writes Fezensac. At Davout's headquarters in the monastery at the Doroghomilov Gate his reluctant chief-of-staff General Baron *L-F. Lejeune* – that future painter of elegant and colourful battle scenes – is daily having to organize ever stronger expeditions. On 17 September, while the fire had still been raging, one of his subordinates had sighted 'a herd of cattle, hidden in a marsh between two forests ten miles away'. And instantly orders had come to Le Roy[2] to take a mixed detachment from the 85th Line and go and grab it. At blush of dawn next day, with a soldier to guide his party, he'd set off:

'At 9 a.m. we got to the edge of the marsh. I had it searched by two detachments of 50 men each and two officers who, each following his own side of it, were to join up at the other side. In the event of their seeing the herd or meeting with any resistance they were to warn me by firing shots or by beat of drum.'

While the remainder of his detachment rests, Le Roy goes up to a nearby isolated church, 200 yards to his right, between himself and the Moskova, and sees, about five miles away on the left bank, in the direction of the city, several foraging horsemen who're returning at a brisk canter, apparently pursued. On his own thickly wooded and deeply ravined river bank he can see nothing. Yet the existence of a church seems to indicate a number of small communities. By and by a Russian peasant appears, but doesn't notice him; and at the same moment a drum roll tells him someone – or something – has been captured without resistance. Half an hour later the head of a very variegated herd of animals appears – oxen, cows, little ponies, sheep and pigs. 'Having massed them together, we set out to our left and followed a track which the livestock seemed to follow of their own accord.' Sure enough, it leads to a village by the river, and into the court-yard of a 'pretty château no Frenchman from the Army had as yet visited'. Deciding to halt for a couple of hours to rest his men, he notes that he's now about seven and a half miles from his camp. He's just starting to count the captured herd when his son, a sergeant in the 85th, brings him one of the château's inhabitants.

> 'He'd arrested him just as I, together with three others, was getting out of a ferry. He tells the major he has evacuated his family to anoth-er of his properties and has come to see whether the invaders have any knowledge of it, and if not, to rescue some of his possessions. "Monsieur," I told him, [says Le Roy pompously, stretching truth fur-ther than it was ever stretched before] "The French soldier only makes war on armed men. You have nothing to fear. And if all Rus-sians had done as you have, the countryside our army has passed through wouldn't have been ravaged."'

With these words he sends off 50 men to explore the other part of the vil-lage on the far bank of the river, which laps the edge of the château's gar-den. Muskets and lances have been found in the village – the former of Russian manufacture, the latter simply long rods with a long nail or knife blade at the end, the kind the Cossacks are using:

> 'I assumed they belonged to peasants who were being incited to rise against us, and that the persons we'd just arrested were leading the insurrection. I tacitly decided to take these gentlemen to Moscow: and, what strengthened me in this resolution, two of them seemed to be disguised Russian officers. The elder was about forty, the youngest about twenty. They were wearing French-style tail-coats, hussar-style boots with spurs, had little moustaches and round hats. The other individual had a serious air, a malicious eye, and the muscles in his face never stopped twitching. He was dressed like the first ones, in French clothes, a furred cap, big and roomy trousers strapped under-foot. I was going to question them when the master arrived. I was astonished to hear him speak Russian to the fellow with the sinister face and to hold his cap in his hand, while the other didn't take his hat off. His son said: "This gentleman has just had a meal prepared and we've stewed it up."'

And in fact the Russian invites all the detachment's officers to refreshment, 'apologizing for not being able to treat us as we deserved. He'd also provided beer for the men.' Le Roy – with his embonpoint, he's a man who relishes his victuals – thanks him and orders an officer to follow him to the table of a pretty room which seems to have lost half its furniture.

'There's an old cooked ham, a quarter of cold mutton and sausages, two dishes of dessert, wine and liqueurs. At first, having decided to leave in good time, I was loath to depart. But unable to resist our host's insistence I took my place at table opposite the eldest of them, and didn't lose sight of a single one of his movements. I kept an eye on him like a cat watches a mouse, without his noticing it; because the main door of the dining-room, which was behind him, had been left open and to all appearances I was watching what was going on down in the courtyard. So I had one eye on him and the other on the château's courtyard. Beside this man sat an old tippler of a captain of the 33rd Regiment, who got thoroughly tipsy. Next was the young man with the little moustaches, speaking German to his neighbour. Then another Russian, all of whose manners struck me as military. From time to time he looked at the man sitting opposite me and smiled.'

Le Roy also notices that the number of servants waiting on them is steadily growing. Some have moustaches, while others are bearded peasants. His neighbour tries to reassure him by saying they've come bringing more provisions in case the French would like to stay the night. At 4 p.m. Le Roy goes down into the courtyard and orders a captain of the 17th Light Infantry – his party, regrettably, has been taken from several regiments – to form an advance guard with the herd and not leave the road. Vodka in great bowls has been served to the men and by now many of them are drunk. Going back into the dining-room, Le Roy peremptorily asks the four Russians to be so good as to accompany him to Moscow. 'The poor devils seemed thunderstruck – and this confirmed me in my idea that they all spoke French.' He threatens to use force if they resist. 'The first young man asked if he could go into the next room and get his clothes. I consented, ordering the drunken captain to go with them.'

Now Le Roy assembles his detachment, meaning to place his four prisoners in the middle of it, and calls up to the officers he's left in the dining-room to bring these gentlemen, whether they like it or not.

'I was just about to mount my horse, when the sergeant of the Moscow outpost came and told me he'd seen a couple of groups higher up river, which some horsemen were fording. He was sure they were Cossacks. I was just going to go and see, when the officers came out of the château and approached me, laughing. They told me the Russians, having gone through several rooms, had asked the old drunk to wait for them while they went into the little room – saying they'd only be

long enough to fetch their coats. Of course they'd escaped by another passage that lead out of it into the garden.'

Le Roy, furious, decides to ask permission to return next day with a battalion of his own regiment – the 85th – to search the château and capture its
occupants. Guided by the flames and smoke of Moscow 'the detachment,
having doubled its advance guard, returns to its encampment at 9 p.m.
with its herd of cattle, sheep, pigs and ponies.'

But were those four Russians newcomers who'd come to fan the flames
of an insurrection? Or were they in charge of one that's already been organized? He can't be sure. 'In either case the hidden weapons would have justified my arresting them,' he concludes. And the moral? 'Always prefer a
detachment made up of men from your own company or regiment to ones
supplied from different units.' But he'd accomplished his most important
task: to get his lowing, mooing, bleating, neighing booty back to camp
before nightfall. General Friedrichs comes and promises him a light cavalry escort and men from his own unit to return next day and wreak
vengeance on the fugitives and their château,

> 'not because they'd run off, but for having assembled a lot of men
> strange to the village, as well as some soldiers. If I'd let myself be
> lulled by their fine promises what happened two days later to a
> detachment of the 108th regiment would have happened to me.'

Luckily, next day (19 September) he's suddenly ordered by Davout to take
his battalion to the outskirts to support the Chasseurs of the Guard on the
Kaluga road:

> '"I'm sorry, my dear Le Roy", he said, "you can't go back to look for
> what you left behind out there either on the road or in the marsh.
> Soon we shan't have any meat, even for our sick and wounded. I'm
> going to send a detachment of 300 men from the 108th under a
> bright and efficient captain called Toubie."'

Le Roy hands over the livestock to his general's ADC, 'keeping only two
pretty little Russian horses to carry my baggage'. But Toubie and his party
aren't sufficiently on the *qui vive*, and are massacred.

As the days pass, then weeks, such marauding expeditions are having to
range ever farther afield and be provided with ever heavier escorts. Far
from responding to de Lesseps' appeal to 'come out from the woods where
terror retains you' and sell their 'superfluous' produce to market, the peasants are (as Le Roy had suspected) forming themselves into efficient guerrilla bands. Hardly a day goes by without at least 300 French or Allied
soldiers being snapped up by the Cossacks or by bands of guerrillas. 'The
circle is daily being drawn tighter around us,' a French officer writes
home,' – but his letter too is intercepted by the Cossacks:

'We've having to put 10,000 men with artillery into the field outside Moscow to forage, and still can't be sure of success unless we fight. The enemy is gaining the energy we're losing. Now audacity and confidence are on his side.'

A despondent General Gelichet, posted at a point some forty miles from the city, writes that every order he gets is only making him

'want to resign my command. As for the victuals you ask from me, the thing's impossible. The 33rd would be helping us out if it still had the horses killed the day before yesterday. As it is, it has only two head of cattle left.'

Even on 30 September Césare de Laugier has written in his diary that 'the colonels of the Royal Guard are taking turns with the Army of Italy's generals of brigade to direct and command such flying columns. The good and intrepid Colonel Moroni, the vélites' colonel, being more than once detailed off for this kind of job, I, by virtue of my rank, am having to go with him.' And goes on:

'So yesterday about 1,000 infantrymen, 200 troopers and two pieces of cannon were placed under Moroni's orders, to attempt a reconnaissance along the Tver road, as well as to protect numerous Saccomans' [Sacs-au-mains = bagmen] bringing with them carts and pack horses. The greater part of the villages we passed through were totally deserted, and had been searched from top to bottom by earlier reconnaissances. Between Czerraio-Griaz and Woskresensk, about 28 versts [20 miles] from Moscow, we'd reached the extreme limit of our earlier excursions. In the plain a few sparse villages and country houses which, albeit abandoned, were still completely intact and witnessed to the sudden flight of the inhabitants. There we camped for the night.'

The Italian vélites realise that they're in the presence of enemy troops. But at dawn they form two columns and pursue their way without troubling themselves:

'And in fact the enemy withdrew as we advanced. We passed through more villages without trouble, guaranteed as they were by the chain of posts set up by cavalry and infantry. The heat was excessive, and a magnificent forest spread out beyond the advanced posts to the right, where I was. Accompanied by some NCOs, I wanted to push on that far.'

But then something surprising happens:

'I'd only gone a few paces when I heard voices. Alone, I walked calmly over to the side the noise was coming from. There I saw through the trees, in the middle of the wood, a clearing where there was crowd of people, men and women of all ages and kinds. I came a few steps closer. They looked attentively at me, but without being either scared or surprised. Some men, whose manners and faces didn't augur any good to me, came toward me.'

The vélites' adjutant-major signs to them to keep their distance, but calls over

'the one of them I'd recognized as one of their priests. Then, using Latin, I asked him politely to tell me whether this was the population of the villages just now occupied by our troops. "We are", the pope replied gravely, after looking closely at me, "part of the unfortunate inhabitants of the Holy City whom you've reduced to the state of vagabonds, of paupers, of desperates, whom you've deprived of asylum and fatherland!" As he said this, tears ran down abundantly from his eyes. At that moment his companions began advancing with threatening gestures. The priest managed to calm them and ordered them back. Whereupon they remained at a certain distance, to hear what we were saying.'

The priest says he cannot conceive what 'barbarous genius, what inhuman cruelty' can have animated Napoleon to set fire to their venerable capital. Césare de Laugier says he's got it all wrong ... No, no, says the priest. It's he who's deceiving himself. There's no question but that Napoleon was the author of the fire:

'While we were talking I was able to examine at my leisure this crowd of unfortunates who were gradually coming closer to us. The men's masculine, energetic, bearded faces bore the impress of a deep, ferocious, concentrated pain. The women's air was more resigned, but it was easy to guess what anxieties they were going through. Untroubled by my paying so little heed to what he was saying, the pope went on with his sermon. Swept along in some line of reasoning, he happened to touch my horse and lay his hand on the pommel of its saddle. Seeing how moved I was, he redoubled the violence of his words. For my part I was lamenting the fate of so many unhappy families, women, old men, children, who, because of us, were in such a pitiful state. And this thought made me forget the danger I was so imprudently exposing myself to.'

Suddenly one of the Russians comes up to the 'pope' and, 'with a look of sovereign scorn' says something in his ear. Suspicious, the Italian officer begins to walk away:

'But then the pope asked me whether I was a Christian, a question which only half surprised me, as I knew we'd been represented to the Russian people as a band of heretics. The moment everyone knew I'd said I was, I saw all the faces looking at me with greater interest, and the conversations grew more animated. Then the pope took my hand, pressed it affectionately, and said: "Get going as fast as you can. Ilowais-ki, reinforced by the district's militia and some completely fresh caval-ry, is advancing to attack you. By staying here you're exposing yourself to every danger. And do what you can to prevent the acts of impiety your leader and your comrades are making themselves guilty of!'"

Before going back to his men, de Laugier makes a last effort to convince the kindly priest of his error; tells him that he and all his flock can come back to Moscow without the least risk. But his interlocutor accompanies him to the fringe of the forest, 'and didn't leave me until he saw the NCOs appear, who'd come to look for me'.

The priest's warning turns out to be correct. 'A long column of cavalry had appeared near the Liazma. Other Cossacks and armed peasants were coming up along the Dmitrovo road.' Some foragers are running back to the Italian lines as fast as their legs can carry them. Many of the them, pur-sued by Russian scouts, have abandoned their carts or horses, already laden with plunder:

'The Dragoons of the Royal Guard advanced. The Marienpol Hussars made ready to receive them but, disturbed by the artillery fire, beat a retreat, carrying away the Cossacks, who'd imprudently advanced and had exposed themselves, not without some rather serious losses.'

By now it's 4 p.m., too late in the day to come to grips with this enemy. So Colonel Moroni, his foraging operation – apart from the few carts and horses the foragers had abandoned – being completed, gives the order to march off home:

'But being followed closely by the enemy and forced to escort a numerous convoy, he thought it dangerous to make the whole move-ment en bloc. First the wagons and other impedimenta filed off as far as a wood to our rear, then the troops followed in the best order.'

This is the signal for the Russians'

'best horsemen to attack, uttering shrill cries, and firing some shots, but without daring to come too close. Hardly was the convoy lined up properly along the road which passes through the forest and the sharpshooters had been placed on its flanks to protect it if attacked, than our columns abruptly faced about, and marched against the enemy. Seeing this, the many groups of armed peasants soon began to flee, throwing away their weapons as they crossed the fields. The cavalry followed their example. Night was already falling. Then two vélites rejoined the detachment. They'd got lost in the woods while looking for me, and the pope I'd spoken with had saved them from the hands of the Cossacks by hiding them until we'd come back.'

Not all foraging expeditions, the vélites' adjutant-major adds sombrely, operating under the same conditions, are being so successful.

Young Lieutenant Paul de Bourgoing, he of the fancy fur, has to interrupt his struttings to and fro in front of the two actresses General Delaborde has taken under his wing, and sally out with some wagons and 50 men of his own regiment, the 5th Tirailleurs-Fusiliers of the Young Guard, to see what he can find in a village on the left bank of the Moskova – its right bank has already been occupied by the various Guard cavalry regiments. He's just entering a village dangerously close to the Russian outposts when the tocsin sounds and a fusillade breaks out between his men and some peasants who 'aided by some Russian soldiers lodging with them, defend their cows and sheep'. Seeing one of his officers and five men beat a hasty retreat, dragging a cow with them and followed by a compact mass of peasants, he orders his men to fire. The Russians reply with well-nourished musketry. A corporal falls wounded in his arms, spattering him with his blood. From all sides armed peasants and Cossacks come running or galloping across the plain. Now the whole detachment, carrying its badly wounded corporal on a cart, has to beat a hasty retreat. Already night is falling, and it's necessary to find the bridge across the river. Which they do – receiving timely support from a company of voltigeurs. The corporal dies on the forage cart.

Altogether, such sorties are producing less and less. By the second week in October no escort under brigade strength, or stronger, has much chance of bringing in a convoy of foodstuffs. Baron Lejeune, struggling with all the paperwork needed to reorganize I Corps and set it to rights, is finding

    'these last days very hard. Our foragers no longer brought us anything back, either for the men or the horses. Their accounts of the perils they'd run were scaring, and to listen to them it seemed we were surrounded by a network of Cossacks and armed peasants who were killing all isolated men and from whom we ourselves would only escape with difficulty. These perplexities made the task of restoring order as soon as possible in the army's organisation extremely laborious, both for the corps commanders and their chiefs-of-staff. The days and nights were all too short to cope with so many difficulties and I hardly had time to see anything more of Moscow than the very long street leading from my suburb to the Kremlin.'

War Commissary Kergorre puts the matter in a nutshell:

    'Even if we had had enough provisions to spend the winter here, we should still have had to retreat, for absolute lack of forage. What would we have done without cavalry, without artillery, in winter quarters in the land we'd conquered, without communication with France?'

Large-scale reconnaissances are being made, some even at divisional strength. On 27 September the 18th Line, part of Ney's III Corps, had

102

moved into town to occupy the German quarter, where there are 'still some good houses left standing'. Though Captain Bonnet finds himself poorly lodged, this inconvenience is more than made up for by his being promoted *chef-de-bataillon*, i.e., major. But on 3 October, III Corps, too, has to send out a

'strong reconnaissance of élite companies. I'd a command. The marshal led us to Bogorodsk, a little town 48 versts [35 miles] north-east of Moscow in the direction of Vladimir.'

And there, for four days, they 'lodge in the houses, a trifle anxious for the strong point we'd set up, and without news of the army. The road being intercepted, we guarded ourselves with greatest care.' But next day (6 October) they hear that the rest of III Corps is now on the same side of the town. All Ney's units except Colonel Fezensac's 4th Line have marched as far as Bogorodsk. On about 10 October Fezensac hears that

'a division of IV Corps made a movement on Dmitrov on the Tver road. Meanwhile Marshal Ney seized Bogorodsk, 36 miles from Moscow, on the Vladimir road. We spent several days erecting huts around this little town, as if to spend the winter in it. This pretence was perfectly useless. It fooled neither the enemy nor our own men. I didn't go to Bogorodsk. At that moment I was in an expedition commanded by General Marchand on the banks of Kliasma between the Vladimir and Tver roads. Part of my regiment went with me. The rest had followed Marshal Ney. The enemy, faithful to his system, withdrew as we approached. General Marchand had a blockhouse constructed at a point where a detachment had been carried off by a regiment of Cossacks. The command of this little fort had just been entrusted to a very intelligent officer when suddenly Marchand received the order to return with his whole detachment. Anyone could see that the army was about to quit Moscow, since it had ceased to defend the approaches.'

Not until 13 October will Bonnet leave Bogorodsk and get back to Moscow the following morning – only to go down with a fever.

LOVELY AUTUMN WEATHER

A theological assumption – 'so this is the famous Russian winter?' – parades and promotions – a mortifying setback for Lejeune – a fragile courier service – Abbé Pradt's difficulties in Warsaw – Muraldt visits Berthier – the Canaries at Smolensk – trophies – evenings at the theatre

Although the nights are becoming chilly, the weather's beautiful. Golden autumn days succeed one another, with the clear blue skies one only finds in the far north. Stopping briefly at the 4th Bavarian Chevaulegers' bivouac out at Petrovskoï for a visa, a Russian who's obtained a permit to visit his estate tells von Muraldt, 'The weather's so lovely for the time of year, one is tempted to believe God is with the Emperor Napoleon' – 'a theological assumption', von Muraldt remarks, 'belied by the outcome'. Unless, that is, illness is a mark of divine favour. For it's now, he sees, men are beginning to fall ill:

'Sicknesses, particularly dysentery,[1] appeared ever more violently. Few of our men were spared, and even among the officers only the youngest and strongest escaped this torment.'

Again and again Caulaincourt, who after all has spent four winters at Petersburg as French ambassador, warns Napoleon of winter's imminent onset. In vain. And his frankness gains him no thanks. Napoleon makes mock of Caulaincourt's fears. Even after the third week has passed without the least sign of any reply arriving from the Tsar, he's exclaiming: 'So this is the terrible Russian winter M. de Caulaincourt frightens the children with!'

'The weather was so fine and the temperature so mild, even the locals were amazed. On his daily rides His Majesty remarked very pointedly when I was present "the autumn in Moscow is fine and even warmer than at Fontainebleau."'

As for notions that the Russian army is disintegrating or demoralized,

'he continually ridiculed the stories told by the King of Naples, even though they fed the hopes he wanted to entertain, in spite of the reflections he must have had.'

Each day at 1 p.m. there's a splendid parade in the Kremlin courtyards. Reviewing the Old Guard infantry on Thursday 6 October, Napoleon turns to Narbonne:

'Well, my dear Narbonne, what do you say about such an army manoeuvring in bright sunshine?'

'I say, sire,' replies that gentleman of the *ancien régime* and one-time minister of war to the Republic, 'it's had a good rest. Now it can take the road so as to occupy its quarters in Lithuania, leaving the Russians their capital in the state they've left it in.'

Promotions and decorations rain down. Pion des Loches, promoted major, is overjoyed when two brother officers bring him his commission, the more so, he says, as their compliments are obviously sincere. Now he's to command the 1st Company of the Old Guard's Foot Artillery together with the 2nd Company of Foot Artillery of the Young Guard, plus a park and its train. 'It was mainly from this time I kept open house. We were rarely fewer than seven or eight at dinner.'

Next day Roguet's Young Guard division is reviewed. On 8 October there's a 'general parade'. On the 10th the turn comes to Compans' division of Davout's I Corps; and Sous- Lieutenant Dutheillet of the 57th Line is promoted full lieutenant[2] for his heroic assault on the first of the Bagration *flèches* at Borodino. Also, he says, because Compans' division is suffering from a general shortage of officers.

(In sharp contrast to the state of affairs among Ney's Württembergers, where *Karl von Suckow*, rejoining divisional headquarters in the Kazan district, with his convoy of 400 more or less recovered Borodino wounded, finds there's such an excess of them that any number have to be detailed off to follow the army 'as amateurs'. There are, in fact, very few Württembergers left. The day before Compans' division goes on parade one of its generals, Scheler by name, writes home to his king from the Kazan suburb:

'the infantry in a state to bear arms number no more than 490 men, but we're expecting a convoy of convalescents. The artillery still has 385 men. The four cavalry regiments together 444 men. General Breuning's condition is hopeless. The extraordinary homesickness so many people have been stricken with and which there is no medicine for is consuming his strength. All we're getting from the French administration is some ammunition. What we're above all short of is vigorous horses. The French have taken no measures for subsistence or to renew the equipment, or else only bad ones. Nor is anything being done for the hospitals.')

Best of all, Pion des Loches' promotion entitles him to a wagon of his own for the homeward journey:

'As captain I'd had one wagon for myself and my lieutenant, half filled with my troops' effects and reserve shoes. Now I was major I had a wagon to myself, smaller it's true, but sufficient for my victuals for a retreat of three to four months [which he immediately gets busy filling with], a hundred cakes of biscuit a foot in diameter, a sack holding a quintal of flour, more than 300 bottles of wine, 20-30 bottles of rum and brandy, more than 10 pounds of tea and as much again of coffee, 50–60 pounds of sugar, 3–4 pounds of chocolate, some pounds of candles. Then, against the event of a winter cantonment on the left bank of the Niemen, which I regarded as inevitable, a case containing a rather fine edition of Voltaire and Rousseau, Clerc and Levesque's History of Russia, Molière's plays, the works of Piron, [Montesquieu's] Défense de L'Esprit des Lois and several other works such as Raynal's Philosophical History, bound in white calf and gild-ed on the spine. Further, for 80 frs I'd bought myself one of the most beautiful furs that have been brought back from Moscow.'

Alas, for at least one superior officer that day's parade of 10 October is far from being a happy one. Lejeune, the future painter of battle scenes, a man who on occasion can find that 'in war a heart moved by bellicose exal-tations is endowed with a sensibility more exquisite than at any other instant in life,' has wearied of the unending paperwork involved in being Davout's chief-of-staff, an appointment he'd never wanted and even begged to be excused from. Until Borodino Lejeune, like Fezensac, had been one of Berthier's 'lady-killers' – prancing about in the gorgeous uni-form he'd designed for his colleagues. But Berthier, Fezensac tells us, never fails to help his staff officers up the ladder. And now – apparently without waiting for the Emperor's signature – the army's Major-General has presumed to give Lejeune command of the 57th Line. The upshot, as witnessed by Lieutenant Dutheillet, is utterly painful:

'Candidates for the cross of honour were very numerous. I recall that the Emperor, coming to the regiment's front – it was very much reduced – saw at its head, in command of it, Colonel Lejeune, from his [sic] staff.[3] Having asked Berthier how it came about that Colonel Leje-une was in command of the 57th, in advance of his signature, he said: '"Colonel, I haven't taken the command of the 56th from you, I fancy, so as to give you the 57th. Return to the staff, that's where you belong." And to General Compans: "Who's the division's senior major?" "It's Major Duchesne of the 25th." "Have him immediately recognised as colonel of the 57th." Which was done. And in front of the division Colonel Lejeune got the most humiliating of affronts an officer can experience.'

Berthier takes him back and consoles him, Dutheillet supposes. Actually, as Lejeune himself laments – though he makes no mention of this no doubt extremely painful incident – he has to resume his arduous duties under Davout. But young Dutheillet must have known who his colonel was, and there can be no reason to doubt his account of an episode altogether char-acteristic of Napoleon's drastic ways at parades or his phenomenal photo-graphic memory for who's who in the army.[4]

These parades, of course, although perhaps primarily designed to keep up morale in a situation everyone knows is more and more worrying, are more than ceremonial events. Though Napoleon is being lavish with rewards, as Césare de Laugier notices, he's also scrutinizing each division with a view to its efficiency in a nearer future than his dinner guests suppose. Nor is he deceived by his own praise of the fine weather.

At first communications with France and western Europe have functioned well:

> 'The post-houses were fortified. The courier service, which I'd organised at the campaign's outset, was given special attention. The despatch case containing despatches for the Emperor was arriving regularly every day from Paris in 15 – often in 14 – days. The service's punctuality was truly astonishing.'[5]

Even so, though he won't admit it, Napoleon's concern for the mail's daily arrival shows how aware he is of being out on a limb:

> 'He was always impatient for his courier's arrival. He noticed the delay of a few hours, and even grew anxious, though this service hadn't ever broken down. The Paris portfolio, the packets from Warsaw and Vilna, were the thermometer of the Emperor's good or bad humour. It was the same with all of us. Everyone's happiness hung on the news from France. Small consignments of wine and other objects arrived. Officers, surgeons and administrative officials also came to join the army.'

The service, Caulaincourt goes on,

> 'was carried on by postillions relayed from post to post between Paris and Erfurt, from Erfurt to Poland by couriers stationed in brigades [teams] of four at every hundred miles; in parts of Poland by relays of postillions, across the frontier and through Russia by French postillions personally selected by Count Lavalette [head of the post office]. They were mounted on the best post-horses, and placed at my service. There were four to every relay, and each relay covered from 15 to 21 miles.'

Engineer-Colonel Serran, covering all the hundreds of miles through Lithuania and Russia on his way to Moscow from Spain, had been less impressed; he thought that

> 'nothing would be easier than to intercept them, leaving us isolated, very much weakened, with rather a lot of cavalry in a pitiable state, an enormous amount of artillery matèriel, 600 miles from any friendly country.'

He'll turn out to be right. 'A few isolated men,' Caulaincourt hears one day, have been 'chased or captured. One courier was delayed almost 15 hours, which worried the Emperor extremely. Every quarter of an hour he asked me, also the Major-General, whether we'd heard anything about what had caused the delay.'

Caulaincourt profits by the occasion to

'renew the demand I'd been making ever since we'd got here for an escort for the courier, even if only a couple of men. But to establish this at all the relays would have entailed a considerable detachment of troops, and the cavalry was already considerably reduced in strength. So the Emperor dismissed the matter, saying it was an unnecessary precaution as the road was perfectly safe.'

Well, it isn't.

'Three days later the postillion driving the courier to Paris escaped several gunshots beyond Mojaisk and was chased for a couple of leagues. Whereupon the Emperor lost no time in sending out the detachments I'd asked for.'

Even so, Caulaincourt's initial self-congratulation that it 'was as easy to travel from Paris to Moscow as from Paris to Marseilles' is rudely disturbed when Cossacks capture the courier returning from Moscow for Vilna and Paris:

'Other points along the Smolensk road were similarly intercepted by enemy parties, with the result that all sure communication with France was cut off. Vilna, Warsaw, Mainz and Paris were no longer daily receiving their orders from the great Empire's sovereign master.'

And back at Gumbinnen, the last town on the Prussian frontier before Kovno and Vilna, where a courier should pass through daily, the district governor Schön has just reported on 7 October to the Prussian chancellor Hardenberg in Berlin that

'since 1 October not one courier has arrived here from the general headquarters, nor any official news of the capture of Moscow, nor even a letter from Moscow.'

All he has to go on are rumours from Vilna that the city had been set on fire. 'According to these the misery reigning in the army is beyond any idea. Already people are talking of the Emperor Napoleon's coming back.' And when on 10 October the Vilna courier at last arrives, after taking five days, he brings news that 'the fire of Moscow is a lie'. Not until 15 October will any official news, despatched on 17 September 'not from Moscow, but from a bivouac in front of Moscow, arrive from IHQ. 'That the journey has taken so long is said to be due to the lack of horses between Moscow and Smolensk and to the Cossacks who are troubling the road.' The very first despatch from Moscow itself won't pass through Gumbinnen until 24 October, having 'taken four weeks because it has had to be escorted from Moscow as far as Smolensk'.

Napoleon's choice of *D. G. Dufour de Pradt,* Bishop of Poitiers and Arch-bishop of Malines, for the post of ambassador plenipotentiary at Warsaw – a post, one would think, of utmost importance – had been so odd as to be inexplicable. Ever since July, when he'd thought of sending the pro-Polish Narbonne from Vilna to replace him because of his blunderings with the Polish Diet, Napoleon has been bitterly regretting it. According to Mme de Rémusat, that acute observer of human nature, Pradt

> 'had intelligence, and knew how to intrigue. His language was at once verbose and piquant. He had some humorous small talk, held liberal opinions and too cynical a way of expressing them. He was mixed up in many matters without achieving much success in any. He even man-aged to wrap up the Emperor in his words; perhaps gave some good advice; but when he'd managed to obtain the right to implement it, spoiled everything.'

That Pradt's an intriguer, Napoleon – who'll describe him afterwards as 'my spy on the clergy' – knows very well. Hadn't he caught him out, repri-manded him at a levee, but pardoned him? 'I made a mistake, but God pro-tected him.' Yet it's this weak reed Maret, at Dresden[6] in May, at his orders had suddenly been ordered to go to Warsaw as minister plenipotentiary. Whereat, Pradt says, he'd felt 'a mortal chill in my veins. There I was, ambassador in spite of myself.' His task had been 'to push the Poles into transports [of enthusiasm], avoiding delirium'. And above all to produce '16 million Poles on horseback' to fight their arch-enemy – a task which, as Napoleon sees it, should have been as easy as putting a match to a barrel of gunpowder. But ever since the July day at Vilna[7] when he'd refused to re-establish the Kingdom of Poland, and even told one of the Diet's emis-saries, in confidence, that he might 'at any moment make peace with Alexander', his Polish affairs have been going agley. Such blowing hot and cold had

> 'produced exactly the opposite effect of what he'd hoped it would. They'd gone there all fire, and come back as ice. Their coldness had spread to Poland and since then no one has managed to set fire to it again.'

Pradt, uncomfortably resident in a Warsaw more astoundingly poverty-stricken than anything he'd ever imagined, has found Poland 'foul and primitive' and the Polish administration no less so:

> 'I was bewildered by the gap I found to exist between the real state of Poland and the picture I'd been given of it. Anyone who'd wished to follow Napoleon's line of march had seen him create for himself an imaginary Spain, an imaginary Catholicism, an imaginary England, and an imaginary nobility, even more so an imaginary France; and now he'd made himself an imaginary Poland.'[8]

Since 1806 the Poles have been supplying the French armies with thousands of men. Currently, Pradt estimates, 85,700 of them are serving in various corps – a figure utterly out of proportion to a poor duchy, of Napoleon's own creation, with only five million inhabitants and whose trade, consisting almost entirely of fat grains that couldn't be stored very long and whose outlets – Turkey, Danzig and Russia – are being strangled by Napoleon's invasion of Russia together with the detested Continental System and the British blockade:

> 'The Duchy's revenues amounted to 40 million francs. Its expenses exceeded 100 million. The deficit for 1811 and the first few months of 1812 amounted to 21 million.'

No one in Warsaw has a penny to bless himself with. Every day Pradt is keeping open house – without ever being invited back, for the simple reason no one can afford it. Vandamme's[9] name, particularly, is hated throughout Poland. His Westphalian troops of VIII Corps, and the Saxons of IX Corps, passing through in June and July, had murdered and pillaged and ravished:

> 'All these horrors had their roots in the system, as absurd as it's inhuman, of waging war without magazines. This system has become the flail of the armies as of the peoples, has killed the art of war and relegated almost all those who follow this once so noble profession to the category of ferocious animals. He who in this way has depraved the generous hearts of warriors and by so doing has multiplied a hundredfold the calamities inseparable from war, has merited the curses of the human race.'

Jérôme[10] had been as endlessly loquacious as – and no less demanding than – his imperial brother. As for General Dutaillis, the French commandant at Warsaw, Pradt regards him as a ruthless brute. Even back in October 1811 there'd been talk of reducing the Polish armed forces by a half, and a great review fixed for 7 November had had to be cancelled – 'because the soldiers had no shoes'. Yet, though everywhere in Europe the harvest has failed, with starvation as the result, the Duchy has already provided 25,000 horses for the campaign. Ordered, via Maret at Vilna, to get hold of 10,000 more cavalry horses, Pradt tried to – 'I say tried, because that number of horses suitable for cavalry didn't exist.' Maret, Duke of Bassano, is Pradt's *bête noire*. Every day he's sending him peremptory letters from Vilna – in the seven months of his so-called embassy Pradt says he got 400 of them – telling him to

> 'keep out of politics and supply the army's needs. I was delighted whenever a day passed without one arriving by the post. The Duke of Bassano [Maret, Napoleon's foreign minister and plenipotentiary at Vilna] was the Emperor's monkey, one of the flails of our age. Every-

thing about him has to be flattered, admired, even down to the duchess's little dog, of whom it's been said "that dog has made many an auditor, many a prefect".'

Maret, Pradt says, 'didn't have the art of abbreviating interviews or discussions', of sitting too long at table; of wasting hours chatting up the ladies while men with urgent business have to sit outside for three or four hours waiting in his antechamber; of 'turning night into day and day into night', and never getting down to work in his office until midnight 'amidst an infinite number of portfolios without order or classification'. In a word, he detests him. Otherwise Maret's reputation is of quite another order than Pradt's. According to the young Duchess Marie-Charlotte Eugénie de Reggio, who has just joined her severely wounded husband Marshal Oudinot at Vilna, Maret

'like Count Louis de Narbonne, wore his hair in the old style. He carried himself and his well-powdered head very straight. He was tall; his manner was grave; his movements were slow, his words rare and always well-considered. Taken as a whole, he was imposing.'

Particularly so, perhaps, to the ladies on whom he, according to Pradt, lavished so much time in long chats.

The farther away any corps or unit is, the less the words of the master are likely to be put into effect. One day von Muraldt, the youngest of the 4th Bavarian Chevaulegers' officers and the only one to speak good French, is sent into town to Prince Eugène's headquarters in

'one of the few surviving palaces. It was situated in a street that hadn't suffered as much as most from the fire.'

While there he's sent in the middle of the night to the Kremlin, not very far away, with a despatch to Berthier. What Eugène wants to know is how he's to send letters and despatches to General Wrede, commanding the Bavarians of St-Cyr's VI Corps, at faraway Polotsk, whose excellent cavalry had been seconded to Eugène at Vilna in July. Though Muraldt doesn't realise it, he's exceedingly lucky the Bavarian chevaulegers aren't with their wretched compatriots who, Wrede has reported back to Maret at Vilna in September, have 'a perfect mania for deserting' and are dying in large numbers from typhus. The night is pitch black. Though he takes a French chasseur to guide him, Muraldt soon gets lost among the ruined streets. The chasseur pretends to know his way about, but after half an hour of straying hither and thither the young officer realizes he doesn't, and that they're lost. Now and then they bump into marauders, who've also lost their way. 'We'd wandered about for a couple of hours when we at last met a patrol of Guard Horse Grenadiers, who put us on the right track.' So they reach the Kremlin, 'brilliantly illumined by the campfires of the Imperial Guard all about'. One can just walk in. On the main stairs he encounters Roustam,

> 'who very politely gave me the information I desired. An adjutant announced me. I found Berthier writing at a little table in the centre of the room. In all its four corners secretaries sat similarly writing, and only the scratching of quills disturbed the profound nocturnal stillness in this high-ceilinged, spacious, faintly lit hall. The Prince seemed tired and strained, and only glanced through my despatch.'

So, in his excellent French, Muraldt repeats its question *viva voce*. To this Berthier replies

> 'that no definite information had been recently received from Marshal Gouvion St-Cyr's army corps. Nor were those communications wholly secure. And anyway he'd inform the Viceroy at the first suitable occasion. This answer wasn't at all to my liking. It indicated all too clearly that things weren't as they should be to our rear, as we already partly knew.'

On the other hand Eugène's emissary is delighted when Berthier tells his adjutant to give him some supper,

> 'for just then one could show no greater politeness than to offer someone something to eat. On a big table lay the remains of an evening meal, to which I did all honour – in those days one always went hungry.'

Equally uncertain, even worrying are the behaviour and secret dispositions of Prince Schwarzenberg and his Austrian corps, in faraway Galicia. On the same day that Napoleon had entered Moscow, in that southern theatre of war, Tchitchakov, coming up with his Army of Moldavia – an army which, if French gold had been a match for British, should still have been fighting the Turks – had absorbed Tormassov's force and taken the offensive against Poland. Whereupon an outnumbered Schwarzenberg had retired behind the Bug and, together with Reynier, had forced Tormassov to retire. One day Berthier gets a personal letter from Schwarzenberg whose very politeness seems worrying. On that Caulaincourt, Duroc and Daru are all agreed:

> 'In brief, its sense was the following: "The position is already embarrassing, may become graver. Anyhow, whatever happened, the Prince assured Berthier of his personal sentiments and the value he placed and always would place on him."'

He expresses no such devotion, either real or feigned, towards Napoleon; and certainly feels none.[11] Napoleon sees through Schwarzenberg's letter. Tells Berthier:

"This gives warning of defection at the first opportunity. It may even have started already. The Austrians and Prussians are enemies in our rear. This letter is sentimental twaddle."

Foreign Minister Maret, however, who is keeping an eye on Schwarzenberg's movements, seems perfectly satisfied, as he has reason to be. Napoleon writes to his all-important father-in-law, the Emperor Francis in Vienna, asking him to promote Schwarzenberg field marshal and send him 10,000 more men. He's also beginning to worry about Macdonald's mostly Prussian X Corps and its immense siege train, investing Riga. As for St-Cyr's operations around Polotsk, Napoleon directs Victor to divide his attention between Vilna and Minsk, where he is to liaise with the extremely experienced Polish General Dombrowski, a veteran from '96 and Italy.

Everywhere the Russian numbers are growing.

Smolensk, however, is Napoleon's nearest base and is now becoming the prime object of his attention. It's in that wreck of a burnt out city that such sapient regimental officers as Le Roy and Fezensac are looking forward to going into winter quarters. These, according to Napoleon's new plan, will be taken up along the Molihew–Smolensk–Witebsk line, where the stores assembled at Smolensk, together with yet more supplies being collected at Witebsk, Vilna and Minsk, should be sufficient to feed the army through the winter.

At Smolensk immense food convoys and fresh units have been arriving almost daily from Germany. One such unit is Berthier's own Neuchâtel Battalion. Marched – at his express order not too ruthlessly – from their depot at Besançon, 'the Canaries', as they're universally called in the army because of their yellow coats, are doubtless unique in not having lost a single one of their 666 men *en route*. When they get to Smolensk they're overjoyed to find that their own well-liked commander Colonel Jean-Henri Borset – a middle-aged man of cheerful spirit who loves to join in amateur theatricals, 'especially comedy' – is already installed as the city's *commandant d'armes*; and – again at 'their' prince's special behest – are housed 'as comfortably as possible'.[12]

Not all regiments are being treated so considerately. When the 129th Line staggers into Smolensk on 13 October it will number only 724 men and 40 officers, i.e., be hardly a battalion strong. As for the food convoys, few if any can go a step further. After dragging their wagons so many hundreds of miles their scraggy oxen drop dead and aren't even worth eating.

Indeed the position at Smolensk is far from rosy. That once prosperous city, abandoned by its populace at the time of the battle and the fire,[13] is hardly recognisable. When its new governor, General Charpentier, arrives from Witebsk (where, much to his successor's distaste, he's being replaced by the wounded General *F-R. Pouget*, he finds he hasn't a single mason to 'put the hospitals into good repair, to rehabilitate buildings which could be of the greatest usefulness for troops passing through and the garrison and, in a word, to procure objects of prime necessity'.

Where's the company of artisans, Charpentier writes to Berthier: the one, he suddenly seems to remember, that had accompanied Imperial Headquarters (but his memory is failing him, it was Davout's I Corps) at the campaign's outset? He needs them so badly:

'We could do with 10 locksmiths, 10 masons, 10 joiners, 10 carpenters, 2 coopers, 2 tinkers, 1 hatter, 4 edge- toolmakers, 2 tinsmiths, 2 cutlers, 2 cordwainers, 4 saddlers, 8 shoemakers, 8 tailors.'

In the burnt out houses of the upper town are tile stoves which could be dismantled and re-erected elsewhere. But above all it's becoming difficult to increase the stores. All around Smolensk, as around Moscow, Cossacks are so terrifying the peasants that they won't sell the troops their wares any longer. Charpentier urges upon Berthier his imperative need to keep the '160 mounted men of the 1st Polish Horse Chasseurs' who speak Russian, or anyway the local dialect (a blend of Russian and Polish), in order to keep the Cossacks at bay and deal with the population.

In Moscow Colonel Serran's works on improving the Kremlin's fortifications have largely been carried out by 5 October, for on that day Césare de Laugier has already seen there '12 heavy- calibre guns in battery, while 18 others are ready to be placed beside them.' For their part the Italians have converted

'the prison known as the Ostrorog, situated in the suburbs, into a kind of fortified citadel. The two convents occupied by I and III Corps' depots are to be used for an identical purpose.'

Yet all these fortificatory works, it seems, are at least in part a blind, intended to throw dust in the army's – perhaps also Russian – eyes. For at about that same date, 'at the time he'd decided to send Lauriston to the Russian camp', Secretary Fain, taking down letters and orders to Berthier in his self-invented shorthand, has already realised that Napoleon is already beginning to plan the army's departure:

'From then on he'd been incessantly busy. We'd seen him imperatively assign 15 October as the last date for evacuating the wounded. As early as 9 October the trophies he wanted to honour France with had been packed up and loaded. Among them were the flags taken by the Russians from the Turks over a hundred years ago, some ancient armour, a madonna which the devout had enriched with diamonds, and the gilded cross from the belfry of Ivan Veliki, which had so long dominated all the domes of Moscow and which the Poles had

often mentioned as the object of the Russians' devotion, even super-
stition.'

Caulaincourt will afterwards seem to recall a report coming in that the Russian authorities had declared the recovery of the gilded iron cross to be the
first goal of all orthodox Russians, and it had been this which had 'fixed the
Emperor's determination' to take it back to Paris and place it on the dome
of the Invalides. Unfortunately, as treasurer Peyrusse either sees or hears,

> 'one of the cables of the crane broke, and the weight of the chains
> dragged down the cross and part of the scaffolding. The ground was
> shaken by the enormous weight of this falling mass, and the cross was
> broken in three places,'

shattering the cathedral dome in its fall.

More important than trophies are the wounded. That same day, 5 October,
Fain hears Napoleon tell Daru:

> '"I want to preserve my freedom to choose my line of operation. How
> many days do you need to evacuate the hospitals?" "Sire, forty-five
> days." "That's far too long. Your calculations are exaggerated. Expe-
> rience shows that three months after a battle not a sixth of the wound-
> ed are still at the ambulances. So first separate out your wounded into
> two classes – those who a month from now will be able to march
> unaided, and those whose trouble would be aggravated by being
> moved. There's nothing you need do about either of these cases. But
> into your second class, on the contrary, you'll enter those invalids who
> can conveniently be transported. These are the only ones you need
> worry about, beginning, as is only right, with the officers. You see, if
> you rectify your calculations in this way you'll come to quite a differ-
> ent result, and we'll gain precious time."'

Meanwhile appearances must be kept up. As the French had penetrated
ever deeper into the soil of Holy Russia, the actors and actresses of the
French troupe, though still under the Tsar's patronage, had felt themselves, like all other foreign residents, being regarded with ever deeper sus-
picion. Not even an attempt to stage an anti-Bonapartist show had saved
them. Their director had been one of a party of foreigners whom Rostopchin had rounded up and deported by barge to the interior. While
some of the company's actresses had followed their gentleman friends to
Petersburg, the homes of those who'd remained had first been pillaged by
the departing Russians, then looted by the French. Her house burnt down,
the 38-year-old *Louise Fusil* has been left with nothing and has only survived
thanks to the asylum given her by Caulaincourt. Certain others of her colleagues likewise.[14]

Another, much more famous, artist who has survived the fire is the Italian tenor Tarquinio. Summoned to the Kremlin to sing to Napoleon, who's fond of Italian music, he's being accompanied on the piano by the son of Martini (composer of the ever popular *Plaisir d'Amour*). Is it he, Tarquinio, who now first mentions to Napoleon the presence in Moscow of the remainder of the troupe? Or Bausset, the Prefect of the Palace? Bausset at all events takes

'the opportunity of mentioning the matter to the Emperor during lunch. He distributed some immediate reliefs, appointed me to superintend them, and ordered me to find out whether, given their present composition, it would be possible to stage a few performances and so provide some slight entertainment for the army lodged in Moscow.'

Though no professional singer, Louise has a pretty voice and has sometimes even sung duets with Tarquinio. Ordered to seek her out, Bausset finds her and one of her fellow-actresses, almost in rags, in some outbuildings of the Galitzin palace. But Louise absolutely declines the honour of singing before His Majesty 'who's a connoisseur'. What she and her colleagues can do perhaps, providing Bausset can find them a theatre and costumes, is to stage some plays and vaudeville pieces.

Fortunately a theatre has survived – evidently not Henckens' 'big theatre', but the one in Count Posniakov's palace. One of the most beautiful in town until the catastrophe, it had been the scene of the city's best productions. Found to be still serviceable, its auditorium is hastily whitewashed, its boxes magnificently draped, and a 1,700-candle candelabrum, brought from some church, is hung from the ceiling. Here, rigged out in the strangest fragments of clothing, the company rehearses in front of an astounded Bausset. The male lead, otherwise naked except for a Russian militiaman's cap, appears in a military greatcoat. Enter the young lover in a seminarist's cassock and a Russian general's plumed hat! The *père noble* at least has some trousers, albeit badly patched. Alas, the Villain of the piece, though shod in superb boots from the days of Louis XIII and a grey Spanish coat he'd saved from the troupe's burning wardrobe, hasn't. Though wearing a red fur-lined jacket which reaches to her knees, Mme Burcet, who seems to be in charge, has neither skirt nor petticoat. The overall effect? In Louise Fusil's eyes, it's as if they're 'dressed up to attend a masquerade ball for lunatics and beggars'. Bausset, shocked, immediately asks Daru to get them something better. Which is done. 'We drew up a sort of repertory,' Bausset, Ségur's superior, goes on:

'In the unhappy situation in which the actors found themselves, nobody had any pretensions. The distribution of parts was very easily done. Never was there a cast more united, more flexible, or easier to manage. Besides, Mme Burcet had a strong influence on them and knew their talents well. I wasted no time in obtaining costumes and suitable premises for their performances. In the Mosque [sic] of Ivan the military authorities had collected everything that had been rescued from the flames, and there, thanks to the kindness of Count Dumas, the army's Quartermaster-General, I found all sorts of costumes. The French actors took velvet dresses and clothes which they fitted to their figures and to which they fastened some broad gold braid which was to be found in quantities in these stores. In fact, they were dressed in great style, though several of our actresses, such was their distress, barely had the necessary linen to wear under these beautiful velvet dresses – at least,'

the over-plump Prefect of the Palace adds hastily, 'that's what Mme Bursay told me.' The actors' ludicrous rags and tatters replaced by odd – if more seemly – costumes, the theatre opens to a packed, virtually all-male, not to say all-military, audience 'at 6 p.m. precisely' on Wednesday 7 October, with a double bill:

LE JEU DE L'AMOUR ET DU HASARD

The Game of Love and Chance, Marivaux's famous comedy of 1730, is followed by

AMANT, AUTEUR ET VALET

Lover, Author and Valet, a one-act comedy by Ceron. 'This was a brilliant début,' Bausset goes on:

'The pit was filled with soldiers, while the two rows of boxes seated officers of all arms. Only a small charge was made at the doors and this was shared among the actors, with nothing but the cost of lighting deducted.'

Audience enthusiasm knows no bounds. The actors forget all their usual rivalries. The orchestra consists of the Guards bands' finest soloists. Mlle Lamiral's Russian dance number – she's been a teacher of dancing and deportment at the Catherine Institute for daughters of the Russian nobility – takes the house by storm. And for eleven successive evenings a very good time is had by all. 'We went on acting', Louise will afterwards remember, 'right up to the eve of our departure, and Napoleon was most generous to us. He rarely came to see the play.' That excellent actor – in his own role[15] – prefers to listen to Tarquinio in the Kremlin. One day when he does come, the Emperor goes on talking through a pretty air Louise is singing and which is making 'a kind of a sensation'. Yet no one claps, because the Emperor is there. Such is the etiquette:

'Napoleon asked what the matter was; and M. de Bausset came and told me to begin again. I was so overcome with emotion I felt my voice was trembling and thought I'd never get through it. I managed to,

117

though; and from this moment this romance became so fashionable that people never stopped asking me to sing it. The King of Naples even asked me to give it him for his band:

> *'With fond farewells a handsome knight*
> *Consoled his sword as he flew to the fight:*
> *"On honour's field love guides my course,*
> *Puts arms in my hands, o'er my life decides.*
> *When victory's mine I'll soon return,*
> *And seek the prize whereto I yearn.*
> *My heart's the gauge of thy constancy,*
> *Thy love proves valour's faith in thee."'* [16]

Such were the pretty sentiments that could move the hearts of Napoleonic warriors amidst Moscow's blackened ruins.

CHAPTER 8

A LETHAL TRUCE

Talking to the enemy – 'the peasants are buying them at 2 silver roubles a head to kill them' – 'we were getting absolutely nothing from Moscow' – Mme de Staël at Woronowo – Wilson helps Rostopchin burn down his château – 'the law of cuck- oldom, from which no one's exempt' – a bad joke – a march on Turkey? – bright frosty weather – 'our enfeebled arms turned the millstone' – 'How will it all end?' – Le Roy loses his son to the Cossacks – 'Bah, they won't attack you'

Hardly less fantastical, perhaps even more so, are the theatrically glamorous costumes of King Joachim I of Naples as he gallops about the disconsolate plain beyond Winkovo, letting himself be admired and chatted up by the Russians. Between him and them there's 'a kind of tacit agreement'. At outposts 'placed a mere 50 yards from each other' Victor Dupuy of the 7th Hussars even sees

'the King of Naples, finding the Cossacks too close to us, go among them, and make them withdraw their sentries and show them where they ought to be. The Russians obeyed. Their generals, even those of the advance guard, whom we'd often had a chance to see, made no difficulties about yielding to the King's least requirements. He really had an air of commanding the whole lot of them.'

On 6 October, the day after Lauriston had gone back to Moscow, Griois had been present at the first of these strange encounters:

'The enemy had come closer and closer to us and his scouts were at pistol range from our own. Murat, informed of this, had the signal to mount sounded all down the line. He summons one of the comman- ders, asks him in an imperious tone of voice by what right the Rus- sians are occupying ground they'd been repulsed from during the affair of the 4th, and orders him instantly to retire.'

The Russian officer declines, saying he must refer the matter to his gener- al; who soon turns up. And is reproached, even more arrogantly, by Murat:

'His anger no longer knows any bounds when the general answers him, in the calmest and most respectful tone, that the space separat- ing the two armies after the affair of the 4th not being occupied by our troops, nothing prevented him from putting his outposts there with orders not to commit any hostile action.'

"This ground belongs to me; I'd driven your troops off it. You should have stayed in the position I'd driven you back to, and you've broken your word by leaving it after the suspension of hostilities. But you're not to be trusted. You respect nothing. Yesterday, when I was visiting my

outposts, one of your Cossacks was so insolent as to fire at me. If my officers hadn't restrained me, I'd have killed him on the spot. What's
more, I summon you to instantly withdraw your posts to their first position, or I'll oblige them to." And at the same time he orders the cavalry to advance and my artillery to arrive at the gallop. "Your Majesty",
the Russian general replies, "is free to do what he likes. I cannot withdraw my outposts, and if they're attacked, they'll defend themselves. As
for the offending Cossack, he'll be severely punished, and I beg Your
Majesty to accept my excuses for this act, which I wholly disavow.'"

Griois and the other officers, much pained to see how violent Murat has
become, are even afraid it may lead to negotiations being broken off
because of 'a misunderstanding that had no importance'. After remon-
strating with him, the generals in his suite interpose themselves *vis-à-vis* the
Russian general,

> 'who relaxed his pretensions. After an hour of debate and at the
> moment when our troops, arriving on the scene, were only waiting for
> the signal to attack, everything arranged itself amicably and we went
> back to Winkovo. I was close to the king throughout this scene which,
> if the possible consequences hadn't been so grave, and but for the
> king's martial air, which gave dignity to his wrathful disorganised ges-
> tures and his Gascon rodomontades, Murat's rage would have been
> really funny.'

All this and much else is being reported back to the Kremlin, where Ségur
is hearing how the King of Naples is

> 'enjoying the admiring glances which his good looks, his reputation
> for bravery and his high rank were attracting. The Russian chiefs took
> care not to upset him. They overwhelmed him with every mark of def-
> erence that could sustain his illusion. If he took a fancy to some bit of
> ground they were occupying, they made haste to give it up to him.'

'This inoffensive behaviour', Dupuy goes on, 'led us to believe peace was
very near. We ardently desired it, for every day our ranks were growing
thinner.'

The magnificent cuirassier companies, for instance, which had entered
Russia 130 troopers strong, are 'now only 18 to 24, so that a division didn't
even reach regimental strength'. Everywhere it's the same story. Arriving
from Moscow, Lieutenant *Mailly-Nesle*, a young aristocrat at IHQ, whose
only notable deed so far has been to be ordered to get Auguste Caulaincourt's heart embalmed after Borodino, is shocked to find his own regiment, the prestigious 2nd Carabiniers, have

> 'lost so many horses I think we weren't more than 100 men in the two
> carabinier regiments all told. We'd left France 1,400 strong, and sev-
> eral detachments had joined us.'

For five days the Carabiniers, in their brass-coated breastplates and superb Grecian-style helmets, have only been eating horseflesh. Though 1,500 troopers are daily being sent out to forage, all they're bringing back is 'a few bales of hay'.

How different from the situation near the village of Woronowo where, twelve miles behind Murat's lines, Zalusky has been given the duty of providing a special escort for the Emperor should he suddenly turn up. There the Lancer Brigade is in clover. Each day they're breakfasting on

'polewka [rice wine] and rice cooked in milk from our own cows, and dining on whole roast pigs or chunks of beef roasted on wooden spits, and then taking coffee from iron pots hung up over an enormous fire, kept up from morning until late at night by the cantinière, or rather several cantinières at once. On the four sides of the hearth, on rugs or bits of canvas, heaps of roasted coffee, of raw coffee, of crushed sugar mounted up. And beside them cups, glasses, goblets – from the most sumptuous in gilded porcelain to earthenware mugs, Muscovite wooden drinking bowls and white metal campaign gourds. Against payment, the cantinière, sugaring it amply, poured out mocca to amateurs of all ranks assembled there and seated on canapés and satin divans with gold brocade, morocco leather, or simply on planks which supported trestles and barrels.'

Alas, nothing of all this, nor anything like it, applies in the Winkovo camp. There the Line cavalry regiments are literally starving. Each time the 7th Hussars have to 'do the dawn'[1] there are

'unfortunate horses which, lying down and worn out, could no longer struggle to their feet and died on the spot. Though Moscow was stuffed with victuals, the men were in the greatest need. The King wrote to the Emperor to inform him of our truly calamitous situation. The Emperor interrogated the ordnance officer carrying the despatch who, to play the courtier, replied that we lacked for nothing – and that was a word too much! The Emperor even got angry with the King of Naples for sending him a pack of lies. This became quickly bruited abroad and the officer received all the reproaches and all the curses he deserved. I shall abstain from giving his name.'

Murat's opposite number on the Russian side is a man who cuts hardly less glamorous a figure than himself. No one, in Wilson's view, is better matched to deal with him than General Miloradovitch, whose

'manner, his tone of voice, gestures, etc., render him superior to Murat in fanfaronade, while his singular courage and the unbounded confidence of his soldiers secure him every respect from the enemy'.

On one such occasion Miloradovitch airily tells Murat:

> 'Really it's an outrage, letting so many of your dead remain unburied, and your wounded lie in that wood. I'll give permission to come within my posts and remove them.'

Other generals, too, are talking to their French and Polish opposite numbers. The Russian

> 'General Korf, a most excellent man, with a fund of dry humour, met General Amande at the advanced posts. Soon the conversation turned to peace. And Amande observed: "We're really quite tired of this war: give us passports and we'll depart."
>
> "Oh no, General," said Korf. "You came without being invited; when you go away you must take French leave."
>
> "Ah!" said Amande. "But it's really a pity two nations who esteem each other should be carrying on a war of extermination. We'll make our excuses for having intruded, and shake hands upon our respective frontiers."
>
> "Yes," replied the Russian, "we believe you've lately learnt to esteem us. But would you continue to do so if we suffered you to escape with arms in your hands?"
>
> "*Parbleu!*" sighed M. Amande. "I see there's no talking to you about peace now and that we shan't be able to make it."'

Peace! It's what everyone's waiting for. And, in the Kremlin, Napoleon is still making a confident outward show of expecting it. Can it be he's really deceiving himself, and thus endangering the army and his empire? Everything possible, Caulaincourt is dismayed to realise, is 'being done to prolong the Emperor's fatal feeling of security and feed his hopes of an arrangement'. Not that he's really taken in by Murat's reports of the Russian army being demoralized or disintegrating:

> 'He continually ridiculed the stories told by the King of Naples. Yet they fed the hopes he wanted to entertain, in spite of the reflections he must have had. "Murat's the dupe of men far more astute than himself. All this talking under a flag of truce serve no purpose except to those who send them, and they invariably turn out to our disadvantage."'

Indeed Murat's position at Winkovo is utterly precarious. Ahead of him, based on its entrenched camp at Tarutino, some three miles ahead of his outposts, he has an ever-growing Russian army, while a couple of miles behind him the road to Moscow runs through a long, deep defile that has a stream running through it and can only be crossed at one point. In the event of a sudden reverse that ravine can be deadly. Furthermore, it's a very strange kind of a truce which only applies 'to the front between the two camps. At least that's how the Russians were interpreting it. We could neither bring in a convoy nor go foraging without fighting. So the war went on everywhere except where it could be favourable to us.'

Not that Murat, any more than General Amande, lacks for warnings:

'Colonel Neninski, whom he'd sent to the Russians, had talked to Platov and other senior officers, who'd said quite openly: "You're tired of the war. For us, on the contrary, it's just beginning. We'll strip you of everything: your wagons, your baggage, your guns."'

And when on 8 October Murat personally asks Miloradovitch to let his cavalry go foraging to right and left, the Russian answers bluntly:

'Why, would you wish to deprive us of the pleasure of taking your finest cavaliers of France like chickens?'

MURAT: "Oh! then I'll take my measures: I'll march my foraging columns with infantry and artillery on its flanks." MILORADOVITCH, ironically regretting not having an occasion to see the French cavalry make a real charge:

"That's just what I want, so I can order my regiments to face them."

Murat galloped off, and instead of his marching the columns to protect his foragers, the Cossacks last night took 43 cuirassiers and carabiniers, and 53 this morning,' probably another example of Wilson's implicit trust in Russian claims. In his lapidary diary Lieutenant Maurice Tascher is noting the

'extreme poverty of the army, which is living off vegetables, horse-meat and unground rye. In the forests the peasants are defending themselves against the soldiers when they try to get some food and forage.'

And not only defending themselves but also avenging themselves on the invaders. Wilson hears how they're 'buying French prisoners from the soldiers for a few francs a head, to kill them'. Himself, though suffering from a painful leg caused when his carriage overturns but in piquant contrast to conditions in the French camp only a few hundred yards away, 'the English general' is relishing 'sturgeon, caviar and large barrels of red and white grapes' given him by Platov's newly joined Don Cossacks. One day he forwards a letter to the ambassador of the Spanish government in exile. Found in the pocket of a French officer of the Swiss Colonel Tschüdi (commanding the 2nd Battalion of the Spanish Joseph Napoleon Regiment in what had been Dedem's brigade), it begs permission to be transferred to the 57th Line (Dutheillet's regiment, still back in Moscow), as he's sure 'his honour will be ruined by the desertion of his men on the first occasion.'[2] Like everyone else, Wilson is by now certain that French morale is at a complete ebb. His only wish is that Bonaparte would 'attack our camp, but I fear he won't. Yesterday 200 French cuirassier foragers were made prisoners. A general came with a flag of truce to remonstrate against the cruelty of the Cossacks in falling upon "poor men only going in search of a little hay!" Sweet innocents! How tender! How humane! how considerate these myrmidons have become!'

And all the time, as Murat's forces are dwindling away, Kutusov's are growing stronger. Each day that passes, no matter how fine the weather, has brought winter a day nearer.

On 9 October Wilson, who has hurt his leg and just heard that yesterday, though the King of Naples commanded in person, 'the French lost 4 caissons on the ground, and a wood and plain covered in dead', takes his carriage and rides out to Woronowo, twelve miles to Murat's right rear. At the junction of the 'fine, broad, well-maintained old Kaluga road' and another that leads westwards to the little town of Vereia and to the 'new' Kaluga road, Woronowo is of strategic importance. Though French troops are probing toward 'this pretty village, bisected by a stretch of water, the village on the hither side, the château and its outbuildings on the other', they've so far not occupied it.

But that's not why Wilson's carriage is taking him there. It's at Woronowo that Rostopchin has his unusually superb country residence. And he has invited 'the English general' over ... to help him burn it down.

Back in August, while everyone had been trembling for the fate of Smolensk, it had been at Woronowo that the governor of Moscow and his countess had received Europe's most famous novelist. Napoleon's most inveterate enemy and leader of the intellectual opposition to his military dictatorship, on 10 May Mme *Germaine de Staël*, had flouted his Geneva prefect's express orders that she be kept under house arrest in her home at Coppet,[3] and taking her courage and her nerves in both hands and, accompanied by her daughter and her lover *Albert Jean Michel de Rocca*, had fled to Bern. There she had taken the German philosopher Schlegel into her carriage and, passing through the recently insurgent Tyrol, had arrived in Vienna. There, though feted as usual – no woman in Europe is as famous as the author of *Corinne* – she'd been horrified to find that, as a result of three successive defeats at Napoleon's hands, the easy-going Austrian regime had been replaced by a quasi-Napoleonic police state of the kind she most utterly detests. Her plan had been to go on to Petersburg, thence to Stockholm, to see her old friend, the former Marshal Bernadotte, now Crown Prince Elect Karl Johan; and thence to England, the country which, next after her beloved France, she most ardently admires for its parlia-

"What a monstrous sight! All those palaces! Extraordinary resolution!
What men!" But of Rostopchin, who'd ordered his police to set fire to the city:
"He fancies he's a Roman, but is nothing but a stupid savage!" The marshal
standing behind Napoleon is Ney.

Moscow in flames, seen from the riverside. It was along this road that Napoleon and IHQ escaped from the Kremlin, passed round the west side of the town and went out to the Petrovskoï Palace.

V. V. Verestchaguin imagines Napoleon being guided through the flames by Davout's grenadiers. In reality it's doubtful whether he ever came so close to the fire. But Quartermaster *Anatole Montesquiou* and his colleagues had 'to protect cheeks, hands and eyes with handkerchiefs and headgear and turn up the collars of our uniforms'.

The Petrovskoï Palace, occupied for three days by Napoleon and IHQ when
the fire was at its height. Its 'Gothick' style reminded Roman Soltyk of Hampton Court and
to Castellane seemed "Greek, truly romantic". It hadn't a single stick of furniture.

Return to the Kremlin from Petrovskoï, 19 October. Caulaincourt found
the scene utterly depressing. The Guard Dragoons' breeches can hardly have been so
white! A few days later one its squadrons was annihilated at Malo-Wiazma.

Incendiaries, real or imaginary, were shot by firing squad in the monastery by
the Doroghomilov Gate where Davout ('the Iron Marshal') and his reluctant chief-of-staff,
the future battle-painter Baron L-F. Lejeune, had their headquarters. – Oil painting
by V. V. Verestchaguin.

'Moscow, September 24, 1812' – one of the scenes drawn by Major Faber du Faur on his
unit's arrival on 24 September. 'In this labyrinth of devastation' he saw remains of the
iron-plate roofings whose fall had been so dangerous to many of our eyewitnesses.

Moscow seen from the south-west by the Württemberger Major G. de Faber du Faur. His fine engravings, based on drawings made on the spot, cover the whole campaign. Left: the River Moskova. Middle ground: remains of half-burnt monasteries.

'Moscow, October 8.' One of the many intact monasteries, whose brilliant colours contrast vividly with the ruins of houses, Faber du Faur noted, was a depot for the 4,000 dismounted cavalry. View 'from the north-west bastion of the powder magazine,' to the east of the city, where III Corps was quartered.

Right: Baron A-J-F. Fain, Napoleon's hard-worked Second Secretary, kept a private journal. Metternich admired him for his probity and intelligence.

Below: Captain Boniface de Castellane, one of Napoleon's orderly officers, was 'so so used to the Emperor's infallibility and his projects succeeding' that he was prepared to march on India.

Below right: Colonel Bacler d'Albe, Napoleon's chief topographer, was, physically speaking, his closest collaborator. Sometimes as they lay stretched out over the map table fixing Bacler's coloured pins they would 'let out loud cries as their heads bumped together'.

Above: Rostopchin was an unbalanced personality. As he left the city, which at any moment would burst into flames, he told his son to look at it for the last time. He and his pious wife had recently entertained Mme de Staël at his château at Woronowo, which he also personally set fire to and which General Wilson thought 'could not be replaced for £100,000'.

Above right: Colonel Lubin Griois, commanding 3rd Cavalry Corps' light artillery, conversed familiarly with Napoleon on ballistics, prided himself on knowing each of his gunners by name and on never ducking when roundshot came whizzing overhead.

Right: General Jean Rapp, Napoleon's battle-scarred and most senior ADC, though many times wounded and aged 41 in 1812, he 'still walked with the jaunty gait of a hussar officer'. Although not recovered from his four wounds at Borodino, he inisted on serving during the retreat.

Far left: The Dutch ex-diplomat and general of brigade Dedem van der Gelder was too critical for his superiors' liking. – From a miniature painting.

Left: Major C. F. M. Le Roy, promoted Lieutenant-Colonel of the 85th Line at Moscow, wrote his memoirs to show the importance of getting one's daily dinner. His son, a sergeant in the 85th, was captured by Cossacks and never heard of again.

Opposite page, bottom: Césare de Laugier, Adjutant-Major of the Italian Guardia d'Onore, an Elban whose diary is always concerned to defend the honour of the Army of Italy.

Below: 'Over 100 ammunition wagons' assembled in October in the open area to the east of the Kremlin's two spectacular churches were so thick on the ground that Faber du Faur found it hard to find a spot from which to draw them.

Davout at the Doroghomilov monastery, in the western part of the city.
Presumably it's his reluctant chief-of staff, Baron Lejeune, the future painter of
battle scenes, who is talking to him.

The Battle of Tarutino where Murat's starving advance guard was only saved by his personal intervention and the Polish Legion of the Vistula. 'Seeing Bagavout's infantry advancing in three squares to cut off our retreat, the King of Naples put himself at the head of some carabiniers and the 5th Cuirassiers, charged and sabred them to pieces.'

Prince Eugène Beauharnais, Viceroy of Italy, commanded the Army of Italy.
He was, said Napoleon, "The only member of my family I've never had to complain of."
But his attitude to his Italians was arrogant.

Right: Leaving Moscow, midday 19 October. Napoleon at the Kaluga Gate. 'The crush in the streets was terrific. The units were crossing each other's path in all directions... more than 500 guns, 2,000 ammunition wagons with their half-starved teams, the endless train of vehicles of all kinds and nations laden with booty and foodstuffs...' All would by and by have to be abandoned.

Right: Marshal Mortier's mines were partly defuzed by rain. But when the others went off they blew part of the Kremlin sky-high and made the 'loudest bang' Lieutenant Paul de Bourgoing would ever hear in his life. Lieutenant-Colonel Le Roy heard it from fifty miles away.

Bringing up the rear on 23 October and turning off from the old Kaluga road to reach the new road, III Corps had to blow up any number of its ammunition wagons, their teams being already utterly exhausted. This one was casually exploded by a gendarme who fired his pistol at it while it was having its load lightened!

Advance or retreat? "That's enough, gentlemen. I shall decide." The scene in the weaver's cabin at Gorodnia. In fact he did not do so until next day, when he was sure the Russian army had once again eluded his grasp. – Oil painting by V. V. Verestchaguin.

Borowsk, 26 October. Ney's III Corps being attacked by masses of Cossacks. "A brief discharge of artillery and a charge by the cavalry of the Royal Guard sufficed to drive them off. At Borowsk our luck seemed to turn. In the afternoon of the 26th we began our retreat." – Engraving by Faber du Faur.

mentary form of government. For a moment, while anxiously waiting in Vienna for her passport to arrive from Petersburg, she'd even contemplated braving the hazards of travel through Turkey and getting to London that way. But then the Tsar's passport had come; and on 14 July , anniversary of the fall of the Bastille and the same day as Napoleon had left Vilna for Glubokoië, she too had – it's the only appropriate word – invaded Russia. How frustrating that her arch-enemy's armies and their thousand cannon should have placed themselves between her and Tsar Alexander! It had added 800 more miles to her journey, a wide detour via Moscow – still supposedly far outside the theatre of war. In fact she'd probably been the last western European to see the ancient city before it had gone up in flames.

Driving out to Woronowo, she'd been entertained by the Rostopchins. Not that the city governor is in the least degree a liberal. A week or two later, to save his own skin he wouldn't hesitate to throw a journalist who'd been disseminating French ideas to be torn to pieces by an infuriated mob. What Rostopchin's 'pious' countess (one day to be the author of the century's most sado-masochistic novel) or their daughter (one day to wed Philippe de Ségur) had thought of their garrulous visitor, we don't know.

From Moscow she'd gone on to Petersburg, and there still more deeply imbued the reportedly liberal-minded Tsar with her ideas. And thence to Stockholm, where her brilliant garrulity is fast wearying the taciturn Swedes as she makes propaganda for their new ruler as putative successor to a defeated Napoleon.[4]

'Situated by the roadside', Rostopchin's château will appear to Dumonceau, that sober-minded and meticulous observer, as

> 'an ordinary country house, of modern architecture, plastered on the outside and having two storeys, four or five windows in its façade, with a door in the middle, enhanced with an attic portico supported by two columns.'

But by then it'll be in ruins. To Wilson, as his carriage approaches it, the still intact château seems very much more impressive, irreplaceable for less than £100,000:

> 'The very stabling was of rare grandeur, surmounted over the gateways by colossal casts of the Monte Cavallo horses and figures which he had brought from Rome, with costly models of all the principal Roman and Grecian buildings and statues that filled a large gallery in the palace, the interior of which was most splendidly and tastefully furnished with every article of luxurious use and ornament that foreign countries could supply.'

Unfortunately Friedrichs' division is fighting its way towards it. And to Wilson Rostopchin's sacrifice of his lavish residence seems a 'magnificent act, executed with feeling, dignity, and philosophy. The motive was pure patriotism. Rostopchin, on hearing the pickets commence skirmishing, and seeing the enemy in movement, entered his palace, begging his friends to accompany him. On arriving at the porch, burning torches were distributed to every one. Mounting the stairs and reaching his state bedroom, Rostopchin paused a moment, and then said to the English General: "That's my marriage bed; I haven't the heart to set it on fire; you must spare me this pain."

'When Rostopchin had himself set on fire all the rest of the apartment then, and not before, his wish was executed. Each apartment was ignited as the party proceeded, and in a quarter of an hour the whole was one blazing mass. Rostopchin then proceeded to the stables, which were quickly in flames; and afterwards stood in front contemplating the progress of the fire and the falling fragments. When at last the Cavallo group was precipitated, he said: "I am at ease." And as the enemy's shots were now whistling around, he and all retired, leaving the enemy the following alarming and instructive lesson affixed to a conspicuous pillar.'

Written in charcoal and afterwards to be read, not to say differently remembered, by many French and Polish eyes and quoted with various pathetic embellishments, it reads, according to Heinrich von Brandt, who'll be arriving in a minute with his voltigeur companies of the 2nd Vistula Legion:

I'VE SET FIRE TO MY CHATEAU, WHICH COST ME A MILLION, SO THAT NO DOG OF A FRENCHMAN SHALL LODGE IN IT. [5]

Dumonceau sees it attached to the left-hand pillar. Beneath it, some French soldier, 'also in charcoal, but illustrated with a drawing' has proffered his (probably obscene) comment. Le Roy, arriving on the scene with the 85th Line, proffers others, expressed with greater elegance and innuendo:

'The newly built château of cut stone, constructed in the Italian style, had a fine appearance, though since the morning it had been on fire. Since it hadn't been able to bite into the walls the fire had concentrated on burning the panelling, furniture and floors. The grand staircase was almost wholly reduced to quicklime. However one of the regiment's captains, Souvigny by name, risked going up to the upstairs apartments and brought back some curious belongings and a roll of letters written in French.'

These, Le Roy goes on gleefully,

'were nothing but the correspondence of Rostopchin's daughter with a certain cousin who hadn't always respected the bonds of relationship, at least so one could suppose from the free and familiar expressions in this correspondence.'

All of which will delight Le Roy, that great hater of aristocrats the more when, many years later, he comes to write his memoirs:

'I'll wager a hundred to one the little cousin is a friend about the house of M. le comte de Ségur, and count though he be, neither intelligence nor wealth, as our good Lafontaine wittily puts it, protect anyone from the law of cuckoldom, before which all ranks are on the same level. And it's not certain it's he who has carried on the direct line of Asia's greatest conqueror.'[6]

Evidently the same notice, also scribbled in charcoal, has also been nailed up on the doors of the parish church, where Le Roy's bosom friend Lieutenant Jacquet, bivouacking there, points it out to him as the battalion's staff settles for the night in the porch:

'But the French had been politer than that boyard. They'd left the two marble statues above the main door standing on their bases. With my own eyes I saw them still there when I left. As for the park and its embellishments, everything had been spoiled by the artillery and its vehicles which had camped in the gardens and occupied the kiosks. The trees had been cut down for the men to warm themselves, since the nights were beginning to be cold.'

When Griois sees

'this stroke of patriotism, so little in our own style and whose heroism has something barbarous about it, it gave us food for thought and a glimpse of what we had to expect in such a country.'

But that isn't how it's received in the Kremlin. Declaring Rostopchin's defiant notice 'ridiculous', Napoleon sends it – presumably in a copy – to Paris, to be printed in the newspapers, where, according to Caulaincourt, 'it made a deep impression on all reflective people, and, in respect solely to the sacrifice of his house, found more admirers than censors'. But Gourgaud[7] fancies he can detect Rostopchin's true motives. Hadn't this Russian count, he asks, burnt down his château simply to escape the reproach of not himself having lost anything in the great disaster he had precipitated?

Bored by having nothing to do in Moscow as the days and weeks go by, Captain Biot, ADC to the wounded General Pajol, offers his services to Murat's chief-of-staff General *A-D. Belliard*. The wise and efficient Belliard, 'the only man who had a hand with Murat', has just been appointed Major-General of the Cavalry, as successor to Auguste de Caulaincourt, killed at Borodino. Now he sends Biot with a despatch to Murat, possibly to inform him of this fact. On the way Biot falls in with a certain General Dumont, who generously gives him his card to take to his valet who, he says, will give him a bottle of wine and a beefsteak; but before he goes on to Winkovo Dumont also takes him to Prince Poniatowski, who sends him on his way.'

The hitherto well-fed Biot is appalled at the state of affairs in the Winkovo camp. He has brought his comrades of the 11th Chasseurs some Moscow chickens, bread, rum and wine. And well he has done so. For by now they're very hungry indeed. The state of things at the Winkovo camp worry him so that he's 'unable to get a wink of sleep' at the 11th Chasseurs' bivouac. 'Men and horses were dying of hunger. Literally. Never any distributions.' Rather than stay there he prefers to accompany Murat on a reconnaissance, where, almost more alarming, he sees at a glance that the over-confident Sébastiani[8] is still being guilty of all sorts of negligence: 'His favourite occupation, Colonel Meuzian of the 5th Hussars told me, was uttering declamations.' Murat sends Biot back to Moscow with a despatch, and probably a letter to Belliard, for they are in frequent correspondence.

Honours, at least so it seems, are flying to and fro between Moscow – where Biot finds his conduct at Borodino has made him a chevalier of the Legion of Honour – and Winkovo. A similar one reaches Griois – but in circumstances that nullify its effect. At a musket shot's distance outside the village, he and Jumilhac and their orderlies are almost daily having to use the flats of their swords to fight off insubordinate soldiers who want to grab their timber cottage and burn it down for firewood. Driven off, they swear they'll come back in the night. But now something much worse befalls. Immediately after Lauriston's visit, Griois, taking advantage of the unofficial truce, has sent his empty ammunition wagons back to Moscow to be replenished from 'the great artillery park'; and with them his orders to his servant Batiste, also left behind in Moscow, to join the returning convoy and bring him his own wagon, his carriage, worn though it is from its long journey from Italy, his victuals and his horses, all of which he'd also left behind:

'Several days had passed since I'd sent off my order; but everything in front of us being calm, I assumed the same state of affairs prevailed between Winkovo and Moscow, and wasn't at all worried that the convoy was delayed. But then, one day at dinner, Lahoussaye, with a laughing air, announced that he'd just received my nomination to the Legion of Honour.[9] At the same time he had some annoying news for me. My vehicles had been carried off by Cossacks.'

At first Griois thinks the idiotic Lahoussaye is only joking. He isn't:

'A quartermaster sergeant of the Train, who'd just arrived, told me that on the second day out of Moscow the convoy had been assailed by Cossacks, whom the escort had prevented from doing it any great harm, they'd only smashed up some wagons and made off with the horses. But just as they were going off they'd caught sight of my car-

riage, with my wagon and lead horses, quite a long way from the convoy's rear, seized it without anyone resisting them,'
and made off into the forest. His carriage is worth 'at least 20,000 frs. The
loss in my situation was irreparable.' It's a stunning blow:

'All I had left was what I was wearing, a shirt in a portmanteau, the
horse I was riding, and another I'd brought with me. But what I
regretted most was my papers and some other objects of little value;
and, above all, my faithful servant Batiste, who I feared had probably
succumbed to fatigue, chagrin and maltreatment.'[10]

His adjutant-major Lenoble, too, had had all his effects in Griois' wagon,
'so we could only console each other. He even went to the place
where the "hurrah"[11] had occurred; but returned with the sad certainty that all was lost. By some kind of fatality this was the only event
of this kind that occurred while we were at Winkovo. Every day
unescorted convoys were arriving without accident from Moscow.'

Not all promotions to the rank of chef d'escadron are as straightforwardly
due to experience and merit as young Victor Dupuy's. For years now –
Henckens had seen it start as early as 1806, in Italy – experienced regimental officers who've risen from the ranks have had to get used to seeing
blue-blooded youngsters from ancient military families advanced over
their heads. Now the 6th and 8th Chasseurs, in Chastel's light cavalry
brigade of 3rd Cavalry Corps, is no exception. On 6 October Lauriston had
brought out with him in his suite two such newly fledged colonels – the
young Belgian count de Talhouët for the 6th and Talleyrand's son, Count
Talleyrand de Périgord, for the 8th Chasseurs, both, 'though still in their
twenties, orderly officers to the Emperor:

'It seems the Emperor had found his dead colonel's temporary successor, Squadron Commander de Feuillebois, a trifle on the elderly
side. It's true young colonels with experience of the great staffs are
necessary for light cavalry regiments,' and young Talhouët, though
he knows 'virtually nothing about what goes on inside a regiment,
had been to a good school to learn the profession,'
sighs Henckens, on poor Squadron-leader Feuillebois' behalf. Swallowing
his cruel disappointment – short of performing some spectacular feat
under the Emperor's very eyes, it's good-bye forever to further promotion
or a colonel's epaulettes – Feuillebois at once recommends to young Talhouët that he avail himself of the 34-year-old but highly experienced Henckens' services. Talhouët, who since being wounded in the shoulder at
Mojaisk on 8 September has been resting in Moscow, turns out to be a
young man with a lot of good sense, and confirms Henckens, though still
not commissioned, in his post as acting adjutant-major to the 6th Chasseurs.

Cuirassier-captain *Bréaut des Marlots* too rejoins his regiment, bringing with him a wagon laden with coffee, sugar and wine:

> 'The wine was soon drunk up, but I still had nearly 600 pounds of sugar and coffee, which was a fine stock even after giving some of it to my comrades. I drank it day and night.'

On one occasion – but only one – some tuns of wine arrive 'without escort and without accident' for 3rd Cavalry Corps from Moscow. And here's a really big surprise for Surgeon *Heinrich von Roos* and his 3rd Württemberger Chasseurs, in the nearby village of Teterinka, occupied by Sébastiani's light cavalry division. At the campaign's outset huge herds of sheep and cattle, prodded on across Europe – some from as far afield as Italy and Hungary – by 'frighteningly inexperienced drovers', had accompanied the regiments; but of course had immediately fallen far behind. Now, all of a sudden, the Württemberg chasseurs and Prussian lancer units are rejoined by

> 'the remains of herds of cattle, cows and sheep we'd assembled at the Niemen. I can leave it to your imagination what state these beasts were in. But they were no less welcome for that.'

Even Murat comes and asks for some proper meat.

> 'We sent him now a sheep, now a haunch of beef or cow. As for ourselves, we made broth of sheep or beef, like tea or coffee. Sometimes it happened, but rarely, that one of the Moscow regiments, knowing how badly off we were, sent us some real tea, some coffee or sugar.'

But the men who've brought the herds have terrible things to relate about the state of affairs in the rear; how on the Borodino battlefield there are

> 'still wretched mutilated creatures crawling about, living off rotting horseflesh with their teeth and fingernails, all black, like wild animals, having nothing human about them but their shape.'

Similar horrors are related by two troopers who'd been taken prisoner at Inkowo[12] on 8 August and who, to von Roos' and their comrades' amazement, turn up disguised as peasants.

One day a begging letter is received via the outposts from five officers who've been captured by the Russians. They want some money. The cash is raised and sent to the outposts. But is never received. This is war *à outrance*. Nothing so stimulates the imagination as hunger! Remain only its imaginings. In the Kremlin the younger officers, always the most optimistic, are discussing how, peace once made, in the spring the French and Russian armies will be marching southwards together against Turkey – or possibly even India.[13] 'We're so confident,' Captain Castellane writes in his journal,

> 'that we aren't discussing the possibility of such an enterprise succeeding, but how many marches will be needed and how long it'll take letters to reach us from France. We're used to the Emperor's infallibility and his projects succeeding.'

Can it be an echo of these fancies that reaches the 2nd Cuirassiers out at Winkovo and causes Regimental Sergeant-Major Thirion's imagination to sprout erotic wings?

'We imagined we'd be taking up winter quarters in the Ukraine, and in the spring the Russian and French armies would march together to conquer Turkey. Each of us already saw himself as a pascha. We made it a duty in advance to restore their liberty to numerous victims shut up in harems. Instead of being herded together waiting for their despotic shepherd to select a favourite, it'd be they who'd toss a handkerchief amid our squadrons. Each of us wanted to bring a beautiful slave back to France. One fancied a Greek, another a Circassian. This one a Georgian, that one a daughter of the Caucasus. These castles – not in the air but in Turkey – helped us to pass a very dreary, very painful time in this camp we'd named The Camp of Famine, a title it merited all too well, since we lacked for everything. No tents. No shelter. Sleeping under the open sky on a little straw, eating horseflesh, drinking river water from the infected stream.'

Surely this disastrous war must soon be over? Is as good as over already? Topics of conversation vary, but are never gay. Some of the officers try to cheer their men up by reminding them it's the great, the hitherto never defeated, Emperor Napoleon who's still in charge. Others are sceptical, accuse these optimists of not revealing their true thoughts:

'The women accused Napoleon of not keeping his promises, "he who lives well-off in Moscow with his Guard and sends us here to die of cold and hunger!" We let these women relieve their feelings by such words, but none of us would have permitted himself to express himself in that fashion.'

Only the weather's superb. Since settling into their cabin Griois and Jumilhac have 'only had two days of rain. On the other day the air is steadily getting colder. By now the 3rd Württemberg Chasseurs are burning down Teterinka's barns, one by one, for firewood. Soon there's

'nothing left of the village but a few rooms for the senior officers and invalids. We only had enough straw to feed the horses. We used it for sleeping on at night and then gave it to the horses to eat. Often the nights were so cold we hid under straw to sleep. And next morning this straw was so sticky with hoar-frost we had to break it to get out. The cadaverous horses and the saddles were white with it.'

Fortunately the sun comes out in the daytime and melts the hoarfrost:

'We cooked what grain, barley, buckwheat we could get hold of. We boiled them until the grain swelled, burst and softened. Then we removed the husk and made soup and thin broth. Part of these grains

were reserved to make bread of, after we'd ground them. This work
was most arduous for our thin and enfeebled arms. Officers and men
alike, we took turns at turning the millstone. Those who wouldn't put
their hand to it had to go hungry. For more than three or four days
my arms refused to do this milling work.'

Von Roos must be wondering what good he'll be for carrying out amputations after a fight. And goes on:

'The saltpetre of our gunpowder, dissolved in the soup, gave it a bitter taste, caustic, disagreeable. It also caused diarrhoea. So we had to
abstain and give up using any kind of salt. For fat we used candles.'

The 7th Hussars, 'very badly established in the utterly ruined village of
Winkovo' are

'living off leaves of tea or cabbage, grilled horseflesh or chicken. Food
and forage were utterly lacking. Strong detachments, taken from our
division and that of General Saint-Germain's cuirassiers [2nd, 3rd
and 9th, 1st Cavalry Corps], went searching for it at distance of 5 or 8
miles, but brought back very little.'

In one of these forages Dupuy loses a horse and a servant, taken by the
enemy:

'The grand'gardes needed more than a third of the men available in
the division. The saddle was hardly ever off our horses – only for a
moment during the day, to let them drink. Yet the Russians were leaving us in peace. Between us there was a kind of tacit agreement.'

As the cavalry's horses dwindle and die, Griois is hearing from the Russian
camp

'musketry fire by sections and platoons, which told us new recruits
were being hurriedly trained. The King of Naples, no doubt warned of
Russian preparations for a new offensive, had ordered all baggage wagons, horses and anything else that might hinder a night action should
be sent back to a village less than three miles to our rear. Next morning, if nothing happened in the interim, they were to be sent forward
again. For the first few days this order had been punctiliously obeyed;
but when it was seen the enemy hadn't attacked and that the only
effect of this precaution was to wear out the horses, it was relaxed.'

Frequent convoys of sick men, too, are leaving for Moscow. 'A month more
of this, and the whole reserve cavalry', says Griois bluntly, will be 'annihilated without even fighting'.

On 10 October the volatile Murat, always capable of falling ill merely from
disappointments or frustration,[14] writes again to Belliard:

'My position is terrible; the entire enemy army is in front of me. The
advance guard's troops are reduced to nothing. And it's no longer

possible to go foraging without incurring the virtual certainty of being captured. Only two days ago we lost 200 men in this fashion. How will it all end? I'm afraid to tell the Emperor the truth; it would pain him. Won't there be officious persons who'll poison my reports? Ma foi, so much the worse. Tell the Prince of Neuchâtel something of this. If only I could see the Emperor! My health isn't at all good, and I'm sure to get ill at the first rains, but let God's will be done. Doesn't the Emperor want to do anything for the advance guard? Send us some flour, or we're going to die of hunger. Give me some news, I know nothing.'

For his part Napoleon is intending to use Murat's cavalry – what's left of it – for a screen to hide a sudden march on Kaluga, taking Kutusov off guard. And His Majesty is becoming exasperated by all the quasi-fraternizations. Now he renews his orders to inhibit all truces or discussions with the Russians, and even orders "any general having intercourse with the enemy to be shot". Though addressed to his distant relative Sébastiani, to spare his brother-in-law's feelings, the order naturally also reaches its real addressee, on whom – Murat writes again to Belliard, the only effect of such a ban on chats at the outposts is to cause him even greater worry:

"For to me they've been an assurance that the Russians won't attack me without warning. This has facilitated our foragings. How unhappy I am, adieu! When will the Emperor make up his mind? What will become of his army this winter?"

Among the infantry regiments supporting Murat at Woronowo is the 85th Line. Its First Major having just died, Le Roy is notified on 10 October that he's been promoted – certainly at Davout's behest – lieutenant-colonel, and is to succeed him. His first duty in his new capacity is to go to Moscow and report to Davout on the regiment's condition. For seven or eight miles Lieutenant Jacquet accompanies him along the Moscow road; but then returns to the regiment. The deserted highway is dangerously exposed. So is a convoy of vehicles coming toward him in the distance.

And now Le Roy, riding along with his trusty servant Guillaume, is in for a terrible shock.

The convoy, bound for Woronowo, turns out to be commanded by the 85th's baggage-master. Its escort, Le Roy sees at a glance – and tells him so – is utterly inadequate. Well, the baggage-master's all too well aware of it:

'"You're right. Yesterday evening I was attacked in the forest and was so unfortunate as to lose four sergeants, on their way to rejoin. They'd laid their weapons on the vehicles and were marching at some little distance from the convoy when some armed peasants and Cossacks carried them off. The worst of it all – for you – is: your son's one of the prisoners. Of course we opened fire. But not being in sufficient strength to pursue the pillagers we decided to guard the vehicles as far as to the next post.'"

Stricken to the heart, Le Roy pursues his way. What can be happening to his son?

'I still had five more miles to go before I got to the wood where they'd been captured. I realized all too well it was too late to help my child. Even so I had hopes of learning something about these unfortunate men's fate. What stupidity! Ah, young people, young people! Soon I reached the fatal spot. The wood was too dense to penetrate. Seeing a road to my right, I told Guillaume to go on along the highway; I wanted to see where this track led to.

"It can lead wherever it likes," the brave lad said to me, "but I'm not leaving you."

"Very well then, come along with me."

'We put our horses to a gallop and soon we saw a big plain. As this track took us not very far from the town, I decided to follow it. Hardly had I done half a mile or so than I came to my senses, saw what danger I was exposing myself to, also my devoted companion. Halting in my tracks I turned to Guillaume and said:

"You've just heard me saying how imprudent my son's behaviour was. Yet here am I, making the same mistake! What are we looking for? Where are we going? What can we do if we're attacked? We'll only get ourselves killed without any chance of avenging ourselves.'"

Guillaume points out that it's safer to be out in the plain where any enemies will be visible at a distance, and that they still have every chance of reaching Moscow before nightfall. By and by they see some infantrymen running toward a tree. Challenged, Le Roy and Guillaume declare themselves. The infantrymen belong to an outpost of the 108th. Lodged in a windmill, they're grinding corn for their division. Their captain, all sympathy for Le Roy's terrible loss of his son, invites them to stay the night.

'We spent a large part of the night chatting together. To avoid any surprise half the troop were under arms, the other rested with their backs against their packs. As dawn was breaking I dropped off a moment.'

Despite all the grinding noises in the mill Le Roy doesn't wake up till 10 a.m. And immediately – extraordinarily, but true to his Lucullan character – he feels

'revived and disposed to have breakfast. My head had cleared of all the bleak notions it had been overcharged with since yesterday. I gave no more thought to what I was leaving behind in Russia. All my wishes turned toward my family, whose sole breadwinner I was.'

Even so, the shock has had a profound effect. For here's a strange thing. All Le Roy's military ambitions have vanished overnight! From now on his only wish, like so many thousands of others', will be to get back to France, and 'on grounds of long service to get a retirement pension ample enough to keep me from poverty, and to which I felt I had a most legitimate right.'

On 13 October Castellane, in the Kremlin, notes in his journal that the eleven regiments of Grouchy's 3rd Cavalry Corps, together, only add up to 700 horses. Griois takes up the refrain. 'Under pain of dying of hunger' his horse gunners are still having

'to off and search for some kind of nourishment, since one wouldn't have found a blade of straw for 30 miles around and since – either because of transport difficulties or the insouciance of the administrations – we were getting nothing, absolutely nothing, from Moscow. There our comrades had an abundance of everything, were living in magnificent palaces, eating succulent dishes, drinking the best wines, while we were having to sustain ourselves on a crude broth, rye cakes baked under ashes, muddy and marshy water. Our foragers were having to go 9 to 12 miles to bring back a little crushed straw or even a little of half-rotten thatch from roofs. Many were killed or captured, and these losses were happening over and over, every day, though we were taking care now to have them escorted by numerous detachments.'

One such foraging expedition, on a very big scale, has gone quite exceptionally far. Colonel *T-J-J. Séruzier*, commanding 2nd Cavalry Corps' horse artillery, had been 'given orders to take command of a strong detachment, taken from all our light cavalry regiments. To these forces I was to unite half my squadron of horse gunners.' But though his column marches for 120 miles and even pushes

'into the Ukraine, it wasn't until in the surroundings of Poltava[15] I found any inhabited countryside. This country is very fertile. I found remounts for the whole of my cavalry and assembled a considerable number of wagons, which I loaded with grain, flour and forage.'

They all get back without being molested; and Séruzier, already rewarded after Borodino with a 4,000 francs pension, finds he's been nominated, not a Chevalier, but a Commandant of the Legion of Honour. 'I was as happy as a brave military man can be.'

By now Murat's situation has become so desperate that he sends his 36-year-old Neapolitan ADC, the newly fledged Colonel *M-J-T. Rossetti*, to Moscow to

'tell the Emperor how compromised his advance guard was, and how impossible it would be for him, should he be attacked, of successfully resisting a much stronger enemy. "Tell the Emperor," the King added, "he shouldn't count on our suspension of hostilities. It's illusory, since on either side we can attack each other after giving only a few hours' notice.'"

The King had only agreed to it, Rossetti's to explain, in order to give his men a few days' rest. But it's

'"solely to the Russians' advantage, since it in no way changes my position, whilst every day the enemy is being reinforced and all day long I hear from my camp the shots of their recruits' target practice."'

At 10 p.m. on 12 October Rossetti sets out with his despatches

'for the Emperor and for Berthier. I reached the Kremlin at 8 a.m. At 10 a.m. I was introduced into the Emperor's office. As he had already informed himself of the contents of the King's despatches, which I'd handed to Berthier, I no sooner appeared than he says to me:

"Well! So Murat's complaining, is he?"

"Sire," I replied, "it's because he's in a very critical situation."

"Bah! With light cavalry one can live anywhere. Not all the surrounding countryside has been devastated. He can draw resources from it."'[16]

Rossetti points out that the countryside is entirely occupied by Cossacks, and that even marauding parties commanded by generals are only bringing back a few bales of hay 'not sufficient for one-fifth of our horses'.

'"Where's Poniatowski?"

"On the other side of the ravine, between Pictrowo and Kroueza."

"Show it to me."

'I showed him on the map the position of V Corps. Having examined the map for ten minutes, the Emperor says to me brusquely:

"What an idea of Murat's, to put himself in a ravine! It's on the Nara he should have established himself."'

Rossetti explains that that's exactly what they'd been intending to do on 4 October, but that the enemy had prevented it with his whole forces, obliging Murat to withdraw to the Winkovo position:

'While the Emperor was walking to and fro, I expounded to him in greatest detail what the King had told me to say. He wore an air of not entirely giving faith to my report. Often he interrupted me, saying:

"Bah! They won't attack you. They're in more need of rest than we are. My army's finer than ever. A few days' rest has done it a lot of good."'

But when Rossetti reiterates that the advance guard is in a 'state of *dénuement* [utmost destitution]', he says:

'"Assure the King that tomorrow I'll be sending him a convoy of flour. Tell him he must absolutely hold his position. Anyway, he won't be attacked; but in any case he must halt and retrench himself at the Woronowo defile.'"

Rossetti's account seems circumstantial enough. But we've caught him out telling fibs before.[17] Can the greatest soldier of the age, emperor though he be, be so preoccupied with other matters that he only now bothers to check up on the exact position of his only major field force, facing the entire Russian army?

Certainly he seems to have left it very late to give Murat any real orders; and even then they seem too vague to be addressed to a field commander of Murat's wavering temperament and fluctuating strategical ideas. At 2 p.m. Napoleon dictates a letter, as always via Berthier:

"On the basis of your reports and the reconnaissances which have been sent in to him, the Emperor thinks the Woronowo position is a fine one, reserrée [compact] and able to defend itself with infantry, which would easily cover the cavalry. If you think so too, you are authorized to take up that position. The Emperor has sent off his horses, and the day after tomorrow the army will reach you to attack the enemy and le chasser [drive him off]. Three days will be needed for the army to reach your level; thus you will only have to spend four or five more days [where you are]; and if you think the enemy's going to attack you or that the nature of things is making it impossible for you to avoid the losses you've been sustaining these last eight days, you have the recourse of taking up the Woronowo position. All the vehicles which you have sent [to Moscow] are laden with victuals. Those being sent off this evening will also leave [again] tomorrow."

The long rambling letter goes on with that air of vagueness which can characterise Napoleon's orders at critical moments, as if partly dictated by a need to pass the buck. And this one will certainly need reading twice. As Napoleon himself, on second thoughts, seems to realize. Has Murat enough sense to adjudge his own situation aright?:

'Make sure to reconnoitre the outlet which could lead you toward Mojaisk, so that if you have to make a retreat in front of the enemy, you would thoroughly know that road. The Emperor supposes that your baggage, your park, and the greater part of your infantry could disappear without the enemy noticing it."

As if still bothered by uncertainty, he asks:

"Is it true that your cavalry when moving back through the Woronowo defile could be covered by your infantry and in a less fatiguing position than the one where it is [now], in flat countryside that obliges it to be always on the qui vive? At all events it is very [surely?] important

to procure your troops food for several days. In Moscow are 1,000
quintals of flour and plenty of brandy at your disposition."

If the advance guard had been commanded by Davout or Ney it's just possible such fuzzy instructions might have sufficed. To Murat, whose cavalry screen is going to be crucial if Kutusov is to be outflanked by a sudden
drive southwards to Kaluga, it can only give an uneasy feeling that, no
matter what happens, it'll be he who'll get the blame if things turn out
badly.

Even Henckens, from his on-the-ground viewpoint as adjutant-major of
the 6th Chasseurs, is seething with irritation to see the Russian army
becoming steadily reinforced and the attack on Kaluga delayed until the
season for it has passed. Say Gourgaud and other apologists what they will,
Napoleon's incisiveness at this moment is far from what it used to be, and
will be again.

While Rossetti is talking to Napoleon in the Kremlin, Murat is lodging a
formal complaint with Kutusov. Cossacks have carried off some of his mule-
teers which have accidentally crossed the agreed demarcation line. If he
doesn't get them back, he says, he'll raise the cease-fire.

That day too Sous-lieutenant Pierre Auvray of the 23rd Dragoons, foraging at a distance of nine miles from his bivouac, runs into Cossacks:

'Hardly have we had time to put ourselves in a state of defence by
forming up a troop of officers and NCO to contain them, while the
dragoons were making off with their loads, than a fight started. We
charged the Cossacks in force to be able to get across a little stream,
where we were mixed up pell-mell with them. Almost all our officers
were wounded. I received two lance-thrusts in my left arm. One young
officer was killed.'

That same day (13 October) Wilson hears more good news. On the
Mojaisk road a convoy of

'350 wagons, laden with Buonaparte's plunder, was proceeding
under the escort of four cavalry regiments and two battalions of
infantry. Three hundred Cossacks charged at night, killed all the
wagons' horses, rendered the column immovable and have given
advice to 3,000 men under General Docturov, who has marched to
profit by the occasion.'

Three days later at roll-call Surgeon Heinrich von Roos finds his regiment
of Württemberg chasseurs consists of one major, five lieutenants, four
sergeant-majors, five NCOs, a handful of medical personnel ... and only sixteen chasseurs. Next day (17 October) Wilson and Murat both get off their
horses at the outposts 'to have a fairer gaze at each other'. But on Murat

sending an officer, 'I desired Captain Fanshaw [his ADC] to request that he would return to his line.'

Between this true-blue English officer and gentleman and an upstart king who was born an inn-keeper's son, at least, there are to be no dealings.

And anyway the time for parleying is past.

CHAPTER 9

PREPARATIONS FOR DEPARTURE

Napoleon reads a novel – 'They even said he was mad' – convoys go astray – too many cannon? – handmills – reconnoitre another return route – the wrong François – a first fall of snow – 'in twenty days' – Napoleon's concern for the wounded – rules for the Comédie Française – what are the poets doing? – 'an officer arrived post-haste'

Do Napoleon's orders to Murat betray a lack of inner certitude? Perhaps. Ségur, always concerned to give a critical turn to his drama, describes, doubtless exaggerates, his state of mind:
'In the midst of that terrible storm of men and the elements massing all round him, his ministers, his ADCs see him spend these last days discussing the merit of some new verses he'd just received, or drawing up regulations for the Comédie Française in Paris, which took him three whole evenings to complete.[1] As they know perfectly how anxious he is they admire the force of his genius and the ease with which he shifts his attention and fixes it on whatever he chooses. All one noticed was that his meals, until then so simple and brief, were taking longer. He was trying to numb himself. Then they saw him, to satisfy a craving [*s'appetissant*], pass long hours in a half-reclining position, as if stunned [*engourdi*] and, a novel in his hand, waiting for the dénouement of his terrible history.'
But Caulaincourt belies all this. And so does Gourgaud. Though no less critical than Ségur will be, the Master of the Horse is finding
'the Emperor's activity to reorganise his army and prepare it for new combats really extraordinary and it was giving the heads of each arm a lot to do.'
A lighted candle in his first-storey window assures the army that its all-puissant emperor is ceaselessly busy. Any number of his orders are in fact dictated in the small hours. In Prince Baratinsky's palace Planat de la Faye hardly has a moment to leave his desk, has to sleep on the floor at nights on a catskin fur, explaining to his six ill-educated artillery captains, feverishly transcribing and delivering Lariboisière's orders, that, in Russia, proper beds are rare luxuries. On one of his daily tours of inspection, Napoleon suddenly appears in Lariboisière's 'light and smoke devices' department. He's been informed that its personnel have only been able to produce 10,000 rounds during the last fortnight. Peremptorily he orders them to step up their output to 6,000 a week, 'and send them to the Kremlin for storage as soon as they're ready'. Cannonballs picked up on the field of Borodino, too, are arriving by the

cartload. "*Mon Dieu*," sighs the depressed Lariboisière who, after his son's death at Borodino,

> 'no longer uttered a word at table. "Haven't we already much too much for our teams? And what does the Emperor think we'll bring it all back with?"'

In Caulaincourt's, Pion des Loches' and many other people's opinion, too, the army already has far more guns than it has horses to drag them. But when someone, probably Lariboisière, suggests 'part of them should be left behind', the ex-gunner emperor explodes:

"No. The enemy would make a trophy of them!"

Altogether he's very touchy about trophies. After all, *something* must be brought home from this unexampled but so far fruitless campaign. As to leaving some of the guns behind, Gourgaud scorns the idea:

> 'At the time when it was getting ready to leave, the army still had 600 pieces of artillery and their teams, fully supplied. They had been reinforced by the horses of the Bridging Train which it was intended to leave behind in the Kremlin [in fact, they weren't left behind]. So it couldn't enter the Emperor's head to abandon part of his artillery to the Russians. It would have been a mistake so much the greater as he was expecting a new battle.'

By now, not everyone is as confident in the Emperor's judgement as Gourgaud. Planat hears other generals besides Lariboisière, whose 'gaiety, full of good-nature and seasoned with a light dose of the malice we'd known in him, had totally disappeared',

> 'expressing these fears openly and in a fashion less respectful toward the Emperor. They even went so far as to say he was mad and wanted us to perish to the last man. On this occasion, as later, I noticed that the most injurious remarks against the Emperor always came from the Prince of Neuchâtel's staff. The Emperor wasn't ignorant of this, and didn't like them'

– the blue-blooded young gentlemen, that is, who form an aristocratic little club of their own, whose members refer to him in private as 'Monsieur Bonaparte' and, it's felt, look down on the rest of the army. 'The most one could expect of them,' writes Count *J-C. Beugnot* in another context, 'was they weren't insolent to you.' Major *Marcelline Marbot*, currently serving with Oudinot's faraway II Corps near Polotsk, is even more sarcastic. They did nothing all day, he says, but play cards and dice, 'winning or losing several thousands of francs with utmost indifference'. Nor is Fezensac, who until after Borodino had been one of them, much impressed by all this administrative activity:

> 'Nothing much was being sent to the advance guard, either. Yet every day the Russian army on the banks of the Nera was getting stronger.'

As for chronically overworked Berthier himself, Ségur sees he isn't
'doing much to second his chief in this critical circumstance. He
didn't recommend any new precautions and waited for the least
details to be dictated to him by the Emperor.'[2]

The daily parades, of course, have continued. On Sunday 11 October it was
the turn of Gérard's [formerly Gudin's] division to be reviewed in the
Kremlin; on the 12th Morand's. Certain of its officers, commanding its
quarters of the town, fail to turn up. Likewise their detachments 'not knowing where to go'. By now Captain *Charles François'* leg wound, sustained on
the eve of Borodino, has healed sufficiently for him to burn one of his
crutches – no matter what heroic acts men have performed, only the
crutchless may appear on parade before the Emperor:
'For the sixth time I was proposed for the Cross and another reward.
The regiment took up arms, went to the Kremlin where the Emperor
reviewed it, along with the other regiments of the 18th Division.'
Five lieutenants are promoted captains, six sous-lieutenants are made lieutenants and ten NCOs sous-lieutenants:
'Three officers' crosses and 40 crosses of the Legion were accorded
and a grant of money to the regiment's worst battalion commander,
obtained by dint of sheer importunities. Not that it did him any good,
because he left his bones behind in the retreat. Colonel Bouguet was
promoted general and replaced by a major from the Young Guard.
The Emperor asked Colonel Bouguet where I'd been wounded. "At
Schevardino, and he's one of our old dromedaries from Egypt." The
Emperor came up to me and said: "What are you asking for?" My
colonel didn't give me time to reply, and declared "The Cross!"
"Granted," replied the Emperor. Having done so many campaigns,
I'd been going to ask for a money grant, which would have been
granted. But my colonel, though wishing me well, did me wrong.'
And even then François' nomination somehow gets overlooked – or rather,
is sent to the 13th Light by mistake, where there's another Captain
François, and is only retrieved after much trouble. (What the other Captain François felt history doesn't relate.) That day, it seems, one whole regiment has been late on parade; for on the morrow Davout writes
apologetically to Berthier, wanting to know whether this was really so, and
if so which regiment it was, 'so that I can punish the colonel'.

Three days later, on 13 October, there'll also be an oversight, presumably in 'Monsieur' Salomon's department.[3] Only 185 letters notifying
Davout of the promotions made at the parade of two days earlier are sent
him, instead of 187, and 'immediately forwarded to the military men
they're intended for'. Perhaps His Serene Highness the Prince of Neuchâ-

tel will look into the matter, try and find out what the difference is due to? But one of these commissions, anyway, is 'for an officer of the 85th'. Who can he be, if not our friend Le Roy? For Sergeant *Vincent Bertrand*'s regiment, the 7th Light, there are seven promotions and no fewer than 32 crosses – the 12th Line gets what must be an all-time record of 37.

What state is the army in? What kind of an army is it now? Artillery-inspector *H. J. de Paixhans*, one of Lariboisière's ADCs, is one of the many individuals who've been turning up in Moscow during the last few weeks, a delay due in his case to a gammy leg. The first thing that's struck Paixhans is the army's youth, even in the cavalry and artillery, and the large numbers of merely nominal Frenchmen:[4]

> 'Dutchmen of all ranks had come to poison the artillery units. All had been poorly and hastily trained. As for the NCOs who'd been promoted 2nd lieutenant, they'd come from a class become too feeble for its proper functions, as a result of the enormous consumption of men during the previous years.'

In the artillery train, four horses, their harness and a load of ammunition are being entrusted to two feeble conscripts. Most divisions, Paixhans notes, are only at quarter strength, a mere two to three thousand men, 'the other three-quarters dead, prisoners, marauders or stragglers [he makes no mention of the all-too-numerous wounded]. There were altogether too many administrators'.

As for the army's morale, Caulaincourt is troubled by the effects of a cult of glory, as opposed to efficiency:

> 'Our men were doubtless very brave, but they were careless and lacking in vigilance, which arose as much from their character as from lack of order and discipline. This was often a subject for serious reflection on the part of the Prince of Neuchâtel and other generals around the Emperor. There were too many young regimental officers. Dash and courage were valued above all else. At all his reviews the Emperor made everything of audacity, courage and luck. No commanding officer was ever brought to account for losses due to his negligence, his lack of order and discipline, even if it had caused the loss of two-thirds of his force.'

Despite the evidently satisfactory appearance of Davout and Delzons' crack divisions when on parade early in the month, Césare de Laugier has already made his own worried assessment:

> 'The many sick and wounded who've come back into the ranks, the new march regiments that have turned up, have more or less given the infantry the same numerical force as they had before the battle [of Borodino]. But the cavalry – and above all the artillery – are in a

deplorable state. I won't speak of the horses of the Guard, which have fought and suffered less than the others and preserved a better aspect; but those of Murat and the light cavalry attached to the infantry units! The poor animals are painful to look at, their end isn't far off. None of them have been able to profit from a moment's rest since the hostilities began! As for artillery's guns, even though their number is already out of proportion to the forces at our disposal, more of them are turning up every day. Just now the army counts 501 cannon, but drawn by scraggy horses incapable of making a long journey. And the same can be said of the horses of the baggage train, ambulances and others. We're asking ourselves how we're going to transport the precious booty assembled in Moscow and already loaded on to wagons; that is, if the Emperor doesn't order them to be abandoned.'

Typical of the whole equine situation, no doubt, is von Suckow's little Russian horse – the one on which he'd tried to keep up with Ney's staff at Borodino. Hardly does it reach Moscow than the poor little animal simply drops dead of starvation. 'For several days it had been impossible to feed him. There wasn't a blade of forage anywhere in the town or its surroundings.'

Not every convoy that leaves Smolensk is reaching Moscow. In late September Napoleon had ordered that no more artillery should advance further than Smolensk, and all artillery and cavalry between Smolensk and Moscow were to be concentrated at Viazma, Ghjat or Mojaisk. After an affair during which some artillery coming up from Viazma has lost its guns, a furious Emperor even cashiers one of the majors commanding it, who promptly blows his brains out. Another artillery convoy, coming from Italy and commanded by a Major Vives, is abandoned by its escort; and Labaume says the guns would have been lost if General Ornano and IV Corps' Bavarian chevaulegers hadn't caught up with the Cossacks as they were carrying them off in the middle of a forest and retaken them. Its commander, too, is arrested.[5] And at Vereia, the 'pretty little town' where Le Roy's men had enjoyed a vast meal just before reaching Moscow, the garrison is suddenly attacked and massacred. Everywhere the peasant bands are becoming more and more active.

The far rear, as usual, is essentially beyond Napoleon's control. There a host of oversights are being committed. Words and acts go their different ways. Where, for instance, are the great stores of rice and other foods which should be arriving at Minsk, but evidently aren't?

October 9: To Berthier: Haven't I said and said again a thousand times to bring up to Kovno and Vilna all the clothing which is at Danzig? So write to Danzig that my orders shall be carried out."

Minsk, with its huge and ever-growing stores of food and clothing, is obviously going to be crucial to the army's survival during the winter. Why hasn't a great mass of clothing for which he has 'paid out at least several hundreds of thousands of francs' reached Minsk from Kovno? "Explain this mystery to me." Two days later (14 October) he will order Maret at Vilna to send the rice he's had collected from all over Europe "even from Trieste" to Minsk via Grodno: "Two thousand four hundred and fifty quintals of rice, sent off from there, have arrived at Cracow. They should have been embarked on the Vistula on 12 September."

An instance of his attention to details – a detail one would have thought, in this case, should have been the business of Dumas or Daru – is his almost obsessive preoccupation with some handmills, ordered for the army, and long awaited.[6] On 6 October he'd dictated:

"The Emperor to M. Maret, Duke of Bassano. Forty portable mills left Paris by post on 6 September. It is now 6 October. So they should have passed through Vilna. I have exhorted you to inform yourself on the progress of this convoy. It is my intention that you shall withdraw one of these mills to serve as a model. Have it operated under your eyes, and let me know how much [corn] it has ground in 24 hours and how many men successively have done this work. I want you to have 50 of these mills constructed at Vilna on the basis of the one you use as a model. As soon as you have had two or three made, you will send one by post to Warsaw for Durutte's division, and one to Königsberg for Loison's division. In the same way you will send one to Minsk for 50 to be made. I assume there are workmen in the countryside who will do it promptly. You must also send one to the Duke of Tarente [Macdonald] to have some made on this model at Mittau.'[7] For the rest, having taken this model, you will let this convoy continue its march, for it's getting very late for me to receive it. A second convoy of 160 of these mills, loaded on four ammunition wagons, left Paris by post on 16 September; it must arrive before long. If the first one has already passed through [Vilna], you will carry out this operation on the second. From this second convoy I authorize you to hold up six, which you will send by post coach to Marshal St-Cyr; perhaps he'll be able to have some made at Polotsk. Anyway he will be receiving a greater number on the third and fourth convoys."

On 10 October Davout acknowledges the letter Berthier 'at the Emperor's orders' had done him the honour of writing him, to the effect that

'portable mills have left by post from Paris for the army, where they should arrive any time now, and that it was His Majesty's intention that, on these handmills' arrival, ten should be distributed to each of the five divisions of I Corps. I have informed the troops under my orders of this mark of the Emperor's solicitude.'

No detail is too small to escape his photographic memory. In a list of officers who have died of typhus in the Vilna hospitals he spots a certain artillery surgeon by name Déchy. Hadn't he, en route for the Niemen in June, severely reprimanded that dedicated officer for bringing his 14-year-old son to Russia?[8] True. And straightway an order goes off to Berthier to give the orphan a grant and arrange for him to be escorted back to France, where he's to get the best possible education.

What Napoleon is envisaging isn't a retreat ('a word', Dedem has been reprimanded when he'd used it, 'unknown in the French army'); or if there is to be one, it must be heavily disguised as a new offensive. His plan – confined no doubt as usual to himself and Colonel *Bacler d'Albe* ('and perhaps to Berthier') sticking his coloured pins into the great map laid out on the big table in the middle of his office – is as follows. Marching out southwards, he'll either strike at Kutusov or bypass him; march on Kaluga and Tula; destroy the arms factories there ('the largest in Russia'); and, passing through the Ukraine, meet up with a column, made up of 'march regiments, isolated and disbanded men, men who've recovered their health' and amounting to '12,000 infantry and 4,000 cavalry, to which have been attached 12 cannon' coming out to meet him from Smolensk. Commanded by the veteran general Baraguay d'Hilliers, the column is to be held ready to leave at a moment's notice. Falling back on Smolensk and its huge stores – supplies which, if the Emperor's orders have been properly obeyed, should be enough to sustain the Moscow army throughout the winter – he'll put the army into winter quarters 'along the Molihew–Smolensk–Witebsk line'.

Secret orders are drawn up for a departure on 20 October.

"*M. le Prince de Neuchâtel.* The Smolensk highway being exhausted, it's necessary to reconnoitre routes parallel to it at two or three leagues into the countryside, where there should be resources, villages, at least some shelters. These deviated routes must be tangent with the central points of Doroghoboui, Viazma and Mojaisk."

And the same day, again, to Marshal Victor, at Smolensk:

"Retain at Smolensk all infantry, cavalry, artillery detachments, the convoys, vehicles, and in general everything that presents itself in isolation to pass through. With all you've thus retained you'll immediately form a column of ten to twelve thousand men. Give it twelve cannon and victuals for ten days. Summon General Baraguay d'Hilliers to Smolensk and put him in command of this division. Place under his command and protection all the vehicles accumulated for the army, and hold this column in readiness to leave by the new route which is to be reconnoitred. Thereafter other columns will be formed. Six thousand men can pass everywhere."

From now on it's his intention, the Emperor goes on, that

"only despatch riders, the army's trunks, staff officers on mission, and certain urgent objects, such as the 500 portable handmills arriving from Paris, the first delivery of which should have reached Smolensk, shall reach us by the old route. Thus relieved, the old route will remain open for evacuating the wounded and for everything return-ing from Moscow to Smolensk. None of the heavy convoys from Smolensk to Moscow are to pass that way."

For weeks now Fain has been hearing 'everyone telling the Emperor the temperature didn't usually fall below zero in Moscow before mid-Novem-ber.'[11] Evidently he believes them; or anyway wants to; for he still won't lis-ten to Caulaincourt, wise from his winters at the Petersburg embassy. But on 13 October (the day of Davout's polite little reprimand to General Headquarters), there comes a first light fall of snow, which, to Caulain-court, 'seemed to bewilder him':

'After a few excessively hot and fine autumn days, the weather has changed abruptly and turned cold. Today the first snow has fallen,'

Césare de Laugier notes in his diary. And Fain hears the Emperor exclaim:

"Let's get a move on. In twenty days we must be in winter quarters."[12]

Is it the nightly performances at Count Posniakov's refurbished theatre, or a calculated impulse to let Paris – and Europe – know that, though so far away, he's still fully in control of everything, that causes Napoleon, despite all these more urgent demands on his time, to devote two (not, as Ségur says, three) whole evenings to drawing up new statutes for the Comédie Française?[13] – and theatrically address them from Moscow? The regulations (which are still in force) run to 100 paragraphs. On that ominously snowy morning of 13 October he signs them. And next day, in front of his generals – who, Nar-bonne notices, 'either out of modesty or indifference listened without saying anything' – holds forth at length on literature and the drama.

'The Kremlin's drawing-room occupied by the Emperor, underneath the Tsarina's state apartments, was illumined by great chandeliers. The Emperor was striding to and fro. Everyone around him was silent. M. Daru, the intellect most apt to [discuss] all topics but also the gravest and the one most attentive to the army's serious needs, was just then overwhelmed by a thousand cares; and wasn't present.'

But Narbonne is, and will immediately afterwards dictate it all to his secre-tary Villemain:

'Doubt and worry were obviously weighing heavily on all minds, hardly leaving them the strength for such mental relaxation.'
Suddenly Napoleon turns to Narbonne, that courtier of the *ancien régime*, and says:

"'I ought to have consulted you, my dear Narbonne, before sending off my decree of this morning, about the very matter we're talking about. I'm sure you greatly loved theatre in your youth and were a great connoisseur. It's true, I believe, it was above all comedy, the manners of the great world, Célimène, Mlle Contat.'"

Which is true. 'As he quickly threw out this last name a faint twitch of a smile seemed to mask the Emperor's grave features'.[14] His own preference, he goes on seriously, is for Corneille and high tragedy, where:

"'at the moments of supreme decision great men are truer than the crises which develop them, we aren't burdened down with all the preparatory details and conjectures, often false, which historians give us. But the gain to glory is so much the greater. For, my dear fellow, there are any amount of miseries in a man, fluctuations, doubts. All these should vanish in the hero.'"

For his own part, he goes on, amidst his generals' glum or perhaps faintly shuffling silence, he's

"'grateful to Tragedy for making some men grow, or rather giving them back their true stature of superior beings in a mortal body.'"

But what, he'd like to know, are the poets of his own reign doing? Where are their modern heroes? Why aren't they bringing Charlemagne on stage, or Saint Louis? Or, above all, Peter the Great,

"that man of granite, hard as the stone courses of the Kremlin, who founded civilisation in Russia and who a century after his death forces me to this terrible expedition."

The assassination of the rebellious Strelitz guards only a few yards away from where he's speaking had been like his own 18th Brumaire. There in Peter the Great, if they like, was a genius!

"People haven't realised that he gave himself what even the greatest man born to a throne lacks: the glory of being a parvenu. Peter the Great voluntarily turned himself into an artillery lieutenant, like I've been, to learn about ordinary life and rise by degrees to greatness. Even so, what setbacks there were to that fortune and that genius! Can you conceive how such a man, at the head of the army he'd created, could let himself be invested on the banks of the Pruth, starved out and almost captured by a Turkish army? Such are the inexplicable eclipses in even the greatest men. Yet the man of genius always recovers himself after a mistake, as after a misfortune."

Amidst this tumult of ideas, Villemain scribbles that night,

'M. de Narbonne hesitated to reply. In it he saw, among the dreary realities of the moment, a shock effect of speculative attention and free reverie taking command of this powerful intellect; or perhaps an illusion of security which he, in his disquietude, wanted to extend to the minds of the others.'

With an effort Narbonne replies that ever since Peter the Great Russia has been full of tragic memories. Napoleon ripostes:

'"Let's act in such a way as not to augment them."

Peter had lifted Russia out of chaos, but not provided it with an intellectual tradition. He'd found it barbarous, and it was still semi-barbarous. By force of numbers he'd defeated Charles XII of Sweden at Poltava,

"but less by his own genius than by that king's own fault. If Charles XII, that prince who was more a soldier than a general, hadn't advanced so far into Russia, or had retired in time and gone on carrying out his invasion manoeuvres even in the depths of winter, he'd never have been defeated."'

It hadn't been Tsar Peter's tactics, Narbonne boldly points out, that had been victorious. But the climate. The innuendo isn't lost on Napoleon, who replies with alacrity:

'"I see what you're driving at, my dear Narbonne. Talked to about theatre, you reply with politics. For the rest, the two things do sometimes touch each other. But don't worry. We shan't make Charles XII's mistake. It's been written in history to preserve us."'

He's been obliged to wait awhile here in Moscow to see what effect 'those two thunderbolts, the battle of the Moscova and the taking of Moscow would have. I had reason to believe in a peace. But whether it comes or not, there's a limit for us.'

Either he'll take the army "which by and large has rested up" back to Smolensk and while the fine weather lasts put it into winter quarters in Lithuania and Poland: or else he'll follow Daru's advice

"which I call a lion's: collect provisions here, kill and salt the injured horses and pass the winter in Moscow which is still a town, and in the spring resume offensive warfare – though I don't incline to this project. One can go far. But one mustn't be away from home too long. I feel Paris calling me even more than Petersburg tempts me. So, my dear fellow, you can be content. With or without a peace, we'll soon be leaving."

Next day he sends for Mathieu Dumas and asks him whether most of the wounded aren't already on their way to Smolensk. And when he hears they aren't, realises 'how much time has already been wasted, and that he must make haste to cope with the innumerable cares of so perilous a retreat'.

On one of those days, if Ali's memoirs are to be trusted, Napoleon falls to 'discussing with Duroc the best sort of death. The best, according to Napoleon, was to "die on the field of battle, struck down by a bullet". For his part he feared he wouldn't be so happy. "I'll die", he said, "in my bed, comè un' coglione."' On St Helena, where he will, he'll say: "I should have died after entering Moscow."

In fact the evacuation of the wounded – according to a recent report there are still 12,000 in Moscow – is a major problem. The medical administration, Caulaincourt sees, has 'ceased to exist except on paper'. But transport wagons must be found for all but the most severe cases, who are to be gathered together in the main hospital, with their surgeons, and be left to the tender mercies of the returning Russians. Altogether Napoleon estimates he has only 800 to 900 wagons in Moscow, and he has no intention of sending them to the rear filled with the sick and wounded. "The walking wounded can conduct their comrades." But any wagon arriving from Smolensk may be used for the purpose; and I, III, IV and VIII Corps are ordered to drum up between them a further 200. The 60 furnished by I Corps and the 40 from III Corps

'are to leave tomorrow and the day after. They're to be loaded with flour, brandy, wine, medicines, which are to be sent to Mojaisk and above all to the convent,'

i.e., the great Kolotskoië Abbey, three miles from the field of Borodino, where the wounded had been assembled, and where – so Césare de Laugier hears – a secret order has been given for all the muskets assembled after the battle to be burned.

"General Ornano will have them escorted. Arrange for these convoys to leave in a regulation manner and carry to those hospitals the help they so badly need. Begin the evacuation with the officers. Express my dissatisfaction to the pay commissioner in charge at Mojaisk,"

he adds. Also to his war commissaries (among them no doubt the hardworking Bellot de Kergorre) and the Administration's agents at Kolotskoië,

"for never writing to let me know the state of affairs in their hospitals. Lastly, send an officer and an agent of the Administration to find out exactly how many sick there are at Mojaisk, at the monastery, and as far as Viazma, so that I can in all circumstances know what sacrifices would have to be made should our operations mean we must abandon those establishments."

As for the large numbers of wounded still in Mojaisk itself, he writes sharply to Berthier that, having provided Junot and his VIII Corps and "the other route commanders with the men they've asked for to be able to master their surroundings", he intends that his intentions shall be carried out:

"Therefore the commandants shall have the countryside scoured for thirty miles around and in this way collect a good number of peasant carts to serve for the evacuation of our wounded. You will render the duc d'Abrantès [Junot] responsible for having all the wounded evacuated to Viazma, and the commandant at Viazma [Poincaré] to have them evacuated to Smolensk. In a word, whatever happens, my intention is that eight days from now there shall not be a single one of our wounded at Mojaisk, Raza, the Kolotskoïë abbey, or at Ghjat."

Davout, who has already written to Berthier on 10 October pointing out that despite the 'great number of weapons existing at the abbey and Mojaisk, the commandants at those places are still letting unarmed men pass through', is having difficulty in supplying enough wagons for the wounded. On 13 October, however – the day of the first snowfall and after 'a detachment of the 108th Line in General Friedrichs' division has been attacked by Cossacks and armed peasants in the village of Cigadaiewo' – he has given orders for all his sick and wounded to leave;

'and I hope those of the 1st, 3rd and 5th divisions will be able to be transported by the means at our disposal. But it is indispensable that the Intendant-General shall supply transportation for those of the 2nd [Dufour's] and 4th divisions, detached with the advance guard, who are much more numerous than the others, and have no means of being brought here.'

A recommendation which causes Berthier to write on the morrow to Belliard, telling him the wounded are to set out 'for Vilna or Smolensk'. Those who after resting up a few months at Vilna find themselves in a state to go on campaign again will report to IHQ. Those others who, by reason of the nature of their wounds, aren't in so favourable a state, will be authorized to go back to France. 'This arrangement, however, only applies to generals, colonels and battalion commanders.' What is to happen to the irreparably wounded subalterns, NCOs and rank and file he doesn't say.

There are also the army's cadres. At Smolensk some officers – even some of the Canaries' rank and file who've served out their time – are being sent back to France to form them for the new units to be raised from next year's recruits.[15] On 12 October Lieutenant Dutheillet of the 57th Line has heard that each regiment has been

'ordered to send a battalion of cadres to each corps' depot, to train the recruits who'll be coming in. As lieutenant I was included among the officers to be sent off, even though my commission still hadn't been sent to me. All these cadres hardly added up to 700 or 800 men. We left Moscow on 14 October, I think, taking with us General Nansouty, who'd been wounded and was in command of us. There were also a great number of generals and officers of all ranks, sick or wounded, whom we were charged with escorting.'

One of the convoy's wounded, Lieutenant Brandt of the Vistula Legion, will suppose afterwards that

'if I hadn't left a few days in advance but been forced to make the retreat with the regiment, I've every reason to believe I, in the state of weakness I was in, would have succumbed to its fatigues, if I hadn't been killed by the enemy's iron.[16]

Another – unwounded – member of the convoy is Daru's cousin, dragoon captain Henri Beyle, of the Food Administration. As yet the future novelist Stendhal's sole ambition is to write comedies – while in Moscow he's been labouring over one more called *Letellier*, as unactable as all the others – live in Paris and keep mistresses. But now, as the long train of jolting and groaning wagons, laden with its cargo of sufferers, sets off down the Mojaisk–Smolensk highway, all he has to keep his spirits is his (to us rather irritating) gift for persiflage.

On the day when it had snowed, Césare de Laugier and his comrades, still out at Petrovskoï, had begun asking one another which route they'll be returning by, 'will it be the road we came by, or will we pass through the south-western parts of the [Russian] empire?'. He has heard that 'only staff officers on mission, and *estafettes* [express couriers]' are to leave for Smolensk by the Mojaisk road'. Now he hears that

'in the evening of the day before yesterday, the Emperor's horses left for an unknown destination. All the wagons are laden with food. Yesterday General Borelli, ADC to the King of Naples, left again with the Emperor's secret orders for his master.'

Next day he hears that the convoy carrying the trophies is leaving, escorted by a force under the wounded general Claparède. And during the night of 15/16 October Laugier writes in his diary:

'The Italian detachment at Czernaiagriaz has been ordered by the Emperor to come back to Moscow, but without its cavalry. Broussier's division, the Dragoons of the Royal Guard, placed out along the Smolensk road, are moving towards Fominskoië.' 16 October: Orders to Marshal Victor to send some artillery horses to Viazma 'to collect the ammunition wagons and artillery vehicles abandoned along the road and take them back to Smolensk.' 17 October: Today, general distribution to the whole army: leather, linen, bread and brandy. This wise measure, which would have been most useful if it had been taken a little earlier, comes too late. The ranker is throwing away everything he can't use on the spot; and anyway, he's already too heavily laden and I'm afraid this distribution may be a pure loss.'

But then, on the 18th, something dramatic happens.

The usual parade, this time mainly of Ney's III Corps, is to be held at 1 p.m. Lieutenant-Colonel Le Roy, as he now is, has given up his original intention of asking Davout to let him stay with the regiment for the rest of the campaign. At 10 a.m., after drawing his march orders to leave for the 85th's depôt at faraway Coblenz, he goes to the Kremlin to say goodbye to some friends in the Imperial Guard:

'Many units had already assembled there. They seemed to be dismounted cavalry.[18] I asked to speak to Captain Gouttenoire of the Chasseurs of the Old Guard, who'd come from the 108th and who was a close friend. I found him on guard at the entrance to the palace where the Emperor was lodged.'

Gouttenoire tells Le Roy the Guard's under orders to be ready to leave within 24 hours. And that all the sick and wounded have left for Smolensk. 'As I've said already,' Le Roy goes on,

'there were dismounted troops marching in two ranks, portmanteaux on their backs, wearing big boots, armed with reserve muskets, carbines, musketoons and pistols. All these men seemed to me very heavy and in no state to sustain an action, being entirely foreign to the new service being exacted of them. It was even likely that instead of being of any use they'd end up by embarrassing us.'

"You can see from this movement they're thinking of retreating," Gouttenoire tells him. "This morning we've heard gunfire in the direction of the advance guard on the Kaluga road. And we're waiting impatiently to hear what's happened. So, old comrade, if you leave for France it'll be with us.'"

Le Roy replies that this will be much more to his liking than running all the risks of travelling on his own. He's just listening to local gossip and looking at the big Ivan Bell, lying there in three pieces after its fall from the tower, [19] when

'the Emperor came out of the palace to go on parade. He was walking by himself, eight to ten paces ahead of his staff. His expression was preoccupied. Coming out of the castle courtyard, he turned left and went towards the troops assembled a few paces away. I slipped in among the officers of his suite to watch the parade, which began at once. The troops were ordered to make several forward movements.'

Unfortunately, Major Guillaume Bonnet, as he now is, still suffering from the after-effects of the fever he'd contracted out at Bogorodsk and unable to keep his legs. So though the 18th Line, also part of Ney's corps, are being reviewed and the usual expectations are running high, he has to ask his colonel for permission to withdraw. 'My absence was the reason why he couldn't get me the cross.'[20] General Pajol, on the other hand, commander of the 2nd Light Cavalry Division, has more or less recovered from his broken arm; and together with Captain Biot, his ADC, has just attended Napoleon's levee. Also present on parade is Cesare de Laugier with

'some battalions of the Imperial Guard, the Royal Guard, and Pino's Division. We were drawn up in battle order in the Kremlin's first courtyard. The Emperor was passing us in review. The time was perhaps around 2 p.m. They were about to distribute the rewards the troops are so avid for, when suddenly Colonel Béranger, ADC to the King of Naples, turned up, chapfallen [*les traits décomposés*] and with a worried air.'

As Béranger demands to speak to the Emperor, Biot too recognizes him:

'He hardly took time to shake my hand in passing, and said to me in a low voice: "Things are going badly!"

Instantly

'the review stops. The Emperor withdraws into Peter the Great's apartments.'

What has happened?

CHAPTER 10

BATTLE AT WINKOVO

*Sébastiani surprised – 'They halted not four paces from us, uttering wild shouts' –
a wounded Murat saves the situation - Bréaut des Marlots' single-handed fight –
'This spoils everything' – immediate departure – a merry dance – Wilson is furious
– dead cats in Murat's kitchen – Louise chased by starving dogs – a parting shot*

Among the first to feel that something serious was in the wind had been
the 7th Hussars' Victor Dupuy:

'With the grand'garde on 17 October I had under my orders Captain
Decalonne of the 8th Hussars and 100 men from the division's various
units. Having relieved the old outposts, placed my own, and visited the
line of scouts, whence I could see nothing out of the ordinary, I
reported to General Bruyères. He recommended the greatest vigi-
lance, and told me that, by all appearances, we would be attacked during the night. I went back to my post. I had half the horses constantly
bridled up by turns and didn't neglect my patrols. The night passed off
quietly. At dawn I again visited my whole line with Captain Decalonne.
Everything was in order on our side, and we saw nothing on the
enemy's to make us fear a sudden attack. I left the mounted guard and
reported to General Bruyères, as was the practice each morning.'

At first light of dawn on that misty morning of 18 October, Griois,
'stretched out alone on a bench in our smoke-filled room,' is

'deeply asleep when I was awakened by the noise of firing. To begin
with I assumed this must be the Russian recruits practising. But soon
the noise seemed to be closer than usual. I open the window beside me
– i.e., push up a little wooden shutter like the ones used in hen-hous-
es. And on the ravine's further side see our sentries exchanging shots
with enemy sharpshooters. Everything was lying in a dense mist.'

Perhaps it's just some Russian patrols who've approached too closely in the
fog? Hardly, because

'from other points, too, the firing could be heard; and all over camp
the trumpeters were sounding 'To horse!' So it must be serious. I
order my artillery to harness up, send my servant and vehicles to the
rear, and with my adjutant and orderly officers go to the camp's forward edge. Already our pickets are falling back on their regiments,
formed up in battle order.'

Dupuy finds the rest of Bruyères' light cavalry division outside his bivouac:

'"Go back quickly," he said as soon as I approached him. "This is the
critical moment. Stand your ground as well as ever you can!" And, in

fact, at that moment we heard some carbine shots in the distance.'

Dupuy immediately sets off again as fast as his horse can carry him:

'When I got to the middle of the plain I saw my grand'garde being vigorously driven in by Russian dragoons. I flung myself into the middle
of the scrum, trying to rally my men. Deceived by the Russians' white
mantles – our Prussians and Poles had similar ones – I'm in the midst
of them, shouting at the top of my voice: "Halt! Rally!" when a Russian trooper, letting his sabre dangle by its strap, tries to seize my
horse's bridle, saying to me in French: "Surrender, Monsieur!" At the
same moment Brigadier Wolf of the 7th Hussars came rushing toward
me, shouting: "They're the enemy!" Wolf and I let our sabres play on
the man who'd attacked me and on other enemies who were coming
on the scene. Then, thanks to our good horses, in three bounds we
were out of reach and amidst some of our own men who'd come up
at the sound of my voice! Whereupon I rally my men. Then our
defence gets organised. We begin firing in an orderly fashion, only
yielding ground yard by yard, thus giving the division time to fall back
on General St-Germain's cuirassiers beyond the ravine.'

But Griois ('happily for us Lahoussaye was so ill he wasn't able to mount
his horse') is having trouble with his horse-gunners:

'I don't know how they'd chanced to get hold of some brandy that
day. But I noticed it as, at the first musket shots, I went to the park,
assembled my companies and ordered them to mount. Already that
corn-brandy [vodka], a veritable poison, was affecting several of the
men. Even the officers were tipsy. One of my best captains, usually a
model of sobriety, fell almost senseless at my feet as he was speaking
to me. Another was in more or less the same state. How to get my
orders understood, still less carried out, by men who'd lost their presence of mind?'

Despite Murat's anxieties and warnings the sudden onslaught has taken
Sébastiani completely by surprise. At 6 a.m. 'just when we least expected it'
Sous-lieutenant Pierre Auvray of the 23rd Dragoons sees,

'roundshot, fired at the chasseurs camped in front of us, come bounc-
ing into our shacks. We were still abed. Our horses were unsaddled.
In the midst of the roundshot, which were causing havoc, each of us
rushes to mount his horse, and we abandoned some of our possessions.'

And still Dupuy, out there in the plain, isn't out of danger. His horse, shot
in the right shoulder by two Russians from behind a thicket, falls, with him
beneath it:

'The animal expired with a plaintive sound. The Russians rush to
grab me, but I get up promptly. Some of my hussars surround me.

One of them dismounts and helps me unsaddle and unbridle my unfortunate horse, while the others keep the Russians at bay. This done, I order the hussar to mount his horse again, give him the furniture of mine to carry off, and keenly regretting the loss I'd just sustained of my good old companion, leave on foot to go and get another. For me this was an immense loss, above all in these circumstances – at the moment when we were about undertake so long and arduous a retreat and it was utterly impossible to make it good!'

The signal for the Russian onslaught, writes Séruzier, commander of 2nd Cavalry Corps' horse artillery, had been

'a shell fired at my bivouac. I'd ordered the "To Horse!" to be sounded, the officers struggled to get to their posts. But each of them was surrounded on all sides by a cloud of Cossacks. One could hardly see a thing, and at that moment I'd hardly 15 men around me. My foot and horse gunners, unable to get my orders, set about defending themselves with their usual courage. But this time, lacking co-ordination from a commander-in-chief, for a long while it was nothing but a mêlée, where in the end we were overwhelmed by superiority of numbers.'

To his surprise Séruzier keeps hearing his own name being shouted among the Russians all around him:

'Afterwards I've come to know that Count Orlov was in command of the part of the attack aimed at my troops. Furious at the success of my expedition into his domains as far as the surroundings of Poltava, he'd sworn to get me, and given the Cossacks orders to capture me alive. In my first despair at having let myself be surprised I tried to get myself killed. Not succeeding and seeing my men gradually rallying, I began to hope of escape if I managed not to be recognised. So I got someone to give me a neck-band to cover my decorations, and managed to reach a mass of gunners who'd got together and were looking for me.'

Putting himself at their head, he drives off the Cossacks, and is glad to find the fright they've given him is worse than the damage inflicted.

The Russian attack by Bennigsen, who, supporting Wilson's insistent demand for action, has carefully if not brilliantly planned a surprise led by Bagawout, Dupuy sees, is being made 'simultaneously all down the line'. It all but succeeds. Bennigsen's idea is to march his infantry divisions to the defile at the French rear and, while Davidov's cavalry engages Murat's, cut it off. This is why, behind the line of light cavalry, Captain Bréaut des Marlots of the 3rd Cuirassiers (2nd Cavalry Corps) has just been about to go off foraging when

'a cloud of Cossacks fell upon us. The 4th Cuirassier Division, the whole of Segin's troops, were already overthrown and were retiring in disorder. My lieutenant said to me: "See that, Captain? But look! They're quite close." My horses were unsaddled and I told my servants: "Quick, get my horses ready. I'll deal with this one," – the one I meant to mount. And, against my better knowledge and knowing nothing can be done properly in a hurry: "Don't be scared, they won't get this far." Finally we formed up in line of battle. The guns are firing grapeshot at us, nothing stops them. I'd had my lead horses hurriedly taken to the rear. We're forced to retire, but in good order. Musket balls are falling among our ranks like hail.'

'By and by', Griois goes on,

'the mist lifts and allows us to see Russian masses advancing on us, manoeuvring as they come. I aim my gunfire at them, the Russian gunners reply; and the battle is raging all along the front.'

Dupuy: 'The 2nd Cavalry Corps, camped to our right, didn't get off as lightly as we did. It lost all its vehicles and a lot of men. Above all my old regiment, the 11th Chasseurs, was very badly cut up.' And Bréaut des Marlots:

'An hour later we were being taken in the rear, from the front and, shortly afterwards, from the flanks. We had to fire on all sides. Everywhere we saw only Cossacks, the earth groaned under them. But their great numbers didn't intimidate us, and if we saved ourselves in this encounter we owe it to our staunchness. We retired in good order.'

By 10 a.m., Auvray of the 23rd Dragoons goes on, other troops have come to their assistance,

'and about time too, because by then we were in so difficult a position that the roundshot and shells were enfilading our ranks from both sides, and we were on the point of giving way.'

But Orlov hasn't only been trying to capture the depredator of his estates. At the head of the first Russian column – there are three – he's been ordered to turn a wood on Murat's left, the one held by Sébastiani. Murat's right flank, against the banks of the River Nara, consists of Poniatowski's Poles; and Murat himself, in the centre, has been dangerously cut off from both forces by the steep Winkovo ravine, with the Czernicznia stream flowing through it. The whole position, as Rossetti had pointed out to Napoleon in the Kremlin, is utterly precarious. Séruzier goes on:

'Sébastiani's troops managed to form up on the Woronowo road. Immediately the enemy cavalry, supported by infantry, tried to cut him off. But the King of Naples, jumping on his horse, arrived at the head of his reserve. Twice he charged with his usual dash and forced the Russians to leave him master of the battlefield. Six battalions of Russian grenadiers tried to support their cavalry, but a second charge decided the matter.'

Murat's 'reserve' seems to consist largely of the tiny relics of the 1st and 2nd Carabiniers, which Lieutenant Mailly-Nesle had been dismayed to find added up altogether to no more than 100 mounted men:

> 'The 1st Regiment charged this cloud of cavalry very valorously, despite several batteries which were taking it in flank. But as the regiment's horses could only trot and were in no greater strength than an ordinary company, they were repulsed, lost a lot of men, and came to rally behind us. But then we were completely surrounded by enemies who flung themselves at us, brandishing their Cossack lances and uttering savage shouts. However, though we were perhaps not more than 60 men, we remained motionless, shouldering our sabres. This countenance astonished them and they halted not four paces from us, uttering a thousand insults, roaring like wild beasts and firing at point-blank range. So enraged were they with us that after firing them they flung their carbines and pistols in our faces. General Sébastiani and our colonel were out in front of us, their horses' rumps in our ranks.'

Suddenly the young aristocrat finds his arm is paralyzed. He's been shot in the right shoulder. And is ordered to retire – and his withdrawal from the ranks causes a supporting body of cuirassiers to do likewise! By and by he's joined by other wounded officers, among them 'the colonel, peppered with bullets, sabre cuts and lance-thrusts, but happily without having received any mortal blow'. Shedding his heavy cuirass, with its distinctive yellowish copper overlay, Mailly-Nesle receives from two Poles 'a sky-blue pelisse lined with white hare skin, and under a red velvet bonnet lined with astrakhan, dressed like a Cossack, makes off peacefully' to the rear.

But the carabiniers have put up a resistance that's prevented the Russians from cutting the Moscow road. Rossetti sees 'repeated charges by General Müller's cavalry on our left flank driven off and put to flight' thanks to Murat's personal intervention, and Müller himself is killed:

> 'Then the King, seeing Bagawout's infantry, too, advancing formed up in three squares to cut off our retreat, puts himself at the head of the Carabiniers, commanded by General de France, and of the 5th Cuirassiers, and charges the squares and sabres them completely. Bagawout himself remained on the battlefield, mutilated by sabre cuts. The King is wounded, but doesn't leave the fighting. My friend General Gry, captain in the Guards, is killed; Colonel Bonafoux and Captain Bauffremont, ADCs to the King, are wounded. I have my colback sliced in two by a sabre cut.'

Murat, so inept in so many other respects, is more than justifying his reputation as an incomparable leader of cavalry on the battlefield.

'Murat's charge,' writes *M. R. Faure*, 1st Cavalry Corps' medical officer, 'which the King of Naples led in person, was so impetuous that in an instant two of the enemy columns were broken and cut to pieces, while the [Polish] Zayoncek Division attacked the enemy from the other flank with the bayonet and drove them off.' At one moment Murat himself has been within an inch of being captured by some Cossacks but in the nick of time managed to take refuge in a Polish square:

'A mass of heavy cavalry was coming toward us at the gallop, as if to charge. But about 50 paces away it halted abruptly. There was a moment of terrible silence, during which all we heard was the pant- ing of their horses. Then the Russians, no doubt seeing from our atti- tude that they'd do themselves no good, turned bridle and went off in as good order as on parade.'

A Pole, a cousin of Brandt's colonel, having saved his life, Murat instantly rewards him with a barony and a life pension.

Auvray goes on: 'Such carriages and ambulance wagons as might get in the way were burned, and once the passage was free we carried out our retreat towards Moscow.' Griois sees Murat laughing at the haste with which some soldiers, 'after first sharing the contents', are burning, at his orders, two of his own carriages which 'not having retired quickly enough' are jamming the road.

At about 3 p.m. Sébastiani's badly mauled cuirassiers notice that the can- non fire is abating, and 'the enemy didn't seem to be so intent on follow- ing us'. But now Bréaut des Marlots' blood is up. Being humiliated by a lot of Cossacks is something that's half-turned his head:

'I'm at the rear of the regiment which, at no more than company strength, is marching in column of troops, and I no longer even have a company to command. I'm chatting to my comrades about all these things, stressing my disgruntlement at seeing brigands like Cossacks putting the wind up a lot of soldiers. The whole division is marching en bloc. At that moment, 200 yards off, I see four Cossacks pillaging a vehicle. I seize my chance. Say to the commandant: "I want to prove that four Cossacks are nothing to one good soldier." Galloping over I manage to put them to flight, pursue them for 300 yards and chal- lenge the officer, who speaks German, to cross swords with me. He swears he'll kill me. I laugh in his face. I run at him. He throws him- self among his Cossacks. The commandant (a brave soldier) comes to my aid. Since he's not well enough mounted to stand a charge, which can't be long in coming, I beg him to retire. He believes me, and retires. As soon as I see he's out of danger, sure my horse will move faster than theirs and without consulting my courage, I fling myself among the Cossacks to get them to charge and, as they do, retire.

When I've retreated for 200 yards, I look behind me and see they're advancing in file and at a distance of nearly fifteen yards from one another. I turn about, fall on them, slash up the face of the first and, without pausing, do the same to the second. The third takes flight. I pursue him, the point of my sword at his back. But unfortunately my sabre is worthless, can't even pierce the sheepskin he's wearing. Others come and surround me. One thrusts his lance at my head, shattering my helmet and knocking it off. I catch it by its mane, just as another passes his lance through my thigh. I'm so excited I feel no pain, am only furious with my sabre. Again I throw myself among them. Already I'm being seconded by other men who're coming to my rescue – by now there are some fifteen Cossacks. We force them to retreat for almost a mile, and night comes down.'

In his private battle Bréaut des Marlots has lost one of his best friends, a captain who wasn't sufficiently up on the Cossacks' mode of fighting:

'The colonel reprimanded me, saying I always wanted to play the hussar. My wound, though deep, turned out very well. I tore off the front of my shirt to bind it up.'[1]

The 6th Chasseurs, in the 3rd Cavalry Corps, have also defended their 'position foot by foot, hoping to be supported by the cuirassiers, our reserve, but in vain. After the very indecisive fight we'd seen to our amazement the Russian army take up its position again at Tarutino, so that we were free to go and look for our cuirassiers.' But when Henckens and his comrades get to Woronowo, 'to our great surprise there they were, in great disorder, having been taken by surprise by Cossacks that morning two leagues to our rear'.

There or some other 'village ten or twenty leagues from Moscow' Coignet, sent from the Kremlin with despatches for Murat, also sees:

'some routed cavalry. Our men, mounted bareback, had been surprised while attending to their horses' sores. I couldn't see Prince Murat. He'd escaped in his shirt. It was pitiable to see these fine cavalrymen running away. I asked where the Prince was. "If he's been captured," they said, "they've taken him in his bed." And I could find out nothing. The Emperor heard about it afterwards from Nansouty's ADC.'

For the fourth time during the campaign Sébastiani, above all, has lived up to his nickname. As for the French right, Griois thinks the Russians could easily have turned it 'if they hadn't aimed their opening effort at the left, held by Sébastiani's Cavalry Corps'. Grouchy's 3rd Cavalry Corps, stationed on the right, hasn't fared quite so badly.

By evening various people and units are claiming to have saved the situation. Hearing about the affray, Dedem in his mill near the Kazan Gate even gets the impression that it's all been the work of the feeble remains of Dufour's infantry division. And others will claim it was the Poles of the Vistula Legion. Otherwise the King of Naples has been in his element, and is very definitely the hero of the otherwise miserable occasion. He has even been wounded, for the first time since Egypt in 1799. A lance, says Thirion,

'pierced his side and Tartar-style pelisse, which however covered his clothes and prevented anyone from seeing they were stained in blood. He didn't speak of this wound, which was anyway a light one, and only at the day's end did he have it examined by his doctor.'

The advance guard's losses have been more than considerable. Biot's first glance had seen everything in its true light. From the nearby wood, which Sébastiani hadn't bothered to occupy, the Cossacks had been able to watch everything that had been going on 'even in his headquarters'. Besides 38 out of 187 guns, lost largely for lack of horses to draw them off, Sébastiani has lost some 1,200 to 1,500 men killed and as many again made prisoner – all chiefly, so it would seem, because of his fecklessness; but also because Murat had delayed until that very morning his permission to withdraw in good time to Woronowo. To all intents and purposes it's the end of 1st Cavalry Corps; and though Grouchy's and Latour-Maubourg's two cavalry corps are still in order, their horses are on their last legs. Several generals, too, have been killed, among them General Déri, Marshal of Murat's Palace, 'and General Baltier, chief of Poniatowski's artillery, had been taken'. Poniatowski himself has been hurt in the knee. No one doubts that it's been Murat's presence of mind and physical energy, together with Claparède's and Latour-Maubourg's divisions, that has saved the situation: 'We were saved,' writes Surgeon Roos, whose 3rd Württemberg Chasseurs have been annihilated (a shell had burst beside the place where he'd been getting a night's uneasy sleep under frost-packed straw),

'thanks to the ability and resolution of Murat, who put the cuirassiers and other debris of the cavalry to admirable use. If the Russians, instead of attacking us at dawn, had waited until 10 a.m. or midday, by which time half our troops would have been away foraging, they could have seized our camp without firing a shot.'

Russian losses are about equal to those of the French. Bagawout, who'd executed the entire attack, is dead. Wilson, beside himself with fury at what he regards as Kutusov's lackadaisical way of seconding it,[4] is at the same time delighted at Murat's discomfiture. 'All his silver, equipage, bed, etc., even his plume, seen flaunting in the fight where it had been hottest, were taken,' he crows delightedly into his diary that evening:

'The French camps were quite disgusting. They were full of dead horses, many of which were prepared as butcher's meat.'

Even dead cats, he hears, have been found ready for the cookpot in what had been the King of Naples' headquarters. But all His Britannic Majesty's representative himself picks up among the debris are 'a few amusing letters', chiefly from the fair sex. Among the prisoners is a nephew of Napoleon's War Minister Clarke. Wilson does what he can for them. And goes on, not a little smugly:

'Elliott, Gen. Clarke's nephew, assures me that for the last twelve days he has been living like the rest of Murat's army on horseflesh without salt, and without any bread. As Elliott was plundered of all his money, etc., I gave him a hundred roubles, had his wounds dressed and filled his vacant interior with a good dinner, breakfast, etc. I know that Gen. Clarke had been very civil to many English prisoners, and perceive that he is a friend of Lord Hutchinson's. I was therefore moved to show kindness to Elliott, as well on public as on private grounds. The Cossacks are now so rich they now sell the most valuable articles for a little gold, as that alone is portable in addition to their stock. They must have gained yesterday an immense booty.'

And here comes another source of satisfaction. Earlier that day – presumably before Béranger's arrival – Napoleon had sent Lauriston back to Murat with a new letter to be forwarded to Kutusov. It reads:

"General Lauriston has been charged to propose to Your Highness that arrangements should be reached that would give to the war a character conformable to the established rules of warfare, and ensure measures that shall minimise the evils the country must suffer such as are inevitable in a state of war."

This time it's another of Murat's ADCs, Colonel Berthémy, who – rather unseasonably – has to deliver the letter in Kutusov's camp, where everyone's celebrating what they will claim as 'a great victory'. According to Anstett, an *émigré* who'll report the conversation to the Austrian chancellor Nesselrode, whose agent he is, when Berthémy presents himself before Kutusov (who 'has the upper hand in the conversation') he doesn't so much as let him open his mouth.

Cossacks are an unpredictable people. That evening, Griois will hear later, they invite Sébastiani's wretched gunners, whom they've captured with their guns, disarmed and bound, to a grand party:

'In joy at their triumph and already drunk as lords, they wanted to celebrate with national dances. They wanted everyone to take part and, remembering their prisoners, invited them to join in the general rejoicing. At first our poor gunners had no idea of anything but refreshing themselves; but little by little, restored by the good treatment lavished on them, they joined in the dancing. This conduct drew upon them the Cossacks' esteem and tender feelings, and upon the reciprocal benevolence reaching its height, our Frenchmen again donned their coats and shakos as well as their weapons, shook their new friends warmly by the hand, who embraced them, and each took leave of the other in a friendly spirit certainly not shared by their sovereigns. And that was why the gunners rejoined their division.'

By no means are all the French and Polish prisoners as fortunate. And Wilson, who's been on horseback for eighteen hours, adds a terrible postscript:

'More prisoners are momentarily brought in. Above 1,500 are now before our eyes, in wretched condition, with teeth chattering, etc. The peasants have bought numbers from the Cossacks, at two silver roubles a head, to kill them ... Another general is killed. Five guns and two standards are among the trophies, but the most consolatory is the rescue of 300 wounded Russians, in a church which the enemy had just fired.'

This, then, is what, in essence, Murat's downcast ADC Colonel Béranger has to report to Napoleon at the Kremlin. News which causes him instantly to advance the Grand Army's departure from Moscow, planned for 20 October, by twenty-four hours:

'"*Moscow, 18 October 1812. Mon cousin,* give the order to the Prince of Eckmühl to move his headquarters this evening to beyond the Kaluga Gate, and there place his infantry, his artillery and all his military equipment, as well as his baggage, in such a fashion as to leave tomorrow at daybreak for *une forte journée* [a hard day's marching]. He is to leave a guard at the entrenched convent [by the Doroghomilov Gate] until the Duke of Treviso [Mortier] has relieved him, should there be reason to.'"

Ney gets exactly the same order. So does old Marshal Lefèbvre. He's to have the Guard infantry bivouac outside the Kaluga Gate "in a square around the Emperor's lodgings". Likewise Eugène, together with an extra instruction: He's to "place himself *une lieu* [an hour's march] ahead, so as to be able to leave first."

First and foremost this insult to French arms must be wiped out. On no account must Europe think he's fleeing from Moscow after an ignominious defeat. His plan now, Napoleon writes to Maret, Duke of Bassano, his Foreign Minister and plenipotentiary at faraway Vilna, is to march southward towards Kaluga; defeat Kutusov or push him back; and then march via the Ukraine "into the square which lies between Smolensk, Molihew, Minsk and Witebsk. The operations will then be directed on Petersburg and Kiev" in the spring. "In affairs of this sort," he adds in a wry postscript, "the outcome often turns out very differently from what has been envisaged."

In a flash everyone's preparing to leave. 'A moment after' Béranger's arrival, the Guardia d'Onore has been

'ordered to return to our respective quarters and get ready to leave on the spot. So it's good-bye, doubtless, to the last hopes of peace! Hastily, we return to our quarters, fold up our gala uniforms, and with pleasure put on our marching coats. Everything's topsy-turvy. Joy at leaving can be read in all faces. Only one thing troubles us: to leave behind us some comrades who're no longer able to walk. Many of them are gathering up all their strength to follow us.'

Le Roy goes to Davout's headquarters in the convent by the Doroghomilov Gate

'to take his orders and thank him for the protection he'd given me by having me promoted lieutenant-colonel. I found him just as he was mounting his horse to go to the Emperor.'

Davout tells him:

'"Oh, my dear captain," (that's what he called me) "go and make haste and rejoin your regiment. Tomorrow it'll receive orders to march for Malojarosl-la-Wetz [Malojaroslavetz] on the Kaluga road. I hope we'll go a fair part of the way in each other's company."'

Davout wants to send him back to France to take over the 85th's depot and train its cadres. Which suits Le Roy down to the ground. The lingering thought that his son is being dragged away, maltreated by Cossacks, perhaps being tortured to death by enraged peasants, has cured him of all thirst for promotion; even if, as Caulaincourt puts it,

'those who trained the men at the bases and kept things going obtained no recognition if they weren't with the Grand Army or hadn't taken part in such or such a battle and a brave lieutenant-colonel who, after fighting twenty campaigns, was back in the depot was forgotten, just because he'd had no chance to contribute brilliant deeds to the successful affair of the moment.'

Le Roy has had enough of brilliant deeds. Major Pion des Loches, too, had been at the parade where

'III Corps was reviewed by the Emperor at the same time as a great number of dismounted men of all arms. After an orderly officer had brought some news, the review ceased and Marshal Lefèbvre enjoined me to prepare to leave, following on after the [Foot] Chasseurs of the Guard. Such an order made us wonder what its cause could be, and we soon heard that the King of Naples had been vigorously attacked in the neighbourhood of Moscow and lost what little cavalry remained to him.'

At 4 p.m. the newly promoted artillery major marches out:

'Under my orders I had the 1st company of Old Guard foot artillery, commanded by Captain Lavillette, with Messieurs Dumas-Catturet and Aubertin under him, and the 2nd Company of Foot Artillery of the Young Guard, a park, a train, and a medical officer, and a sergeant-sous-aide in the Train.'

The Army of Italy, too, is marching out:

'At 5 p.m. drums beating and to noisy music, we pass through the streets of Moscow ... Moscow! Which we'd so longed to get to, but were now leaving without regret. All we thought of was Italy, our own folk, whom we were going to see again after such a glorious expedition. On the Bridge of the Marshals, the sight of the Kremlin and the fine buildings on the Moskova's banks that had been saved from the fire drew a last glance. Finally, the troops, laden with loot, leave Moscow and take the Kaluga road. Soon the silence is broken and, at a marching pace, we begin singing, telling stories. Everyone's happy.'

Bourgogne and his fellow-sergeants of the Fusilier-Grenadiers had been

'reclining like pashas on ermine, sable, lion skins and bearskins amid clouds of East Indian tobacco and rose petal smoke and enjoying a flaming punchbowl of Jamaica rum'

when the duty clerk had entered and told them to prepare for instant departure next day:

'We gave the Muscovite women and the two tailors their share of the booty we couldn't carry away. They threw themselves on the ground to kiss our feet twenty times – never had they imagined such riches.'

Captain François of the 30th Line, though still limping about badly on one crutch with two musket balls still in his left leg and any number of bruises (fortunately, though he can mount neither of them, he's got two horses), defies – wisely as it'll turn out – the regimental surgeon's wish to send him to hospital; and prepares, he too, to leave for ever this Moscow they should have left at least three weeks ago.

Superintending at dinner that evening, Bausset sees that the Emperor's so agitated he can hardly sit out his meal. Has he only now, the obese Prefect of the Palace wonders, tumbled to the real nature of his predicament? Various reports are coming in of the Winkovo affair and causing him – evidently in front of Caulaincourt, Berthier etc. – to criticise himself 'for having stayed in Moscow without inspecting that position:

'"It means I must see everything with my own eyes. I can't rely on the King. He trusts in his own bravery. He leaves things to his generals, and they're careless. The King performs prodigies of valour. Without his presence of mind and courage everything would have been lost."'

Above all he's determined to

"wipe out the effects of this surprise. It mustn't be said in France that a check like this has forced us to retire. This upsets all our plans. It spoils everything. The honour of our arms must be re-established on the battlefield."

On no account must it seem – least of all at Vienna and Berlin – that the Grand Army is being forced to retreat as a result of this skirmish, as he calls it in his letter to Marie Louise.

In Moscow the evening is warm and beautiful – so warm and pleasant that Dedem van der Gelder, in his mill near the Kazan Gate, dines with some fellow-officers 'in front of open windows'. But all over the ruined city some 3,000 foreign residents, as well as Russians who feel they've compromised themselves by collaborating with the invaders are piling every trans-portable chattel on to carts and carriages and making for the Kaluga Gate.

Getting home late to her lodgings in the outhouse of Prince Galitzin's palace, after a successful performance of *Les Amants Protées* ('Lovers in Their Various Guises'), Louise Fusil has just sat down to repair her 'Petronilla' costume for a forthcoming production, when a fellow-lodger, a French officer, enters. 'Armed from head to foot', he advises her and her friend to get going. In two hours, he says, the army'll be leaving Moscow. Other French officers have already pointed out to her how furi-ous the Russian soldiery will probably be with all foreigners who remain behind – 'the women above all aroused their compassion, because some couldn't find any horses and others had no money to pay for any'. Though this is exactly her own predicament she decides to leave. She'll go as far as Minsk or Vilna, she thinks, and there await calmer times before returning to Moscow. Hurrying through the already deserted streets, she's 'examining with a sort of fright this town, where I saw only ruins,' when

> 'suddenly a pack of dogs threw themselves at me. They were so hun-
> gry they ran after me to devour me, flung themselves at my shawl and
> tore it to pieces; also my dress which, however, was wadded and of
> rather strong material. My screams drew the attention of a peasant
> armed with a thick stick. I still shudder when I think those dogs might
> have been rabid.'

Everyone who has a carriage is setting out in it. War Commissary Bellot de Kergorre, for instance, who's come up to Moscow from Mojaisk and has filled his with

> 'bread, wine, sugar, everything we could carry away, even a mattress –
> it was so full only one person could get inside. I was far from expect-
> ing the host of miseries we were going to suffer; but I was sure we'd
> lose our horses from fatigue and hunger, and from the first day I
> meant to get used to walking. Nothing was more fearful than the
> crossing of this great city, in the midst of its ruins and by the light of

a few stars and of a few dying fires vaguely illuminating the remains of palaces. Only the noise of our wheels broke the silence.'

But then Louise has a stroke of luck:

'One of the Emperor's orderly officers, a nephew of M. de Caulain-court, put his servants and carriage at my disposal. It was a very fine dormeuse [a light carriage in which one could sleep]. I also kept my furs, knowing very well I might need them. It was beautiful weather and I was far from foreseeing the disasters to follow: because if I had, nothing would have induced me to leave Moscow.'

But for ten Russian soldiers it's the end of life's road. Obviously innocent of any part in burning down the city, they've been 'left in prison, hapless victims of their obedience to their superiors and the orders of a madman, as the Emperor said,' where Berthier has been sparing them. Now, evidently without a thought as to what effect it must have on the fate of the 4,000 non-transportable wounded assembled in the Foundling Hospital,[5] Napoleon vents his frustration by ordering the hapless ten

"to be shot as incendiaries. Let the execution take place in the morning, without drawing attention to it."

– a written order which, to Wilson's intense fury, will be found left lying in a cellar in the 11th *arrondissement*; and become the basis, perhaps, of the execution scene in Tolstoy's *War and Peace?*

CHAPTER 11

TAKING FRENCH LEAVE

A lovely sunny day – a host of vehicles – the loot of Moscow – effectives – a crawling army – a bizarre spectacle – Bourgogne lightens his pack – 'the Romans gave civic crowns' – why no courier? – 'the loudest bang I've heard in my life' – Griois gets a fresh wardrobe – the rumble of the guns

At 2 a.m. on 19 October the exodus begins. It's just such anoth-er golden autumn day as the one, 35 days ago, when they'd first gazed in amazement from the Sparrow Hill at the still intact city. Prince Eugène, who has 'given himself all possible trouble to reor-ganize his corps' ('but Davout too had given himself a lot of trouble on I Corps' behalf, to prevent the catastrophe he'd begun to foresee') is in the van:

'The Italian Guard was superb. The Emperor has sent it off first, with orders to take the Mojaisk road, then throw itself to the left and get to Malojaroslavetz by the Old Kaluga Road.'

After the Army of Italy comes I Corps. The crush at the Kaluga Gate is stu-pendous. Slowly, chaotically, throughout the forenoon, IV and I Corps surge out between its twin stone pillars: 'All day it was as much as we could do to get out of town,' Le Roy will recall, 'so encumbered was the road.' After Davout comes Ney. His reserve artillery only reaches the Kaluga Gate at about 1 p.m., just as Napoleon appears.[1] Major *G. de Faber du Faur*, com-manding III Corps' 12-pounders and artillery train, promptly sketches the scene – a grenadier grabs a private carriage's startled horse – Caulaincourt, Duroc and Berthier in immediate attendance – surely that's Duroc to whom a plumpish Emperor, apparently imperturbable, is talking as he walks one of his Arab greys forward through the throng? A few yards behind, to add a touch of lighter blue amidst the Imperial Staff, under the warm hazy sky, Gourgaud's uniform gets him into the picture, as it will into so many others.

All day the divisions move slowly out between the Kaluga Gate's monu-mental pillars. Last out is the Imperial Guard. Surgeon Roos sees it go by, both foot and horse:

'The men marched past in columns, well aligned, proud and hand-some, alert and smart like troops leaving their winter cantonments. Each of them carried three or four white loaves attached to his knap-sack and a bottle of brandy hanging from strap of his sabre or car-tridge box. They were followed by a convoy of baggage such as has never been seen in any war.'

Though Pion des Loches' two companies of Young Guard foot artillery leave in the afternoon, the Foot Chasseurs won't get out of the gates until midnight.

If the army had been characterized at the Niemen by the 'vast, the unprecedented host of vehicles it was dragging after it', the evil is now many times worse. Assembling the 1,100 men of his 4th Line in a sandy space beside Prince Galitzin's huge town palace 'as big as the Tuileries', Fezensac has already been shocked to see some overladen carts and carriages being abandoned:

'They were burning such foodstuffs as we couldn't take with us, and we saw provisions being burnt under our eyes that perhaps would have saved our lives.'

And Dedem is no less shocked to discover that

'when we left there was enough of it left in the stores to nourish 20,000 horses for six months. Leaving Moscow I saw a storehouse whose immense long vaults were filled up with sacks of fine flour. It was left to be looted. And yet eight days previously I'd had difficulty in obtaining a sack of crude flour.'

Now, reaching a hilltop outside the town, Fezensac looks out over

'the immense caravan, reminiscent of the conquerors of Asia, marching several vehicles abreast. The plain was covered with these immense baggages, and on the horizon Moscow's bell towers bounded the picture. We were ordered to halt at this spot, as if to let us contemplate a last time the ruins of this ancient city, which soon disappeared from our sight.'

The caravan is indeed immense. It strikes Davout's paymaster Captain Duverger as

'a bizarre spectacle: this disorderly caravan of every kind of vehicle, military carriages, little carts, calèches, droshkis, most of them attached to little Russian horses, painfully dragging themselves across a sandy plain – this hotchpotch of individuals from all countries and both sexes isolated in the crowd by completely different interests and languages, mechanically following the impulse given them by necessity. The French who lived in Moscow, even the Germans, had left the city – they were afraid to expose themselves to the barbarians' reprisals if they remained. So they'd fled, taking with them wives and children and a few fragments of whatever they'd possessed.'

The Kaluga highway is broad, but not broad enough. An otherwise anonymous Captain von Kurz sees the vast baggage train crawling along it and beside it in no fewer than ten parallel columns:

'Most officers owned a cart, but the generals had half a dozen. Supply officials and actors, women and children, cripples, wounded men, and the sick were driving in and out of the throng in kibitkas and droshkis, accompanied by countless servants and maids, sutlers and people of that sort. The columns of horsemen and pedestrians broke out on either side. Wherever the terrain permitted they crossed the fields flanking the road, so as to leave the paved highway free for those on foot. But the enormous clutter of transport got jammed up, even so.'

So vast is this host of vehicles, Major *L-J. Vionnet* realizes,

'that their column, alone, took up a space of eighteen miles. It's impossible to imagine what disorder this caused. The soldiers fought to get ahead of one another; and when, sometimes, by chance, a bridge had to be crossed, they had to wait for twelve hours. The vehicles had been well numbered, but even by the second day their order had been turned upside down, so that those whose rank entitled them to a carriage didn't know where to find it and consequently couldn't get at its contents. From the first days of the retreat we already began to lack for everything.'

The strategic and logistic implications of this ball and chain of impedimenta clinging to the army's heels just when every effort should be being made in true Napoleonic style to steal two or three marches on the Russians, certainly aren't lost on Davout's unwilling chief-of-staff. Not that Lejeune isn't himself one of the officers responsible for it:

'I'll give you an idea of my own position in this respect – I who was one of the officers most interested in travelling without impedimenta! I still had (1) five riding horses [essential for a staff officer]; (2) a carriage drawn by three horses and carrying my belongings, as well as furs to wrap round me at our bivouacs; (3) the wagon laden with staff documents, maps, and the kitchen utensils for the officers and clerks – this was pulled by four horses and weighed down by the clerks, the cook, the oats, sugar, coffee, flour, and some scarce bales of hay; (4) the secretary's horse; lastly (5) the three horses which I'd harnessed to my sister's carriage: she'd gone on ahead. All this made a clutter of six vehicles and twenty-five horses, and yet they scarcely carried the essentials! The traces kept on breaking. Halts held up the march. Sand, defiles, marshes – all caused delays. And the army took twelve hours and often longer to cover the distance that one vehicle on its own would have covered in two. The Emperor was very much upset by these delays, and ordered that every vehicle not essential for transporting the few provisions we carried should be burnt and the horses be used to pull the guns. This very wise but severe measure was but feebly enforced. The Emperor had one of his own carriages burnt, but the example wasn't compelling enough and found no imitators.

There were too many people who had an interest in evading it.'

'Despite our foreboding of the mischief awaiting us,' Fezensac goes on,
'each of us was determined to carry off his own part of the trophies –
there was no employee so insignificant he hadn't taken a carriage and
packed up some precious objects. For my part I had furs, paintings by
the great masters (rolled up for easier transport) and some jewellery.
One of my comrades had loaded up an enormous crate of quinine.
Another a whole library of lovely books with gilded spines and bound
in red morocco, including Demoustier's *Letters to Emilia*. I hadn't forgotten my comforts either: rice, sugar, coffee. In my reserves I counted three great pots of jams, two being cherries, a third of currents.'

Even such a veteran as Major Boulart of the Old Guard artillery is
'carried away by the mania for having a carriage. In my wake I had a
very fine brand-new coupé, given me by a general who didn't know
what to do with it! Didn't I even commit the same folly of buying horses to harness it to? This elegant coupé contained sugar, tea, furs and
some magnificent editions of books, and in my delirium I supposed
I'd be able to bring part of those objects back to France.'

Marching on his own at the Italians' heels, Lieutenant-Colonel Le Roy too
sees how
'most officers were having themselves drawn along like Russians do,
in light carriages with four horses abreast. Each carriage had to keep
its rank on the road and was unable to change direction, that is unless
the drivers wanted to take off at a cross-roads to rejoin their army
corps. But the road only had to narrow in a defile for these gentil-
lesses [pretty toys] to turn over and get left behind.'

The 28-year-old war-commissary Bellot de Kergorre, walking along beside
his heavy-laden carriage in the wake of IHQ, notices that 'to the tilt of their
light cart the troupe of actors who were following us had affixed the words:
"First actor to S. M. I. R." [His Majesty the Emperor and King] ... "First
valet" ... Sad recourse against accidents en route!' For his part, Kergorre is
marching with the Intendant-General's headquarters, where, to add to all
the private plunder, General Count *François Roguet*'s three regiments of
Guard Grenadiers are escorting the Treasury wagons, including the imperial loot. Bellot de Kergorre:
'I was carrying away trophies from the Kremlin, including the cross of
Ivan, several ornaments used at the coronation of the tsars, and a
Madonna enriched with precious stones, which had been given by the
Tsarina Anna in 1740 in memory of the victories won over the Poles
and the capture of Danzig in 1733. The treasure comprised silver
coins or bullion melted down from the large amount of silverware
found in the ruins of Moscow. For nearly 40 miles I had to pick my

way through the army's procession of horse-drawn vehicles. Every one was laden with useless baggage.'

And Planat de la Faye, marching with the artillery staff, notices in particular how 'the number of *cantinières* with carts had grown enormously'. Their vast pillage isn't merely bogging down the army 'just when it most needed to be mobile'. It's also

'beginning the army's demoralization, or, more correctly, that of the French troops – the German and Dutch troops had already commenced their career as pillagers and scroungers at Viazma'.[2]

Though it may not seem so, a certain priority has in fact been given to foodstuffs. Most of the baggage train, Biot realises, is transporting 'farinacious foods, biscuit, rice, wine, coffee, tea, sugar and rum'. And Dr Réné Bourgeois, too, is glad to see that all vehicles except the artillery wagons are carrying forage for the horses and victuals, 'flour, wine, sugar, coffee, tea and liquors'.

Even so, the stupendous caravan reminds Captain Labaume, riding onwards with Prince Eugène's staff, of Virgil and Livy's descriptions of 'the destruction of Troy or Carthage'. And Boulart, consoling himself that this isn't a retreat but an offensive towards the south, is reminded of 'the ancient Persian armies in their expeditions against the Greeks'.

But how strong are the army's actual effectives? Prince Eugène is in the van with 20,000 infantry but only 2,000 cavalry, less than half the effectives that had started out from Glogau in May. His once 13,000-strong 15th Division, for instance, now numbers only 4,000. The marquis *de Chambray,* marching with his guns, will afterwards go closely into the matter and give the army's effectives as:

I Corps 29,000 (originally 79,000)
III Corps 11,000 (originally 44,000)
IV Corps 25,600 (originally 42,400)
V Corps 6,000 (originally 30,000)
VIII Corps perhaps 1,500 (originally 18,700)

Imperial Guard 22,480 (originally 51,300), the original figures being Labaume's. Caulaincourt sets the total at 102,260 and 533 guns.[3]

For the time being Mortier is to stay behind in the Kremlin with Delaborde's division of the Young Guard, Carrière's brigade of 4,000 dismounted cavalry (organised in four battalions), two companies of sappers, four of artillery and a brigade of 500 cavalry. He's to collect all sick and wounded who can't be evacuated and leave them in the Foundlings Hospital:

"After the army has left, the Duke of Treviso will tomorrow cause the municipality to make a proclamation, warning the inhabitants that rumours of evacuation are false: that the army is moving on Kaluga,

Tula and Briansk to seize those important points and the arms factories they contain, and obliging the inhabitants to maintain order and
prevent anyone from trying to complete the town's destruction."
Any destruction that's to take place, notably of the Kremlin and the Arsenal, which is expected to be total, is to be at Mortier's hands.

A great deal of the army's superfluous plunder is already having to be left
behind. Disgusted at having to march at such a snail's pace, 2nd Lieutenant Coignet puts all his little party's possessions and equipment on their
horses and burns their wagon. 'After that we could go anywhere.' The
Fusiliers-Grenadiers of the Middle Guard are bringing up the extreme rear.
And all that first day Sergeant Bourgogne is amazed to see what the army's
leaving behind:
'Being at the very rear of the column I was in a position to see how
the disorder was commencing. The route was cluttered with precious
objects, such as pictures, candelabras, and many books. For more
than an hour I picked up volumes which I leafed though for a
moment and then threw away again, to be picked up by others, who,
in their turn, threw them away. They were editions of Voltaire, of Jean-
Jacques Rousseau and Bouffon's *Natural History* bound in red Morocco and gilded on their spines.'
Ahead of him is a vast mob:
'This crowd of people, with their various costumes and languages, the
canteen masters with their wives and crying children, were hurrying
forward in the most unheard of noise, tumult and disorder. Some had
got their carts smashed, and in consequence yelled and swore enough
to drive one mad. This was the convoy of the whole army, and we had
any amount of trouble getting past it.'
Even by this first evening Bourgogne's pack is beginning to seem much too
heavy. So leaving at dawn next morning and overtaking
'a large part of the fatal convoy, which had passed us while we were
asleep and where we could hear screams in French, oaths in German,
entreaties to the Almighty in Italian, and to the Holy Virgin in Spanish and Portuguese,'
he decides while waiting 'for the left of the column' to lighten it:
'I found several pounds of sugar, some rice, some biscuit, half a bottle of liqueur, a woman's Chinese silk dress embroidered in gold and
silver, several gold and silver ornaments, amongst them a little bit of
the Cross of Ivan the Great – a piece of its outer silver-gilt sheath,
given me by a man who'd helped take it down. Besides all this I had
my [parade] uniform, a woman's large riding cloak (hazel colour,
lined with green velvet. As I couldn't figure out how it was worn, I

imagined its late owner to be over six feet tall), then two silver pictures in relief, a foot long and eight inches high, one of them repre-
senting the Judgement of Paris on Mount Ida, the other showing
Neptune on a chariot formed of a shell and drawn by sea-horses, all
in the finest workmanship, and several lockets and a Russian prince's
spittoon set with brilliants. These things were intended for presents,
and had been found in cellars where the houses were burnt down.'
First and foremost Bourgogne, 'feeling pretty certain I shouldn't be wanting them again just yet', jettisons his regulation white knee breeches.[4]
What else he throws out he forgets to say. But he does tell us what he's
wearing:

> 'Over my shirt a yellow silk waistcoat, wadded inside, which I'd made
> myself out of a woman's skirt; over it a large cape lined with ermine,
> and underneath the cape a big pouch hung at my side by a silver
> cord. This was full of various things – amongst them a gold and silver
> crucifix and a little Chinese porcelain vase.[5] Then there was my pow-
> der-flask, my firearms, and sixteen cartridges in my cartridge case.
> Add to all this a fair amount of health, good spirits and the hope of
> presenting my compliments to the Mongol, Chinese and Indian
> ladies, and you'll have a very good idea of a vélite sergeant of the
> Imperial Guard.'

Hardly has Bourgogne relieved himself of his unwanted loot than

> 'ahead of us we hear firing, and are ordered to set off at the double.
> Half an hour afterwards we got to a place where part of the convoy,
> escorted by a detachment of the Red Lancers of the Guard, had been
> attacked by partisans. Several of the lancers had been killed, also
> some Russians and many horses. Near a cart was a pretty woman
> stretched on her back on the ground, dead from shock.'

Why does Dumonceau make no mention of this? The Lancer Brigade,
detailed off to 'provisionally form the army's extreme rearguard' and cover
its flank in the direction of Podolsk, has come back from Woronowo to
meet it. Soon isolated outriders had approached,

> 'and once well on our way it wasn't long before we ran into IV Corps,
> marching in files on either side of the road and leaving its centre to
> us. We saw they were thoroughly refreshed. The men seemed gay and
> in good fettle.'

The rankers of the Line don't hesitate to poke fun at this Guard regiment[6]
which, no more than the others, hadn't been thrown into the action at
Borodino – and get as good as they give. Then comes

> 'the immense mob, bigger than ever, of parks and baggage of all
> kinds, marching on a front of several files, covering the whole road
> and wrapped in a cloud of dust.'

Not to get entangled in it, the Red Lancers take off to the right of the road. And now, on the second day of the march southwards, Dumonceau is sent off to reconnoitre two or three leagues from the highroad – which is perhaps why he'll afterwards forget to mention the affray of the 20th:

'It was recommended to me that I should march prudently, explore the countryside thoroughly and not let myself get pinched. I got back by evening, not having seen a soul. The population of the villages seemed to have returned to their homes, but kept themselves hidden, so that it was impossible to make them appear to obtain any information.'

Griois, too, withdrawing 3rd Cavalry Corps' light artillery after the affair at Winkovo, sees the Moscow army come by:

'Dense columns made up of troops of the different arms, marching in disorder; the horses weak, emaciated, hardly dragging the artillery. The men, on the contrary, having had an abundance of victuals for the last six weeks, were full of strength and health. Carriages of the greatest elegance, peasants' carts, wagons pulled by little country horses and overladen with baggage, were marching in the middle of the columns, pell-mell with the saddle and pack horses. The rankers were crushed under the weight of their packs. To abandon their booty would have been too cruel. Yet already that day baggage was being thrown on the road and vehicles abandoned. This mass of men, horses and vehicles seemed more like an emigration of a people changing its country than an organized army.'

It must have been Ségur who, as usual, in his capacity of Assistant Prefect of the Palace, has gone on ahead of IHQ and fixed on the 'mean' manor house of Troilskoië, about fifteen miles from Moscow, for its first overnight stay. Nearby is concentrated the Italian Guard cavalry and almost the whole army, except Delaborde's division, left behind in Moscow, and what's left of Murat's cavalry – still retreating from Winkovo towards Woronowo and the main column. Already IHQ has met with 'many of the wounded from the Winkovo affair, of which the Emperor only now heard the details'.

Making his way on a *teleg* [Russian four-wheeled cart] to Moscow to be bled, his thigh shattered by a lance-thrust, is an aristocratic youngster of the Carabiniers: Prince Charles de Beauveau. Son of one of Napoleon's chamberlains, 'he was smiling as though his wound was causing him more pride than pain'. Sure they'll never see Moscow again, Caulaincourt sends one of his father's colleagues, the one-eyed chamberlain Count Turenne, hurrying after him. Turenne brings the boy back. And Caulaincourt obtains permission to place him in one of the imperial carriages.

His arm still paralyzed by that lance-thrust in his shoulder, Mailly-Nesle, too, has been making for Moscow in a carriage in which there are some ladies. But knowing the last convoy of wounded has already left, a gendarme named Gimblaut advises them to go no farther. So their comfortable carriage joins the throng. After the miseries of the Winkovo camp the Moscow army, despite all its loot and the snail's pace it's proceeding at, makes a 'magnificent' impression.

'Almost all the staff officers had dressed themselves in the Russian style. Only the artillery was in a bad state. The good horses had been replaced by wretched little konyas, harnessed up by dozens to each gun. The soldiers had provided themselves with gold and silver. They were clad in the most precious furs. Each officer had a little loaded cart in his suite. The most elegant and opulent carriages were following their convoy of immense spoils. Each soldier was carrying at the hilt of his sabre some silver or at very least silver-gilt cutlery. Most of them had silver ciboria or chalices, which they used with inappropriate familiarity. In their knapsacks others had little statues of Muscovite saints, or a silver egg which they scraped or broke up for their transactions with the cantinières. They marched gaily, singing at the tops of their voices, and their full rubicund faces were evidence enough that they lacked neither for bread nor wine.'

Rapp, reporting fit even though his Borodino wound still isn't completely cured, declines Caulaincourt's offer of one of the Emperor's own carriages and mounts his horse, 'to see if I could stand its movement'. As he does so he sees Napoleon talking to Daru who – in addition to his own duties, that highly cultivated and immensely hard-working man, has just taken over those of Chief Commissary Mathieu Dumas, who's gone down with influenza, worsening to pneumonia. Calling Rapp over, Napoleon says:

"Well then, Rapp, we'll withdraw toward the Polish frontier via Kaluga. I'll provide us with good winter quarters, and let's hope Alexander will make peace."

"Your Majesty seems to have waited long enough," Rapp replies. "The inhabitants of the country are predicting a severe winter."

"Bah, bah – always going on about your inhabitants! Today it's 19 October. Look what lovely weather we're having! Don't you recognize my star? Anyway I couldn't leave until I'd got the sick and wounded evacuated. I couldn't leave them to the fury of the Russians."'

Rapp replies respectfully that in his opinion he'd have 'done better to have left them in Moscow. The Russians wouldn't have done them any harm, whereas now they'll be running the risk of perishing on the country roads.'

But Napoleon, more realistic, won't concede this. As for the climate and winter's imminent onset, 'regardless of what he said to contradict me, his obvious worry showed he hadn't convinced himself.'

Next day Castellane watches Dr Yvan set Beauveau's thigh, an operation the youngster bears with great courage. After which Caulaincourt places him in Mailly-Nesle's carriage, which the two young aristocrats have to share with two ladies, three doctors and a footman.[7]

All that day, the second of his march southwards, Napoleon lingers at Troil-skoië, waiting for the huge numbers of stragglers and vehicles to catch up. Roman Soltyk, waiting there with IHQ's topographical department, thinks the infantry is

'in good shape; the cavalry that had been camped near Winkovo in truth much reduced; but that of the Guard, as also that of the three corps which had been in Moscow, still quite well mounted.'

But here comes a nasty reminder of Russian intransigence. Kutusov's reply to Berthier's – i.e., Napoleon's own – letter of 16 October, delivered to him by Colonel Berthémy on the evening of the Winkovo fight, and suggesting that the laws of 'civilised' warfare be better respected, comes in via Murat's outposts. In it Kutusov "emphasises a truth" whose scope, he's sure Berthi-er (i.e., Napoleon) will undoubtedly grasp, and which he'd already enun-ciated to Lauriston at Tarutino:

"However keenly one may desire to do so, it is difficult to inhibit a nation that is embittered by all it sees, a people who for three hun-dred years have never known war within their frontiers,"

[which is going it a bit strong – the Poles had been in Moscow in 1611-13],

'who are ready to immolate themselves for their country and who are not susceptible to those distinctions as to what is or is not usual in ordinary warfare."

No question, that is, of the "polite political war" Napoleon had intended to wage on his "brother Alexander", to be decided by "a good battle". But a war à outrance, an all-out war, a war to the death.

Both Caulaincourt and Berthier have been noticing a peculiar reluc-tance on the Emperor's part to give up Moscow for good. But now, as if reminded by Kutusov's letter that, as he himself has earlier said, "Moscow is no longer a military, only a political position" and 'forced to it by the loss-es incurred at Winkovo, by the reports on the state of our cavalry, and the realisation that the Russians wouldn't come to terms', he reluctantly makes up his mind to do so. Relinquishing his dream of signing a peace there, he dictates an order to Mortier to evacuate the city. After blowing up the Kremlin and the Arsenal, he's to leave, "either at 3 a.m. on the 22nd or at the same hour on the 23rd, whereby he'll become the army's rearguard".

As for the remaining wounded, "I cannot sufficiently urge upon him," he goes on,

> "to have all the men taken with him who are still left in the hospitals, and to do so he can dispose of and make use of all vehicles he can lay his hand on, such as the wagons of the Young Guard and the dismounted cavalry. The Romans gave civic crowns to those who saved citizens. The Duke of Treviso will deserve as many such as the soldiers he rescues. He should let them use his own and all available horses. That's what the Emperor himself did at St Jean d'Acre. He has so much the more reason to take this measure, because the Emperor promises that as soon as the sick-convoy has caught up with the army, all horses and vehicles free because their loads have been consumed will be sent to meet this need. The Emperor hopes to be able to show the Duke of Treviso his satisfaction at his having saved five hundred men. Naturally he should begin with the officers, then the NCOs and give preference to Frenchmen. He is to assemble all generals and officers under his command and impress on them the importance of this measure."

Thereafter Mortier shall join Junot at Mojaisk where, after picking up all the surviving Borodino wounded, he's to follow on behind the army as its rearguard.

Farther on, ahead of IHQ, some 30 miles from Moscow, Davout's headquarters have halted at another country house, built, 'up to its first storey on a base of cut stone. Having many orders to write out,' his chief-of-staff Lejeune mounts

> 'a magnificent staircase to some apartments which seemed to have been only recently deserted and without having been voided of their piano, harp and numerous chairs, on which lay scattered a guitar, some violins, music, embroidery designs and other lady's needlework. Hardly had I been writing for ten minutes than we felt the smell of smoke. Soon it was so strong it distracted us from our work.'

Leaving hastily again, Lejeune hears 'the window frames crack' and sees the whole building collapse in flames.

Once again the Cossacks are burning everything they can. And not merely burning. They've also developed an alarming swiftness – as Sergeant Bourgogne has already seen – in raiding convoys. After leaving Fominskoië – IHQ's next objective – Prince Eugène's Bavarian cavalry are

> 'riding along the Kaluga road through a wood and General Ornano was riding at the head of the 2nd Chevaulegers at rather a brisk canter, and the baggage and lead-horses, including the general's own, were following on behind the regiment,'

when they have a first taste of it. Partly because Ornano is setting such a brisk pace, and partly so as not to get mixed up with IV Corps' disorderly baggage train, a considerable gap has opened up between the 4th Chevaulegers, some 160 to 200 horse, following on, and their commander and his staff:

'Suddenly a hurrah rings out, Cossacks come dashing out of the forest and fling themselves on the baggage and lead- horses. In a flash they've plundered some wagons, seized a couple of loose horses and stabbed down others – all so neatly and swiftly that almost all of them have vanished into the forest before we've even had time to ride back and draw our swords.'

But they do catch one Cossack. And Ornano – he who'd already given proofs of his incompetence at Borodino – makes himself ridiculous by galloping back,

'shouting and swearing and heaping reproaches on us, and claiming that the captured Cossack's nag, at least, was his. We couldn't help laughing as the wretched nag was led out to him. Hardly had he caught sight of it than, with an oath, he put spurs to his horse's flanks and dashed off swearing.'

By taking the cross-country roads that link the old and the new Kaluga roads, Napoleon's idea is to steal a march on Kutusov. And indeed it's only after he's been marching for three days, on 22 October – four days that is – since Bennigsen's half-successful action, that the first news of the French having left Moscow reaches Russian headquarters.[8] Wilson hears that,

'a French officer, brought in as prisoner, admitted that Moscow was evacuated, that Napoleon was with the column at Ignatowo, but stated that he, the officer, knew nothing of the army's movements except that it was leaving Russia. Messenger after messenger then poured in from all quarters with similar intelligence.'

Wilson says nothing of Kutusov falling on his knees and thanking the Almighty for Russia's deliverance.

But though news of his enemy's movements has taken three days to reach Kutusov, Napoleon's plan of outflanking him and striking for Kaluga still calls for speed. Unfortunately that same day, 22 October, the gorgeous weather, with its golden autumn sun shining down out of pellucid blue skies on the evergreen forests and silver birch woods, suddenly breaks. And by morning next day the ground is 'so sodden we'd great difficulty in making Borowsk in two cross-country marches'. For the first time – but not the last – an abrupt change in the weather has come at a most inconvenient moment:

'Making our way across ploughed land and not everyone being well harnessed up, some 1,500 vehicles had to be abandoned. The winding of the road made it impossible for us to assess the innumerable quantity of vehicles making up the headquarters. The rises in the ground, the ravines, were covered with them over a surface of more than twelve miles. There must have been at least 25,000. We were keeping a width of a couple of miles on either side of the main road, a contour clearly traced by the burning villages.'

The steadily falling rain is rendering the side roads utterly unsuitable for the guns and heavy vehicles. What's even worse, the massive downpour has 'done for the draught-horses', and a good number of ammunition wagons and transports are having to be abandoned:

'We set fire to at least 20,000 sutlers' vehicles and others overloaded with sugar, coffee, etc., which were encumbering the road and hindering our passage.'

That day Kergorre finds his chief, the army's Chief Commissary,

'bivouacked in a swamp. M. le comte Dumas had left suffering from pneumonia. Feeble and old, he was exhausted by his work.'[9] That day Count de Lobau exchanged his carriage for a little one I had. His was superb. It had cost at least a hundred louis; but he was finding it too heavy, and as I had some strong horses it suited me perfectly. I filled it with coffee and sugar, pieces of cloth and cashmeres, etc.'

Much of the day is spent building a bridge over the Nara at Fominskoië while the army – disastrously as it'll turn out, in view of its urgent need to strike south – is given a day's rest. Unfortunately, the ranker, Dr Réné Bourgeois 'not having been able to equip himself with food like the officers, had none at all.' This, only four days out of Moscow, and with at least a fortnight's march ahead of them!

Perhaps even more alarming, Kergorre and his comrades are beginning

'to hear the explosion of artillery wagons being blown up, for lack of horses to pull them. The further we advanced the more frequent these explosions became.'

Already Napoleon's obsession with saving his guns is becoming a handicap. That day the Italians, marching doggedly on ahead,

'cross the Nara. The rain keeps falling, the country roads are bad and it's impossible to get on any faster. At each bridge there are blockages, of men, horses and baggage. Most of these bridges are narrow, hardly solid. Often they sag under the vehicles' weight. Added to the slowness of our march, all these obstacles are tiring the men and finally exhausting the artillery horses. A mass of light carriages are getting broken or unable to follow on.'

As a result of all this, Césare de Laugier, sitting for a moment somewhere out of the rain, concludes in his diary, 'a certain feeling of sadness is hanging over the army'. It has also been this drenching cold night, Caulaincourt sees, that has 'really opened Napoleon's eyes and finally convinced him that he must abandon Moscow' – his original idea having been to retain it as a base while occupying the 'fertile Kaluga province, as he called it'. Now he must above all attack and defeat Kutusov.

And still he won't admit, even to Berthier, that he's retreating.

For three days now the courier has been interrupted and there's been no news from Paris. For Napoleon, with all the affairs of Europe centred in his own brain, its arrival, Caulaincourt sees, is each day's most important event. How eagerly he awaits the leather despatch case, how impatiently he opens it – even, if the key isn't instantly to hand, slashes it open with a knife! The three-day gap, due, Caulaincourt has to explain to an irritated Emperor, to Cossacks having seized the second post-station from Moscow, has been the campaign's longest so far. 'This worried and annoyed the Emperor more than I can express.' And it sets him complaining bitterly, first to Caulaincourt, then to Berthier, about the "lack of foresight, the incompetence and negligence" being shown by Foreign Minister Maret, at Vilna, and by Abbé Pradt, his ambassador plenipotentiary at Warsaw.

As if realising that the army is soon going to be surrounded by swarms of Cossacks who can't be driven off for lack of light cavalry, Napoleon has got it into his head that it's Pradt's job, so far from being an ambassador as he understands the word, to squeeze thousands of non-existent "Polish Cossacks" out of the bankrupt duchy – a job of satrap for which the slippery archbishop is singularly unqualified. In the rain near Borowsk, he's complaining to Caulaincourt that "all his present difficulties and any that might arise from them" are due to the Russians having made peace with Turkey,[10] thus freeing Tormassov's Army of Moldavia to come up in his rear and attack Schwarzenberg and Reynier in Volhynia; also to the Russians' alliance with Sweden, both of which happenings he regards as being Maret's fault.

At 1.30 a.m. on 23 October, the air's shaken by an immense distant explosion. Le Roy is riding along the Kaluga road to rejoin the 85th when[11] 'we hear a violent explosion from the direction of Moscow.' What can it be? Three more follow, the last at 4 a.m. Following an unfamiliar road out of Moscow with Delaborde's Young Guard division, miles away to the west, Lieutenant Paul de Bourgoing, his ADC, hears it too. It's the loudest bang he'll ever hear in his life ...

Only later next morning does Le Roy learn what it was.

Mortier has done his best to carry out Napoleon's instructions. His two companies of sappers have done their work and the Kremlin – or at least part of it – has been blown sky-high. The four stupendous explosions have caused many of the city's surviving houses to collapse from the shock-waves – and the few remaining inhabitants to think it's the end of the world. If the Kremlin as a whole hasn't been wiped out it's been thanks to the drenching rain, which has dampened the fuzes. One French officer who'd approached to find out why the explosion wasn't even greater has been stunned by falling masonry:

'By the first two explosions part of the walls and one of the towers toward the river were destroyed; by the third, the church of St. Nicholas and Moscow's four great bell towers were blown up with tremendous violence; at the same moment the lofty tower of Ivan Veliki, the first of the Czars, was rent from the top to its base, and the cross of the cupola, crowning its summit, buried in the ruin below. The fourth shock,'

the anonymous officer goes on,

'had been by far the most dreadful. The walls of the Arsenal, which were upwards of three yards in thickness, together with a part of the gate of St. Nicholas and several adjacent pinnacles, were blown into the air and shook the whole city to its foundations.'

'The most peremptory orders were given to the detachment occupying the Kremlin,' *J. T. James*, visiting the scene of the explosions next year, will be told:

'With unutterable malignity he had marked out for devastation some of the fairest portions of this proud citadel, that had stood uninjured amidst the times of the conflagration. The barbarous fury of Buonaparte attacked whatever Russian piety had spared, the most after his departure. The mines were prepared, and at two o'clock on the last night of their [i.e., Mortier's] stay this horrid purpose was carried into execution. The ground where we stood was strewed with the relics of the church of St. Nicholas: the great bells that were its chief boast (one of which weighed more than 200,000 pounds) lay scattered in different directions, as they chanced to have fallen at the time; and of the celebrated bell cast by the Empress Anne nothing was discoverable but the ring of the top, so deep was it buried in rubbish.'

Hearing the distant noise of the immense explosions, 'though we were hardly astonished by anything any longer, and expected everything,' Pierre Auvray remarks, 'the army was astonished.'

'When the Russian General Ilowaiki re-entered Moscow on 23 October, he found in the three existing hospitals some 1,400 Russian sick or wounded and 650 French sick or wounded who'd been too weak to be transported with their comrades. Even so, part of these latter were thrown on to carts to be dragged to Tver; but they all perished from cold and misery or were assassinated by the peasants charged with tak-

ing them there, who cut their throats to get their coats. The rest were
left in the hospitals with French surgeons who'd remained behind to
look after them, but they were given neither food nor medicines,'

writes *Frédéric-Guillaume de Vaudoncourt*,[12] a staff officer who will himself be
captured during the retreat.

That day the Italians 'pass through a deserted Borowsk and bivouac an
hour's march further on, near the village of Uvarovskoië'. There Césare de
Laugier hears that:

'instructions have been sent off at 5 this morning by the Major-General [Berthier] to the Duke of Abrantès [Junot, at Mojaisk]. He's to
burn everything he can't take with him and be ready to leave at the
first signal for Viazma. The heads of all units as far as Smolensk are
being forewarned of the army's movement and General Evers is
ordered to leave Viazma with 4 to 5,000 men to open the army's communications with Smolensk via Juchnow.'

It seems to him that the Emperor, after his sweep southwards and giving
Kutusov a bloody nose in revenge for the Winkovo affair, is planning to
rejoin the devastated Smolensk road at Viazma.

Leaving Fominskoië at 9 a.m. IHQ marches all day. And at 7.30 p.m. it
too reaches Borowsk – where a courier finally arrives. Always Napoleon's
first act at such moments is to study the covering sheet, giving hours of
arrival and departure at and from the various post-stations. This one gives
an even more serious explanation of the long delay:

'A body of Cossacks, together with great numbers of peasants armed
and organised as a militia, are cutting off communications beyond
Ghjat – a complication which seems to be spreading.'

He observes to Caulaincourt:

"We're going to be without news from France. But even worse, France
won't be getting any news of us."

Everything's still going at a snail's pace. Nor is the stopover at Borowsk
a happy one. Depressed by the dreary landscape and "these slaves' [Slavs']
wild and terrible appearance which must offend any eye used to other
countries", Napoleon tells Rapp:

"I wouldn't wish to leave a single man here. I'd sooner sacrifice all the
treasures of Russia than a single wounded man. Horses, pack wagons, carriages, everything must be used to save them."

And sends off another letter to Mortier to that effect. 'But of course he
was confusing words and his own will with facts and possibilities.'

A few miles beyond Borowsk is a village that's been occupied by Prince
Eugène and part of IV Corps. Bivouacking his artillery there, Griois is invit-

ed to dinner by General *C. N. Anthouard*, head of IV Corps' artillery, whose acquaintance he had presumably made during the last days of the advance on Moscow, when the wounded Grouchy's guns had been placed at Eugène's disposal. It's several days now since Griois, horseless and carriage-less and, lacking all his captured equipment ('almost everything I possessed') has had anything to eat except 'bread and whatever I'd been able to buy from the *cantinières* one rather rarely ran into and who were regarded as well supplied if they could offer a bit of cheese and ham'. But now, at Anthouard's headquarters, plenty of good wine raises his spirits. Even better, all his fellow artillery officers there, no doubt lit up by the good wines, want to help him make good his loss of all his effects back at Winkovo:

> 'On getting up from table each wanted to contribute something to re-establish my wardrobe. Colonel Berthier [Berthier's 38-year-old son] gave me some cloth for a pair of trousers; another a shirt; another a cravat; the general a pair of completely new boots which seemed to be made to fit me, in the circumstances a gift beyond prize. At nightfall I decided to rejoin my artillery and left, taking with me a most agreeable memory, which I'll never forget.'

But a cold rain is falling,

> 'and when I hid myself away, wrapped up in my greatcoat, under one of my batteries' ammunition wagons, I regretted the warm and well covered resting place I'd just left.'

By now it has taken the army six days to cover the 100 kilometres that separate Borowsk from Moscow – mainly because everyone's clinging to the plunder. But now, what's that in the distance? A vague rumble of gunfire? No matter, it's time for a halt. And Surgeon Roos – no more than anyone else who'd been at Winkovo – he has had a chance to participate in the city's plunder – is amazed by what he sees. That evening there's a sort of fair. Valuables are taken out and displayed, the heavier items for exchange for less heavy ones. A gaping Roos gazes at

> 'the most beautiful carpets I've ever seen, tapestries and wall-hangings and cloths embroidered with gold and silver, pieces of silk of every colour, men and women's clothes, embroidered and brilliant such as are only seen at the courts of princes. One heard it being said: "Such or such a one has so or so many precious stones, another has a case filled with diamonds, another rolls of ducats." I listened astounded.'

And still, somewhere ahead, through the rainy weather, the guns are rumbling.

CHAPTER 12

"WHERE OUR CONQUEST OF THE WORLD ENDED"

Two armies race through the night – 'the only member of my family who's never given me cause for complaint' – Malojaroslavetz – Delzons makes up for lost time – Wilson in action – 22,000 Italians fight 70,000 Russians – Soltyk repeats Napoleon's exact words – Malojaroslavetz lost and retaken six times – Séruzier's exploit

A bare day's march south-south-west of Borowsk the new Kaluga road is crossed by a deep gorge and the River Luja, beyond which a long ravine leads up to some heights and the little town of Malojaroslavetz. It's the only point at which the Russian army has a chance of holding up the French lunge southwards. And it's there Eugène's three divisions are making for.

To the ever-critical eyes of Dedem van der Gelder, the 32-year-old Eugène de Beauharnais, Viceroy of Italy, seems

'almost childishly afraid of the Emperor, whence his need to do even more than he wished him to. He was rude both to and about his Italians. For all his excellent and cautious qualities as a general his haughty tone had soon lost him their affections.'[1]

Planat de la Faye, less critical, sees Eugène as a man

'full of uprightness and loyalty, without political initiative, calm, gifted with consistency and sound judgement. All these qualities made him an excellent instrument in the Emperor's hands, whom he always served with fidelity and exactitude and a devotion without limits.'

"In all my family," Napoleon himself had said of him, "only Eugène has never given me any subject for complaint." And afterwards, to Count *Mathieu Molé*, he'd describe him as "less brilliant than the King of Naples. In one aspect he's less eminent. As a whole he's even a mediocre man, though there's more proportion and harmony in him." If Murat hates Eugène, it's also because of the remorseless feud between Josephine's family and the Bonapartes, to whose coterie Murat belongs by marriage.

Such is the man whose corps is leading the Grand Army. Marching along the Malojaroslavetz road, his 22,000-strong IV Corps is headed by the fourteen French and two Croat battalions of Delzons' 13th Division, reviewed only a week ago, on 17 October, by Napoleon in the Kremlin. The 37-year-old Delzons has a long fighting record that goes back to Lodi; and it had been he who'd launched the initial assault on the village of Borodino. Behind his division comes the Italian Royal Guard, followed immediately by what's left of Grouchy's 3rd Cavalry Corps: its artillery consists of Griois' own regiment's 4th and 5th Companies, attached to the imbecile Lahoussaye's dragoon division, and its 6th Company, attached to Chastel's 3rd light cavalry division (6th, 8th, 25th Chasseurs, the 6th Hussars, a regiment of Saxon dragoons and two regiments of Bavarian chevaulegers). All Grouchy's units, except the artillery, are by now reduced to riding mere nags.[2]

> 'I'd left my bivouac early, and was making for Malojaroslavetz, which was only three leagues away. The Viceroy's army corps had taken the same direction, and most of the units that made it up must already have been close to that town when a cannon shot, coming from that direction, hastened the columns' march. The noise grew louder as we came nearer and announced a serious affair.'

At a certain distance behind him Griois knows Broussier's 14th Division (French and Spaniards) is following on; and, bringing up the rear, Pino's 15th Division (Italians and Dalmatians).

It had been late in the evening of 22 October that a message had reached Docturov, commanding the 2nd Russian army corps, that the French have switched their direct line of advance down the old Kaluga road and are making for Malojaroslavetz. An excited Wilson had pointed out to him the importance – rather evident, one would think – of concentrating there and barring Napoleon's passage. Docturov, however, had irritated him by wasting a lot of time in sending a messenger to Kutusov to get permission to move. But now, all day during the 23rd in drenching rain and during the night, Docturov's 70,000 men have been

> 'straining every nerve to reach Malojaroslavetz before the enemy, whose lights were frequently visible during the night, as the columns occasionally approached within a mile or two of each other, through flat meadow lands country full of brooks and broad ditches, unprovided with any pontoons or other means, except such as could be found on the spot.'

Many of his leading units are being transported in wagons. And soon they've

> 'crossed the Protwa at Sparskoïë and gained the plain which lay in front of [i.e. from the Italians' point of view, beyond] Malojaroslavetz. Everyone was ignorant of the location. There were five main roads out of Malojaroslavetz. And the Russians placed outposts on them all.'

Already, late yesterday evening (22 October), Chastel's light cavalry, Henckens' 6th Chasseurs among them, have entered the town and found it abandoned by its inhabitants. Spreading out on the plain beyond 'in the directions of Tourantina and Kaluga, we here and there ran into regular enemy troops, who were falling back in front of us'. Now, also late in the evening, Delzons' division is approaching Malojaroslavetz. Ordered to march at midnight to get to the bridge at dawn, Delzons – if we're to believe Dedem van der Gelder (but the Dutchman is back with IHQ at Borowsk and so doesn't actually see what's going on, and anyway has a strong tendency to criticize on slender grounds of hearsay) –

> 'thought he had time to let his troops have their soup and didn't get going until 2 a.m.[3] It was this two-hour delay' [Dedem goes on] 'that changed the face of affairs, and decided the fate of the army and the peace. If he'd carried out his orders punctually he'd have seized the position without firing a shot.'

Dead beat from their forced march, Delzons' two leading battalions cross the gorge in the darkness – Cossacks have already demolished the bridge – and struggle up the long narrowing ravine, flanked by rocks, which leads up to Malojaroslavetz. Malojaroslavetz, Wilson will see when he gets there at dawn, 'is built upon the side and summit of a lofty hill, rising immediately above the Luzha (which the enemy called the Lutza)'. Somewhere out in the dark plain Delzons' men can hear the voices of Docturov's scouts, being held off by Chastel's light cavalry; but otherwise see no sign of any enemy troops. Placing outposts and sentinels out in the direction of the surrounding plain, they lie down to snatch a couple of hours' sleep;[4] and Delzons sends back an ADC to notify Eugène, who of course notifies Napoleon, spending the night at Borowsk, that the town has been occupied.

Now it's the early hours of Saturday morning, 24 October. 'Over the river', Wilson sees,

> 'is a bridge. Between the bridge and the beginning of the ravine is a distance of about a hundred yards. The ground on both flanks of the town, ascending from the river, is woody and steep, and the ground on the left is intersected with very deep fissures and ravines, so as to be impracticable for artillery movements from the bank of the river. The whole town is built of wood. Near the summit of the hill there is an open space like a grande place. And near the ravine, at the bottom, are a church and a couple or more houses that command the approach.'

Arriving on the scene Docturov orders

> 'two regiments of chasseurs, supported by two more, to dash into the town and drive the enemy (whom some fugitive inhabitants had reported to have reached and entered it) out of the place, and over the river, which ran immediately below, and to destroy the bridge.'

In Delzons' camp everyone's

> 'asleep except the sentinels, when suddenly, four regiments of [Russian] chasseurs come rushing out of the woods which crown the heights, cause the sentinels to fall back hastily on the outposts, the outposts on the battalions, which taken by surprise, were forced after

putting up a certain defence to abandon the village [sic] and go and
join the rest of the division down in the plain.'

Meanwhile, Delzons or his subordinates have fortified the bridgehead on
the south bank, using the church and some large houses. At the first alarm,
Césare de Laugier goes on, Delzons – whose sappers have also been busy re-
establishing the bridge – has called his division to arms 'and runs to his
men's assistance'. While it had still been dark Wilson has himself taken command of a couple of Russian guns, brought them forward and aimed them
at the bridge:

'Already the Russians had deployed their artillery on the heights and
on both sides of the town, so as to fire on the bridge below them [sic]
and prevent any new offensive. Finally, the Russian cavalry deployed
to the right of the infantry.'

As day dawns Wilson sees

'a large body of the enemy descending the lofty hill on the left bank
of the river to pass the bridge and enter the town. This dense body
was flocking forward as if quite at ease and unconscious of any serious opposition being designed to the passage and occupation.'

Reporting back to Docturov, he goes on,

'the English General galloped with a battery of light artillery placed
under his directions to an elevation which he had selected for its site,
and opened its fire almost within grapeshot of the mass. At the first
discharge there was a general halt. On the second a wavering. On the
third a total dispersion, and every one flew forward or scrambled up
the hill to get out of the reach of this unexpected cannonade. The
movement of the advanced guard was thus checked.'

And indeed Delzons' position is critically exposed. Obviously Docturov's
corps – perhaps the entire Russian army – is coming up to defend Malojaroslavetz and block the Grand Army's advance southwards. 'New Russian
columns,' Césare de Laugier goes on,

'were emerging in compact masses out of the woods beyond Malojaroslavetz and coming up to range themselves in battle order. And in
no time at all we saw forts being raised behind their front that they
were putting in a state of defence even during the fighting, with a
parapet and a ditch.'

His own action, Wilson claims, has

'gained nearly an hour before the Viceroy could arrive in person,
bring up his artillery, and re-establish order: an essential hour for the
Russians.'

Delzons' ADC has of course long ago reached Eugène, who,

'escorted by the Dragoons of the Royal Guard and the Queen's Dragoons, had already got going when he'd heard the sound of the guns.

We were to stand to arms immediately.'

'In about an hour' Wilson again sees 'the enemy, under cover of a heavy fire, recommence the descent of the hill and join the two battalions defending the bridge.' Laugier:

'The Russians' plunging fire was raining down in this funnel where Delzons was immobilized. The Viceroy ordered him to get out of this position at once, cost what it might, and to advance. The road onwards from the bridge follows the bottom of a ravine between great stone blocks, whose summits were occupied by numerous Russian sharpshooters, supported in turn by the masses already encamped on the hill.'

The 'brave and heroic' Delzons, who'd fought at Lodi, Rivoli and the Pyramids, hardly has a moment more to live. Colonel Séruzier, whose guns, standing in reserve and unable to reply because of the degree of elevation required, sees him

'rush to the middle of the mêlée, rally his division and try to repulse the enemy. He was just beginning to resume the offensive when some sharpshooters, ambushed behind a wall, fired at him. He fell dead.'

As do his two brothers, 'one his brigade commander, the other his ADC'.[5] Immediately Eugène sends his chief-of-staff to take over. 'Like the experienced soldier he was, Guilleminot occupied and fortified the church and two houses' at the bridgehead. And when 13th Division is again thrown back this at least enables them to enfilade, at point-blank range, any Russian attempts to counter-attack. It also gives Broussier's 14th Division (18th Light, 9th, 35th, 53rd Line plus the remains of his two Spanish battalions) time to arrive on the scene:

'Each time the Russian troops passed these advanced posts they were fired at from behind, fled in disorder, and ours resumed the offensive to thoroughly repulse them. Prince Eugène keeps demanding the arrival of new troops; but no matter how much these hasten their steps, it seems they'll never get there in time.'

By now the battle for Malojaroslavetz and the French army's advance on Kaluga is becoming a very serious affair indeed. More and more of IV Corps' units are arriving on the scene; and again 13th Division, commanded now by Guilleminot and supported by Broussier's 14th, is trying to force its way up the ravine. Despite all Wilson's firing,

'the enemy pushed up through the streets of the town to the outskirts, when the battle began with a violence which corresponded with the magnitude of its objects and the resolute determination of each party to achieve its own. The enemy was infuriated by despair, the Russians by 'the Moscow cry of vengeance'.

Each repulse suffered by Guilleminot's men leaves the 13th Division's leading units cut off. And from the plain behind Malojaroslavetz, more and more of whose timber houses are in flames, one Russian division after another is turning up and deploying. 'Even the militia who'd just joined,' Wilson goes on,

'(and who, being armed only with pikes, formed a third rank to the battalions) not only stood as steady under the cannonade as their veteran comrades, but charged the sallying enemy with as ardent ferocity. Docturov, under cover of his powerful artillery, which poured shot, shell, and grape on the advancing columns, re-entered and repossessed himself of the whole town as far as the ravine, except the church and adjoining houses which the enemy had garrisoned, and which commanded the ground beyond, so that the Russians could not remain under their fire to contend for the ravine and seizure of the bridge,'

and are therefore thrown back again. Dalmatian and Spanish obstinacy equals that of the Russians:

'The roar and crash of the guns, the rattle of light firearms, the whining and sighing of bigger and small shot, the laments of the wounded and dying, the curses in all languages that were heard during bayonet charges, words of command, horn signals, fifes and drums, and added to all this the wavy motion forward and backwards of the masses in gunpowder smoke that hid friend and foe in so secret a darkness that one could often only make out the enemy positions from the lightning flashes or the advancing batteries – all this made an impression that went through the marrow of one's bones. Anyone who says he goes under fire without an oppressive feeling is an idiot. But the danger being shared, it seems less apparent to the individual. Seeing one's comrades falling to right and left, one offsets it by accustoming oneself to the danger which for every minute that passes drives out all fear, also in the increasing rage that takes pleasure in avenging ourselves on our murderers.'[6]

Not until 10 a.m. has Napoleon first heard the distant sound of the guns. At IHQ's 'first halt' outside Borowsk – probably at the village of Ouvarovskoië – he's taking a light breakfast by the roadside together with Murat, Berthier and Lariboisière and questioning two captured Cossacks. Calling for Gourgaud, he sends him off to Eugène to order him to seize Malojaroslavetz and hang on to it until Davout can come up with I Corps. But already Eugène, before flinging in his third – and last – infantry division (Pino's 15th), has sent back Roman Soltyk, evidently on mission to him from IHQ, to ask for prompt supports. Twenty-two thousand Italians, Dalmatians, Croats, Frenchmen and Spaniards are at grips with seventy thousand Russians; but "all these troops won't be enough to hold Kutusov's army at bay". Somewhere along the twelve miles of road between Ouvarovskoië and the heights above the Luja gorge the two staff officers, galloping in opposite directions, probably run into each other, exchange information.

After successive attempts, however, Guilleminot at last regains the town square. But though Broussier's 14th Division reinforces him he still can't establish any lodgement beyond it. Séruzier, who's been on the scene for some time with the 2nd Cavalry Corps' light artillery and witnessed 'the town being taken and retaken several times by our troops', is beginning to be seriously worried:

'Nothing was decided and we were losing a lot of men. Wanting to put an end to it, the Prince ordered General Pino's [15th] Italian Division to cross the bridge to support Broussier's and Guilleminot's. He asked for my artillery, of which he had utmost need, and he'd placed the Royal Italian Guard and General Ornano's light cavalry in reserve behind the riverbank, at the entrance of the forest.'

And now here's Soltyk, the Polish patriot, expert on ballistics and speaker of fluent French, after galloping into Ouvarovskoië, standing in front of his idol – who promptly sends him back to Eugène:

"He's begun to drink the cup," Napoleon tells him to tell Eugène, "and he must drain it. I've ordered Davout to support him."

On his way back Soltyk overtakes the heads of Davout's column, which he sees are forcing the pace. Finding Eugène – who tends to be as calm and imperturbable in battle as Murat is excitable – exactly where he'd left him, amidst all the shot and shell, he sees that by now 'all of IV Corps except the Italian Royal Guard' are 'heavily and inextricably engaged'. Napoleon's orders seem so abrupt – not to say self-evident – that Soltyk hardly likes to repeat them verbatim to the Viceroy,

'because they seemed to express some dissatisfaction. I just told him the Emperor ordered him to press the attack with vigour. I was about to go on when Eugène turned away with a gesture of marked impatience toward his chief-of- staff beside him, and spoke to him in a low voice. Then, turning to me again, he said with vivacity: "But what did he say, then, when you'd explained to him the difficulties of the position and the enemy forces' superiority?"'

Respectfully, Soltyk this time repeats Napoleon's exact words.

'This energetic order produced the effect Napoleon had expected. The Viceroy went in person to meet the Royal Guard, which at this moment was debouching from the wood, gave it the order to cross the bridge and charge the enemy. And in fact, this force advanced at the double and flung itself at the bayonet point on the position already

seized by the Muscovites. Thus the electric spark I'd brought set fire to the troops and victoriously carried the day,'
concludes Soltyk, and adds: 'From then on I decided never to alter a word of Napoleon's orders.'

Césare de Laugier says nothing about charging the Russians at bayonet point, but leaves us in no doubt as to the Italian Guard's morale:

'It's then he sends Colonel Labédoyère to accelerate our march, and at the same time to inform the Emperor of events. The Royal Guard meets this distinguished officer[7] as it comes down the hillside that dominates the Luja.'

Labédoyère encourages them with flattering words, telling them their comrades are in danger, and they'll miss their chance to demonstrate their own bravery:

'At these words, repeated from mouth to mouth, all the battalions utter joyful shouts. The columns no longer march, they fly, and despite the speed with which our chiefs lead us on, we don't seem to be going fast enough. Military songs are struck up. Joy seems to forget fatigue.'[8]

Reaching the Luja and following its bank they see 'on the left-hand side of the road the Italian reserve cavalry encamped [i.e., General Guyon's 9th and 19th Chasseurs] near the pine wood':

'We hadn't seen our brave comrades since the last days of September. But we knew of their exploits and made haste to hold them in our arms and equal them. The encounter couldn't have been more à propos. Hardly had we spotted them than they come to meet us. They blend themselves with our ranks. Everyone is looking for a friend, a relative. They bring us liqueurs, victuals. We shake hands, we weep with emotion. The idea of the fatherland transports us![9] It's about 10 a.m., perhaps, when we finally join our own men, engaged since early morning.'

Well, perhaps a bit later than that – it must have taken Soltyk at least half an hour to reach Eugène from the point on the hither side of Ouvarovskoië where he'd taken Napoleon's orders.

At last, after furious struggles in the ravine and the town, Guilleminot has managed to bring all three divisions of the Army of Italy into line facing the Russian position at the crest of the hill,

'the 13th's first and the second [Pino's 15th] division in Malojaroslavetz and one in front of the town, and part of the 14th in the suburb, beyond a deep ravine which extends for more than 300 yards, along and parallel with the Kaluga road.'

But not for long:

'Seeing the day's success depended uniquely on the possession of this important point, Kutusov sends the whole of Raevsky's corps to Docturov's assistance. The town is taken, then retaken, even up to three times, Guilleminot and Broussier, obliged to yield to force of numbers, fall back to the bridge, where the Viceroy is, to keep account of the overall movement and prepare reserves. He immediately sends them Broussier's second brigade. Then the action seems to move on. Hardly have the battalions left the houses behind them, hardly have they set out from the central point and appeared in the plain, where they're exposed, than they weaken. Overwhelmed by the fire of an entire army, they become demoralised and fall back. The Russians are being incessantly reinforced. Our files yield and break up. The obstacles of the terrain only increase the disorder. Shells fired from both sides have set fire to the town, built of wood. And this circumstance finally puts paid to the two divisions' evolutions and assaults. For the fifth time they have to fall back. The Russians gain ground, and for a moment the defence is paralysed.'

It's then, Césare de Laugier goes on, that the Viceroy sends in Pino's division.

'The troops, led by their chief, march in closed columns, in good order, silent, unquiet, avid for glory. As for ourselves, all the infantry of the Royal Guard, we're made to remain in the little town to the left of the Luja.'

The fire of a Russian battery on a hilltop to the left of the advancing columns isn't merely causing havoc in their massed ranks; it's also forcing the Royal Guard to keep changing its position. Some of its light artillery is 'as much exposed as any sharpshooters to the enemy fire, and are themselves firing upwards'. Its gunners draw Césare de Laugier's admiration as they force the Russian battery off the hilltop. Crossing the bridge again, Pino's Italians 'get their breath back' and form up again:

'Then the first brigade, Generals Pino and Fontana at its head, move towards the right of the town, to protect the 13th Division; the second, led by the Corsican General Levier, climbs up the other side to take the Russian columns which have repulsed the 14th in the rear. And we're overjoyed to see our Italians seize all the positions indicated to them by the Viceroy, and by General [sic] Gourgaud, the Emperor's ADC [sic], who's turned up on the scene. The 1st Brigade forces its way into the town and drives out the Russians. A horrible mêlée ensues amidst the flames that are devouring its buildings. Most of the wounded who fall are burnt alive, and their corpses, soon calcinated, present a horrible sight. The second brigade follows the ravine under terrible artillery and musketry fire. The suburb is retaken and so are the heights.'

Any number of senior Italian officers are being killed or wounded. By now it's about 1 p.m. And already at around midday Napoleon has arrived on the scene

'and placed himself with his staff on a mound facing Malo-jaroslavetz, above the Luja, to the left of the road and perfectly placed to observe the enemy's movements. He spent more than an hour looking through his telescope, penetrating the enemy's intentions.'

Now Eugène's artillery, two-thirds of it French, with the assistance of men from the Royal Guard, reaches the heights, gets through the town, 'crushing dead and dying men heaped up on the roads, mutilating them horribly'. Though the grenadiers of the Italian Guard remain down by the suburb, its foot chasseurs advance and, reinforcing Pino, dislodge the Russians from the houses at bayonet point and drive them back to the junction of the Marina and Czurickowa roads – a charge which, however, brings them up against a deep ditch out on the plain, concealed by hedges. Shattered by fire from the Russians' right-hand batteries and, charged by cavalry that's 'causing them grave losses', they're driven back into the gardens of the suburbs, where that half of them who have survived dig in. But Pino's 2nd Brigade reinforces them, and a new assault is launched, and this time, avoiding the ditch, they establish themselves in a wood beyond the burning town.[10]

At about 11 a.m. Lejeune had received orders from Napoleon, already within a mile or two of the town,[11] for Davout to quicken his march and move up to Eugène's right. And by now I Corps is beginning to turn up on the heights overlooking the Luja,[12]

'and take up position to the right facing the enemy, all of whose cavalry was spread out over the plain and observing our movements'.

The problem, however, is that there's no room to deploy across the bridge – or rather bridges, for by now Davout is throwing a second – into the confined space beyond. But his artillery is soon in action from the north bank.

Every one of Docturov's regiments, like Eugène's, is heavily engaged; and on the Russian side, too, officer after officer has been despatched to hasten the arrival of reinforcements from Kutusov's main army:

'The killed and wounded exceeded 5,000. The troops, exhausted by their previous marches and seven hours' combat, could scarcely continue the action. At that anxious moment Raevsky's corps came within view and, as soon as it reached the position, was ordered to penetrate into, and carry the town by storm. The "huzzas" of the columns announced to the enemy that they were about to be assailed by fresh troops, whose impulse they quickly found they were unable to resist. The Russian grenadiers carried all before them, and for the sixth time the Russians became masters of every post but the fortified church and buildings adjacent. The Viceroy, alarmed for the safety of the troops left within them and in the ravine, as well as for his bridges, urged forward Pino's division to rally the fugitives and lead another onset. The Russian grenadiers, notwithstanding its impetuous efforts and the flames raging around them (for the town was on fire in all parts), tenaciously maintained their position: and the Viceroy was compelled to send across the river all his corps, except the cavalry, to preserve his têtes de pont.'

As wave after wave is thrown in, Lejeune sees how the formidable Russian artillery,

'sited on the heights in the town's gardens, was sweeping from top to bottom the whole of the road along which we were arriving, without our guns being able to gain the upper hand by firing from below upwards, because they could only be placed in the meadows along the Luja. So all efforts had to be made at bayonet point, on a point so narrow as to permit no flanking movement. All the advantages of numbers and terrain were on the enemy's side. I Corps went into the line at about 2 p.m.'

'Debouching by the village of Maloczina,' Séruzier goes on, 'Davout immediately ordered Gérard and Compans' divisions to cross the Luja,' – Gérard's division deploys to the right of the enemy position, Compans' to the left. Lejeune can

'see the Russians' movements perfectly. We expected Kutusov would take full advantage of his very strong position to block our advance and himself take the offensive.'

'Of all I Corps' regiments,' carabinier-sergeant *Vincent Bertrand* claims, 'only the 7th Light's élite companies came under fire, the rest of the regiment manoeuvred all day.'

But Séruzier's horse artillery has been playing so much the more important role. Immediately upon Eugène's calling for his guns,

'I'd had the trumpeters sound "To horse!". Wishing to turn the Russians' flank, I'd started searching for a ford to get my guns over.'

Finding one, and quite a broad one too, Séruzier carefully reconnoitres it in person, then goes back to his gunners. Since the opposite bank is very steep, he hastily sends across eighteen men,

'each armed with a shovel or a mattock, with orders to flatten it enough for a wheeled vehicle to pass. Ahead of this ford was a little forest, and it was this which had made me choose this ford rather than another.'

In a jiffy they're in the wood; then out of it again and flying 'at a full gallop towards the enemy's rear. And there I am, in battery, sending shells and grape at the enemy.' Even if the Russians weren't already so heavily engaged with the Italians, says Séruzier, they could hardly have seen him coming. And are taken utterly by surprise. Deploying undisturbed in their rear, Séruzier's guns do such 'terrible damage' to their centre that it half-paralyses their resistance to IV Corps, pressing them from the town.

Even so, more and more fresh Russian troops are being thrown in, and the Italian chasseurs' Colonel Peraldi,

'who'd taken over from General Levié, who'd just been killed, supported himself on the little wood, covered against the Russian cavalry. At that moment I redoubled my fire and in less than three-quarters of an hour the victory was ours.'

Finally Lejeune sees how

'Guilleminot and Broussier's combined efforts and, coming up behind them, those of Pino's Italian grenadier division, boldly directed by Prince Eugène, forced the Russians to withdraw into the plain and abandon the town to us, in flames. At once our artillery was able to climb the hill and debouch into the plain; and so it did, while crushing thousands of the wounded, the burnt and dead who were encumbering the street.'

And in fact, Séruzier proudly remarks,

'the Viceroy with about 18,000 men had beaten more than 80,000 Russians; the enemy lost 8,000 men in this fight, and the French [sic] some 4,000. The affair was one of the most brilliant of the campaign.'

Wilson is dismayed to see how 'the Russians in their turn, yielding to the new pressure, retired from the town, and took post at half-cannon shot distance'.

Yet Davout's corps, unable to deploy fully because of the narrowness of the bridgehead, has hardly played any part at all. Not, for instance, the 85th:

'Davout had hastened the march of his corps toward the sound of the guns. But having marched all night we'd got there when everything was over.'

'The day', writes Planet de la Faye, presumably looking on with the Artillery Staff,

'belonged entirely to the Italians [sic] 'and justified the Emperor's praises, which more than once irritated and wounded the pride of the French military men. The French [sic] troops only arrived in the line when the Russians were already in retreat.'

But Guilleminot hastens to reward Séruzier for his special contribution by obtaining for him the Italian medal of the Iron Crown and 'anything else he wanted for his brave gunners'. Thus finished, writes Césare de Laugier proudly,

> 'an 18-hour battle during which a handful of Frenchmen and Italians, at the bottom of a ravine, had stood up to a Russian army, whose positions seemed impregnable.'

In fact about 16–17,000 French and Italians have been engaged, against seven Russian army corps with their reserves, i.e., sixteen divisions, or nearly 100,000 men, of whom some 70,000 were actually in the firing line. 'The Army of Italy', Berthier will write at 9 p.m. tomorrow evening to Junot at Mojaisk, 'has lost some 2,000 men killed or wounded [probably an underestimate] and the Russians 7 to 8,000 [certainly an over-estimate; each side probably lost some 6,500 men]. 'Two Russian generals' corpses have been found on the battlefield and 2–300 prisoners taken.'

From the outset, Dedem will afterwards hear, Kutusov had regarded himself as defeated. 'Kaluga's going to suffer the same fate as Moscow,' he'd declared.

The little timber-built town of Malojaroslavetz certainly has. All that evening and into the night it smoulders and blazes, burning to death the wounded. Its centre, so far as there still is one, cannot even be occupied by the victors. Russians and Italians alike hear the screams of those who are perishing in the flames.

CHAPTER 13

"THAT'S ENOUGH, GENTLEMEN.
I SHALL DECIDE."

A cold night – a crucial council-of-war – 'Fetch the horses, let's be off!' – Napoleon almost captured – 'Napoleon's star no longer guided his course' – an affair on the Smolensk road – 'He was astonished at the wild fury of the fighting' – 'the Emperor wavered for some time' – decision to retreat – Italian exploits rewarded – Dumonceau in action – a pyramid of fire – Griois brings up the rear – a phial of poison

Night falls. Another very cold one. No one is getting much sleep. Least of all Napoleon. After carefully going over the ground with Caulaincourt he has established his headquarters

'in a weaver's hut only a few paces to the right of the main road, at the bottom of a ravine, on the bank of the stream and village of Gorodnia – a wooden house, old, dilapidated, stinking, and divided in two by a piece of canvas.'

'Almost all of us', says the Master of the Horse, 'bivouacked in the open air.' He'll remember the hut as standing 'a couple of miles from Malojaroslavetz, at the entrance of the bend in the Luja'; Ségur as being half as far away. What is certain is that it stands at the cross-roads of the Emperor's destiny.

Kutusov, in trying to overrun the Army of Italy, has had to throw in almost everything he has; but even so, has been fought to a standstill. Loath initially to force a pitched battle, and not turning up with his main army until 4 p.m., the limit of his effort has been to try, unsuccessfully, to drive the Italians out of Malojaroslavetz.

'We blamed him for sacrificing a great number of his men, only to be beaten in the end, and fail of his object. Nor had the Viceroy's success gained our objective for us. We held the field, but Kutusov had given us the slip. So there was no change in our situation. The Emperor spent the night in receiving reports, issuing orders, and, on this occasion, discussing his difficulties with the Prince of Neuchâtel.'

Several times during the night he summons Caulaincourt, Duroc and Bessières to the weaver's hut. Asks them

'whether he should pursue Kutusov, who'd abandoned an impregnable position and probably eluded us? And if he didn't find the enemy drawn up beyond Malojaroslavetz, what route should he take to Smolensk? He had to make up his mind.'

It's perhaps the most difficult and, as it'll turn out, most fateful decision of his career. Shall he *(a)* push on with his original scheme and make for Kaluga, on the correct assumption that Kutusov has no desire whatever to fight another Borodino and will merely go on retreating? Or *(b)* make for Smolensk via Medyn, along a route neither army has yet devastated, but with a repulsed but not defeated Russian army at his heels? Or *(c)* do what he's sworn he'll never do: retreat by the same devastated route he'd come by – a route which offers neither men nor horses anything whatever to eat?

According to Gourgaud it's Count Lobau who, asked for his advice, is the first to offer an opinion. In his view the army must retire as promptly as possible to the Niemen, and by the shortest route – i.e., by the ravaged Mojaisk road. 'He repeated this several times.'

Unwelcome advice! And others disagree. Later Napoleon will disclaim it as his own view – and all the disasters of the retreat came of following it. As mere Assistant Prefect of the Palace Ségur certainly isn't present; and as usual it's impossible to know how much substance there is in his drama-tised dialogue. But, outside the weaver's hut, he may well be hearing what's passing inside it. Murat bursts out that 'if he's only given what's left of the cavalry and that of the Guard he'll overthrow everything and re-open the Kaluga road'. But the Emperor,

> 'raising his head, knocked over this wild talk, saying: "We've had enough of temerities. We've done only too much for glory. The time has come to think of saving what's left of the army."'

Bessières, 'his pride trembling at the idea of having to obey the King of Naples and feeling himself supported' by the others, declares that the transports won't suffice for a further advance. 'And finished by uttering the word *retreat*, which the Emperor approved by his silence.'[1] This is followed by a heated discussion between Murat and Davout, who declares for taking the Medyn road, through unravaged countryside. Bessières and Berthier intervene to calm the two enraged marshals. And Napoleon cuts short the discussion with the words:

"That's enough, gentlemen. I shall decide."

It's the crisis of the campaign. The most crucial decision, perhaps, he's ever had to make.

Although the roads are 'in such a bad state that only part of the artillery had been able to reach their position, and that only with difficulty', night-fall had found both IV and I Corps drawn up beyond the burning town. Sergeant *Vincent Bertrand*'s carabinier company is with the rest of the 7th Light

> 'in our bivouac on the Kaluga road. In the night a sutler's horse ran away, drawing many others after it. Terrible panic. Even generals ran after their mounts; even our stacked muskets are overthrown, many men hurt, or burnt by falling into campfires. All the pickets and first lines flew to arms, so did the Russians facing us.'

Stationed not far away with the 23rd Dragoons, Sous-lieutenant Pierre Auvray[2] certainly isn't the only man to assume they've been attacked. And Bertrand, for his part, has to 'spend the rest of the night standing to arms, pack on back, without even enjoying an hour of the sleep we so badly needed'.

The Russian army may be slipping away, but Cossacks, Caulaincourt goes on,

'were swarming everywhere. If we heeded them less than we might have done, it was because about noon in the same area, but to the left of the road, we'd chased away some new ones wearing crosses on their caps, modelled on those of the Don Cossacks.'

Having just received some reinforcements of Don Cossacks, Zalusky (who should have been in Napoleon's escort, but since yesterday evening he's not been feeling well and has attached himself to another squadron of the Polish Lancers, also at Zielonka, and commanded by Janowski) notices that Platov (who's bitterly mourning a favourite son killed in a skirmish) is

'flattering himself he'd take Napoleon prisoner. He'd surrounded the entire French army, and wasn't always being victoriously repulsed.'

That dark night on the heights above the Luja, everything's confused and uncertain. A little after nightfall the Imperial Guard had withdrawn a little, so as to be closer to IHQ and cover both its rear and its left flank. But having bivouacked in the dark its units hardly know anything about their surroundings.

Towards 4 a.m. an orderly officer named d'Arenberg, one of Gourgaud's subordinates, enters the hut and warns Napoleon that 'in the shadow of night and taking advantage of folds in the ground some Cossacks were slipping in between him and his outposts'. 'An hour before daybreak,' Caulaincourt goes on,

'the Emperor sent for me again. We were alone.

"Things are getting serious," he said. "I beat the Russians every time, and yet never reach an end."

After a quarter of an hour of silence, during which he walked to and fro in his little shelter, he went on:

"I'm going to find out for myself whether the enemy are drawing up for battle, or whether they're retreating, as everything suggests.

That devil Kutusov won't ever join battle! Fetch the horses, let's be off!" As he spoke, he picked up his hat to go.'

All the clock round, Caulaincourt explains,

'there was always one troop of horses bridled and saddled; and the duty picket, which consisted of 20 light horse, was saddled and bridled too. The squadrons in attendance provided the picket and relieved it. On the other campaigns there'd been only one squadron in attendance; but in Russia there were four[3] – half of them light cavalry, half grenadiers and dragoons. The picket never left the Emperor, the squadrons followed in echelon, and saddled up when the Emperor called for his horses. As he did so in haste and without warning, he always set out with only two or three other people; the rest caught up. After Moscow, and indeed since Smolensk, the same squadrons had remained in attendance for two or three days running. Men and horses were worn out.'

Napoleon's just picking up his hat to go when Bessières and Berthier come in. They point out how dark it still is outside, and that, with the Guard having taken up its position after nightfall, no one knows the other corps' exact whereabouts. Caulaincourt, who as always is responsible for Napoleon's personal safety, urges him to wait until dawn. So do Bessières and Berthier. But he's impatient to be off.

Then one of Eugène's ADCs comes and says nothing can be seen of the enemy. Only swarms of Cossacks everywhere. Some of them, not very far away, are thought to have lost their way and blundered into the outposts. Gourgaud and d'Arenberg too, the two *officiers d'ordonnance* on duty, assure him noises of horses on the march have been heard all night. So Napoleon agrees to wait. But 'after half an hour' – Rapp gives the time as 7.30 a.m. – 'his impatience drove him to set out' without waiting for his escort.[4] But what's going on? The road, Ségur sees, is

'encumbered with ambulance wagons, artillery and luxury carriages. It was the interior of the army, everyone was marching on, suspecting nothing. At first, far away, to the right, some platoons were seen running, then great black lines advancing. Then shouts were raised. Already some women and a few camp-followers were running back, paying no heed to anything, answering no questions, with an utterly terrified air, speechless, and all out of breath. At the same time the carriages, unsure of themselves, became troubled. Some wanted to go on, others to turn back. They crossed each other's tracks, jostled each other. Soon it was a tumult, everything was in an utter disorder. The Emperor, always advancing, looked on and smiled, assuming a panic had broken out. His ADCs suspected Cossacks, but they saw them coming on in such good order, that they were still in doubt.'

Rapp resumes:

'Dawn was hardly showing. The Emperor was placed between the Duke of Vicenza [Caulaincourt], the prince de Neuchâtel and myself. Hardly had we left the cottages where we'd spent the night and gone a mile or so than we caught sight of a swarm of Cossacks. They were coming out of a forest ahead of us, to our right. Since they were in quite good order we took them for French cavalry.'

Naturally so, since they're already in the midst of the Guard's bivouacs. One of the three Grenadier regiments is only 300 yards from the road. Rapp hears Caulaincourt recognize the Cossacks for what they are:

'"Sire, they're Cossacks."

"It's not possible," Napoleon replied. Shouting their heads off, they flew at us. I grabbed his horse by its bridle and myself turned it about.

"But surely they're our own lot?"

"They're Cossacks, hurry up!"

"They certainly are!" Berthier said.

"No doubt about it," Mouton [Lobau] added. Napoleon gave a few orders and moved away'

– on to some high ground, 'to be able to see more clearly'. Roustam, as always only a few paces away, sees Napoleon 'draw his sword and await the Cossacks' – out of pride, says Ségur who, despite Napoleon's notorious impassivity at moments of crisis, is a considerable expert at penetrating it:

'So did the Prince of Neuchâtel and the Master of the Horse, and, placing themselves to the left of the road, they awaited the horde. At the same moment, crossing the main road, the horde overthrew everything in their way, horses, men, carriages, wounding and killing the soldiers of the Train whom they dragged away to strip them; then, turning away the horses harnessed to the guns, they carried them off across the fields.'

Soltyk, too, is in the Emperor's suite and reports 'these eye-witness details'. He sees how

'Napoleon, as soon as he heard the enemy were so close, had turned his horse's head and at a gallop rejoined the service squadrons marching behind him, while the generals and officers accompanying him drew their sabres, formed a cavalry troop together with their escort, and without hesitation charged the first Cossacks to approach and halted them.'

Ségur sees

'the chasseurs (only ten or twelve had as yet joined us) already moving forward unbidden to join the advance guard. The light was still so poor we couldn't see further than 25 yards. Only the clash of arms and shouts of men fighting indicated where the skirmish was, or even that we were already at grips with the enemy.'

Rapp says he himself

'advanced at the head of the service squadron. We were flung into disorder. My horse received a lance-thrust six inches deep. He fell over on top of me. We were trampled at the feet of these barbarians.'

Rapp's horse isn't the only victim. So is Berthier's duty ADC, Captain Emmanuel Lecoulteux:

'At the exact moment when he'd killed a Cossack, having snapped off his sword in a Cossack's body and grabbed his lance, he was pushing back other enemies with it. A green overcoat covered his uniform, and together with the lance in his hand it made him look like a Russian officer. A dragoon of the Guard,[5] taken in by this fatal resemblance, plunged the long blade of his sabre into him so deeply that its whole length came out through his chest. Seeing this terrible blow, we all thought we'd lost an interesting [sic] friend.'

Fortunately the Cossacks, who're only interested in plunder, haven't realised who they have to do with:

'Some little way off they caught sight of an artillery park and rushed toward it. Marshal Bessières had time to arrive with the Horse Grenadiers of the Guard, charged them, and took back the wagons and guns they were carrying off. I got to my feet again, someone helped me back into the saddle and guided me back to our bivouac. Seeing my horse covered in blood, Napoleon fearing I'd been hurt again, asked whether I was wounded. I replied that I'd got off with a few bruises. Then he began to laugh at our adventure, which I didn't find funny.'

'If these wretched fellows hadn't yelled so as they attacked, as they always do, to dull their minds to the danger,' Ségur says, 'perhaps Napoleon wouldn't have escaped them. It was Platov and 6,000 Cossacks who, behind our victorious advance guard, had tried to cross the river, the low plain and the main road, carrying away everything as they passed.'

From only a few hundred yards away, Sergeant Bourgogne, too, has witnessed the episode: 'A moment after their scuffle the Emperor, chatting with Murat, laughed at his having nearly been captured.[6]

But though the Guard recapture the guns and the few gunners in Cossack hands, and force them to recross the river, 'we were left with many wounded' besides the unfortunate Lecoulteux. General Pajol, his arm still in a sling – Napoleon had suggested he leave for Minsk with Nansouty's convoy of sick and wounded, but he'd declined – had been riding along on his horse when Captain Biot, his ADC, who, having suddenly fallen sick is riding in their carriage in a kind of torpor, suddenly feels its horses bolt,

'so it seemed to me, in the opposite direction. Only by breaking one of the windows did I manage to get the door open. When I'd got into the carriage I'd kept my sabre by me. As I got out, it got caught in the door, forcing me to run beside the coach. However I managed to get clear. But there I was, all of a sudden, alone at the roadside.'

Fortunately Pajol's lead-horses come along and Biot manages to mount one and re-assemble some scattered infantrymen. Someone tells him a sergeant-major of the horse chasseurs, whose job it is to carry the imperial portfolio and who 'usually rides very close to the Emperor, has received a lance thrust that went through both case and portfolio'.

By now other squadrons of Guard cavalry have come up, including two of the Polish Lancers. Zalusky's squadron commander, Kozictulski, too, has been stabbed by a lance 'for which the Emperor promoted him major in our regiment'.[7] Being Janowski's senior, Zalusky had immediately taken over his squadron when the 'hurrah' had occurred:

> 'We met a regiment of [Line] dragoons, deployed on a broad front and pushing some Cossacks in front of them. Elsewhere we saw a squadron of the Mamelukes hastening up. In the twinkling of an eye, after coming to an agreement with Elie, head of the Mamelukes, we decided to attack the Cossacks through the intervals of the line of dragoons. We pushed them back beyond the Luja until we ran into the regiment of Horse Chasseurs of the [Russian Imperial] Guard.'

Boulart too has passed a bad night:

> 'I hadn't slept much and my head was full of sinister forebodings. Suddenly – it's one or two hours before daylight – terrible shouts are heard in the direction of headquarters, the ear is stunned by them.'

His gunners have jumped to their pieces:

> 'The Guard is ready to level its bayonets on the side the noise is coming from, and I have my artillery in a circle to be able to fire in all directions. However, the noise begins to diminish, becomes more distant, and soon can't be heard at all.'

The fleeing Cossacks, Lejeune sees, have also run into a battalion of the 3rd (Dutch) Grenadiers of the Guard, who open fire on them. 'This tall black line of bearskins made such an impression on the Cossacks that they fled into the forest.'

The Italians' baggage train, too, has 'received a dawn visit from Cossacks'. But they'd been driven off by 'a detachment of the Dragoons of the [Royal] Guard, which sabred and dispersed them'. Among other exploits General Joubert, commander of the IV Corps' baggage train, seated in his light carriage, 'with happy presence of mind had the courage to draw his sword and fight off the Cossacks surrounding it until help arrived'. And Griois' horses, watering down at the Luja in the morning mist, had luckily escaped as the Cossacks had swept through the camps. – Their victory, Ségur concludes,

> 'was short-lived, due to mere surprise. The Guard cavalry came galloping up: and at the sight of them they let go, fled, and their torrent

poured away, leaving, it's true, some nasty traces, but abandoning all it had been carrying off.'

To his life-long satisfaction Rapp will be rewarded for his presence of mind during the affray with a mention in the Bulletin of "the imperturbable courage this general has so often shown". No question, says Caulaincourt, but that if Napoleon had set out earlier, as he'd wanted to, he'd have

'found himself in the midst of this swarm of Cossacks with only his picket and the eight generals and officers who accompanied him. Doubtless we should have sold our lives dearly as one can by hitting out blindly in the dark with light swords. But the Emperor would certainly have either been killed or captured within musket shot of the road and the Guard.'

Among the woods and bushes in the far-flung plain 'no one would have known where to look for him'.

But above all the Master of the Horse attributes the whole terrifying episode to the paucity of the army's light cavalry and its wretched condition:

'In general our men fought well, but were keeping a poor lookout. In no army were the reconnaissance duties so neglected. We seldom covered rear or flank. One Guard battalion was bivouacked barely 300 yards from the spot, and on the same side of the road as where the Cossacks had spent the night.'

Nor is it only at Malojaroslavetz that the Cossacks are swarming in such huge numbers. The previous evening, Captain Henri Beyle, *directeur des approvisionnements de réserve*, escorting his convoy of 1,500 wounded along the desolate and ravaged Moscow–Smolensk highway with 'two to three hundred men' under Claparède, has also been in serious trouble, and expecting the morrow to be his last:

'Just as we were lighting our fires, we were surrounded by a swarm of men who opened fire. Complete confusion reigned. The wounded cursed. We had the greatest difficulty in making them take up their muskets. We repulse the enemy, but we believe ourselves destined for great adventures. We had a gallant wounded general named Mounier, who elucidated the affair. Attacked as we were at that time of evening by a horde of infantry, it seemed probable we were facing 4 or 5,000 Russians, partly soldiers of the line, partly indignant peasants. We were surrounded, and it was no safer to retreat than to advance. We decided to spend the night on our feet and next day, at first light, to form square, put our wounded in the centre, and try to break through the Russians. If hard-pressed, we'd abandon our vehicles, form a small square, and fight to the last man rather than let ourselves be captured by peasants who'd kill us slowly with knife-stabs or in some other pleasant fashion. Having made this resolve, we took the necessary steps. Each man made up a bundle of what he regarded as his least essential belongings, ready to jettison them at the first attack so as to lighten the vehicle. I shared a room with five or six wounded colonels, who'd been unknown to me a week earlier but who on the march had become intimate friends. All these men agreed we were done for. We distributed our napoleons to the servants in an attempt to save a few of them. We'd all become close friends. We drank what wine we had left.'

This is evidently not the same convoy as the one commanded by the wounded Nansouty, in which, says Lejeune,

'we'd already sent back our prisoners, those of our wounded who could be transported and much of the army's clutter to Smolensk. I profited from these convoys [sic] to have my sister sent back to France. I installed her in one of my carriages which I'd had harnessed to three good horses with good grooms, taking care to furnish it with food and furs. She was going to travel under the protection of some of our wounded generals and, even more, under the aegis of providence.'

Nor is it clear which convoy had left first, Nansouty's or the one Lieutenant Brandt is in, with 400 sick and wounded officers and 12,000 men, from the Hospital of St Paul. 'I was with the first convoy, a circumstance to which I probably owe my life.' But it's exposed to the same dangers. This same murky misty morning on which Napoleon has so narrowly escaped the Cossacks, and which Stendhal and his comrades are fearing will be their last,

'we set off on foot, walking beside our carriages and armed from head to foot. There was such a mist that one couldn't see four yards ahead, and we kept on halting. I had a book by Madame du Deffand, and read almost all of it.'

Luckily just then the enemy has other matters on his hands: 'The enemy didn't consider us worthy of their anger.'[8]

Meanwhile, beyond the heap of ashes and calcinated corpses that 24 hours ago was the town of Malojaroslavetz, a kind of tacit armistice prevails. Henckens' chasseurs had earlier been withdrawn to the bridgehead so as not to get in the way of the combatants in what had been almost an infantry battle. But Griois' guns, also linked with Chastel's brigade, have

'taken up position at the town's exit in a plain where there were already several infantry units. We were facing the Russian army, from which only the line of outposts separated us. Only a score of paces separated theirs from ours. Sabre in hand, carbine raised, they were in each other's presence without firing.'

Somewhere out there in the plain Kutusov is giving an order which makes Wilson and almost everyone else at Russian headquarters utterly furious. The Russian army is to withdraw two or three miles along the Kaluga road. In that moment – if he hasn't realised it before – Wilson sees definitively that Kutusov has no interest whatever in what he, Wilson, in his despatches is calling 'saving the universe' – i.e., in British interests. Nor in destroying the Grand Army by force of arms or capturing the Emperor of the French. Only to provide him with 'a golden bridge' – or rather, a bridge of ice and snow – back to the Niemen, 500 miles away. With winter only a week or two off, the best way of getting rid of unwelcome intruders is surely to freeze them out?

Nor is that sly and cynical old roué so lavish of Russian lives as is General Guyot, commander of the Horse Chasseurs of the French Imperial Guard, with those of Frenchmen and Poles. Drawn up near a wood, Zalusky's lancers are being fired on during the forenoon by Russian infantry, and men and horses are being needlessly sacrificed. But when Zalusky suggests they move a little further away, Guyot replies astonished:

"'What's that you say? Don't soldiers only exist to be killed?"

I realised I'd spoken out of turn, and stayed beside him until he chose to move away from the spot.'

Never before has Napoleon been so near to being captured, least of all by a bunch of 'barbarians'. 'As soon as he had a few men around him,' Caulaincourt goes on,

'he went on quickly to reconnoitre the enemy's position beyond Malo-jaroslavetz. He made a very close inspection of the formidable defences which had been carried yesterday, and realised with regret that the enemy had indeed retreated, leaving only a few Cossacks behind.'

Captain Labaume and the rest of Eugène's staff see him,

'arriving with a numerous suite, coldly pass over the battlefield and without emotion hear the dolorous cries of the unhappy wounded calling out for help. Yet, though accustomed from twenty years' experience of the evils of warfare, to which he was so madly attached,[9] he couldn't help being astonished at the wild fury of the fighting.'

As Napoleon and Murat arrive on the scene,

'the King of Naples galloped up to our outposts and energetically gave vent to his dissatisfaction. Why weren't we firing? And he ordered the first vedette he met to fire at the Russians. This signal was repeated all down the line. The "To horse!" was sounded. Our cavalry, which had dismounted, put itself back into the saddle, and we went forward, pushing the enemy's skirmishers and light cavalry in front of us.'

During the whole of the rest of the day, Griois goes on,

'there were several fairly lively engagements. Although surrounded by swarms of Cossacks we always had the advantage. The very fine but cold weather favoured this little war which our cavalry carried on ardently.'

The more so as the handsome, popular and capable Grouchy, though scarcely recovered from his Borodino wound, is again in command, relieving 3rd Cavalry Corps of Lahoussaye's ineptitudes.

Rapp too notices how amazed Napoleon is that the Russians should have withdrawn from such a strong position; and how impressed he is by the courage of 'the militiamen he found mingled with the dead and wounded regulars'. The carnage is immense. The Army of Italy has lost some 2,000 men, or a tenth of those who only a week ago had marched so cheerfully out of Moscow. Ségur is horrified:

'No battlefield was ever of a more terrible eloquence! Its pronounced forms, its sanguinary ruins, the streets, all trace of which had been obliterated except the long trail of dead and heads crushed by the cannon wheels, the wounded still to be seen emerging from the ruins, dragging themselves along with their coats, their horses and their limbs half burnt, uttering lamentable cries: and, finally, the lugubrious sound of the last sad tributes the grenadiers were paying to the remains of their dead colonels and generals – all bore witness to the most furious shock of arms.'

At the entrance of the forest near the battlefield Captain Lignières sees

'an ambulance set up. There was an enormous quantity of amputated arms and legs, tossed hither and thither and also in heaps.'

One of the legs heaped up there probably belonged to Colonel Kobylanski, Davout's Polish ADC: 'having had a leg smashed up to his haunches he'd had to suffer amputation.'[10] Le Roy, also visiting the battlefield, is more horrified by the carnage and destruction than impressed by the victory:

'Everything topsy-turvy. Not a house standing. The dead and wounded all heaped up on top of each other, Russians and French [sic] pell-mell. The first men to be wounded had tried to take refuge in the houses and were all burnt or crushed in them. It was a heart-rending sight, enough to make one detest heroes and conquerors.'

And indeed to what purpose? After putting up a fierce resistance, the Russians have once again made off. Napoleon's 'first impulse was to follow Kutusov, but along the Krasnoïe road.'[11] But by now Eugène and Davout have joined the imperial party. Both, like Berthier, point out

'how exhausting this change of direction would prove to cavalry and artillery already in a state of exhaustion, and that it would lose us any lead we might have over the Russians. The Emperor wavered for some time. As he saw it, the fight at Malojaroslavetz wasn't enough to offset the King of Naples' defeat.'

What one of Docturov's staff officers, a prisoner, has to say, may also be a factor in his fateful decision. The Russian tells not only of Kutusov's dilatory march to Malojaroslavetz, but also repeats what – he claims – the Tsar had said when he'd received Lauriston's peace proposals:

"This is where my campaign begins."

All the night's debates when Napoleon 'had resisted every conceivable argument adduced to decide him' still haven't really led to a decision, Caulaincourt realizes, but 'merely postponed it until he could see for himself whether the enemy had really eluded him'.

By now, it seems, Bessières has joined the party, which is unanimously in favour of a retreat. Caulaincourt too seems to have given his opinion, for he uses the words 'we' and 'us'. Only after the others have repeatedly pointed out that

'if Kutusov wouldn't stand and fight in such an excellent position as Malojaroslavetz he wasn't at all likely to join battle sixty miles further on,'

does Napoleon 'in this unofficial council of war' let himself be convinced. And decides to retreat via Borowsk, 'where part of the troops, most of the artillery, and all the vehicles already were. In view of the state of the horses,' Caulaincourt adds, 'this was a weighty consideration.' But is Napoleon really convinced he's doing the right thing?

'Did the Emperor wish it to seem he was only yielding to the convictions of others?[12] Or did he really believe he might still crush the Russian army and at long last turn the campaign to his advantage before deciding on his winter quarters? I can't say.'

It's certainly the bitterest decision Napoleon has ever had to take. None of his campaigns has ever ended with a retreat.

'Napoleon's star,' says Wilson,

'no longer guided his course. For after the [Russian] rearguard had retired, had any, even the smallest reconnaissance, advanced to the brow of the hill over the ravine – had the slightest demonstration of a continued offensive movement been made – Napoleon would have obtained a free passage for his army on the Kaluga or Medyn roads, through a fertile and rich country to the Dnieper; for Kutusov, resolved on falling back behind the Oka, had actually issued the orders "to retire in case of the enemy's approach to his new position".'

Once clear of Moscow, Ney's orders had been to make a feint with his 11,000-strong III Corps to the left of the Kaluga road, as if coming to

Murat's support; but also, in the event of Kutusov moving faster than the main French column, to fend him off. Now he has closed up behind it as its rearguard and is at Borowsk. At 10.30 a.m. Berthier writes to him:

'It is the Emperor's intention to get back to Viazma via Vereia and Mojaisk, so as to profit from what is left of the fine days, to gain two or three marches on the enemy's light cavalry, which is very numerous, and finally to take up winter quarters after so active a campaign. Consequently His Majesty orders you, M. le Duc, without delay to direct toward Vereia and thence to Mojaisk escorted by one of your divisions, the Treasure, the headquarters of the Intendance, the military carriages, the parks of the army's artillery. With your other divisions you will form this convoy's rearguard and you will leave troops at Borowsk until they are relieved by Morand's division.'

Thus, writes David Chandler in his *The Campaigns of Napoleon*, 'after winning a small tactical advantage, Napoleon in effect conceded a huge strategical victory to Kutusov, who had no wish to fight a further action.'[13]

*

Meanwhile the Italians' exploits must be rewarded. 'The Emperor reviewed us,' Laugier goes on proudly, 'and turning to the Viceroy told him: "The honour of this fine day belongs wholly to you."'

Though Le Roy thinks IV Corps is 'in a pitiful state' he's glad to see Napoleon being 'very generous in rewarding the brave men of this corps, as they deserved.'

For once the Imperial [27th] Bulletin isn't lying, exaggerating or censoring, when it declares:

"This feat of arms is to the greatest credit of the Viceroy and the IV Army Corps. The enemy used two-thirds of his army to sustain his position: it was in vain. In the fight at Marojaroslavetz the Royal Italian Guard, highly distinguished itself."

Lieutenant-colonel de Baudus on the IHQ staff[14] hears for example of

'the admirable conduct in this encounter of General Letort, colonel-in-second of the Dragoons of the Guard. For six weeks this intrepid officer had been sick and was so weak he could only follow the army in his carriage. As soon as he hears his regiment is marching against the enemy he calls for his horse, has himself fixed on to it and once facing the Cossacks, gets back all his energy, follows and directs the movements of his brave dragoons and doesn't relapse into the deplorable state where his illness has put him until the guns have fired their last round. His fiery soul re-animated his dying body, suddenly gave it back the strength his long sufferings had gradually taken from it.'

At 5 p.m., Laugier goes on,

'having visited everything and pushed reconnaissances along the Kaluga road, the Emperor returned to Gorodnia. His discontented air as he went off made us think he was in disagreement with his principal generals and that, if only he were listened to, the battle would begin again. However that might be, we anxiously prepared ourselves for a new fight, and impatiently awaited the signal for it. To our great astonishment, the whole day passed without any order coming.'

Caulaincourt returns with his master to the weaver's hut; 'and from there he issued his orders'. To all who understand their implications – and that's more than a few – they come as a nasty shock. Lejeune and I Corps' staff are

'impatiently awaiting the order to advance, when a most unexpected order struck us with surprise and consternation. The Emperor saw himself reduced to order the army to abandon the Kaluga road and again take the one to Mojaisk we had taken when coming. Napoleon was going to throw us, without any food, back into a desert and on to the ashes we'd left behind us. It was to take from us all hope of finding a scrap of nourishment. This decision afflicted us cruelly.'

The news of the Emperor's close-run brush with the Cossacks has spread like wildfire throughout the army. Already it had reached Colbert back at Ouvarovskoië at midday, where his Lancer Brigade has arrived from the rear and is guarding the Malojaroslavetz road. The lancers had just 'done the dawn' that morning, and the enormous baggage train from Moscow they'd overtaken yesterday was crawling past them through the mud, when they'd been assailed by the very same Cossacks, Chlapowski says, that had just been driven off by the Dutch Grenadiers of the Guard. At about midday Dumonceau has seen them come back, this time in force:

'They flung themselves at us on our brigade's flank. One of the Cossacks, doubtless an officer, shouted out to our lancers, in good French: "Come on, come on, you Parisian fops!"'

But Colbert, all too well aware of Cossack tricks, forbids anyone to take up these challenges. Ordering both his regiments to mount, he makes immediate and judicious dispositions. Whereupon the Cossacks vanish into the forest – only to re-appear suddenly at its fringe on the brigade's right. The Dutchmen's own right is resting on Ouvarovskoië village, with the Poles in echelon to their left rear. Chlapowski gathers some straggling infantrymen of the 300 or 400 'who were all the time passing among us' and ranges them behind a hedge, in a hut, ready to manoeuvre the Cossacks into their zone of fire. 'The lead horses were sent to the rear and drawn up prominently on a slight rise in the ground so as to seem to be a reserve.' After which a troop of the 2nd Regiment is sent out ahead in open order.

They're protected by

'a ravine, parallel with the road and only crossable at a very few
points, which separated us from the enemy, with another to the rear
of the village. In view of the distance at which they'd first appeared
and would have to cross in order to come to get at us, the various dispositions had been taken in good time, the more so as the multitude
in question was advancing at a walking pace, with hardly ordinary
calmness, on a broad front, like a threatening storm.'

Dumonceau estimates their numbers at between three and four thousand,
'over two-thirds more than we had to oppose them'. Suddenly, finding
themselves held up by the ravine, the Cossacks throw themselves *en masse*
to their own right; and outflanking the lancers' advanced party 'fling them
back with savage howlings'. So suddenly do they surround the supporting
squadron it hasn't time to fall back on the infantry ambush. Colbert
promptly sends the 2nd Squadron – Dumonceau's – to rescue the 1st, who
charge home,

'dispersing or overthrowing anything that tried to resist us, and thus
joining the endangered squadron. But at the same moment the flood
of Cossacks had closed behind us.'

Whereupon Colbert throws in the Red Lancers' last two squadrons, all
that's left of the regiment:

'The general shouts "Half-turn about, left, by fours!" – and all the sur-
vivors gallop flat out to the rear, where they execute another perfect
turn, the concealed infantry at the same moment firing volley upon
volley from behind its hedge and taking the Cossacks in flank.'

The ambushers, for once, have been ambushed. Even so, Dumonceau
finds himself fighting for his life with his sabre against Cossack lances:

'This time the struggle was brief, and wholly to our advantage. In a
flash the whole of the regiment's front was freed. But then the field
of combat appeared in its sad aspect. Our losses were unveiled. More
than 150 of our men, recognizable by their red uniforms, were lying
on the ground, among them one of our cantinières. Half were dead
or dying.'

Some, still in their death-throes, are being stripped by Cossacks, whom
their comrades are prompt to drive away. One lancer, pierced through by
seventeen Cossack lances, 'survives for the time being'. Although the Poles
of the 1st Guard Lancers, the élite of the élite, the heroes of Somosierra,[15]
had witnessed this terrible scrimmage, they'd 'only advanced at the last
moment to protect us as we rallied'.[16]

Meanwhile 'the remnants of the 1st and 2nd Cavalry Corps, which had
been on observation on the right bank of the Luja' have

'crossed the river and the battlefield, and, passing along the faces of
redoubts covered with Russian corpses, taken up position about six
miles from the town to observe and cover the Kaluga road and mask
the retreat. We were in this position until evening,'

an anonymous officer of the 16th Chasseurs will recall. Griois, too, has
been summoned to Grouchy's headquarters, 'where I found Marshal
Davout'. The retreat via Mojaisk, the two corps commanders tell him, is to
start at midnight. The enemy mustn't suspect it. And part of his artillery is
to form the rearguard. Griois suggests it might be a good idea

'to take out a dozen guns in front of our line and with them, at nightfall, direct a well-nourished fire at the Russian camp. The marshal
accepted my advice. And when night fell I aimed my gun [sic] at the
enemy fires they, to my great astonishment, replied only feebly.'

The reason, though he doesn't know it, is that Kutusov, too, has begun his
precipitate retreat.

That evening no one is more astonished, or dismayed, at the order
which has just reached them than the Italians. Instead of attacking again,
they're to retreat to Borowsk:

'This very night we're to reach Uvarovskoië, regulating our movements on those of Davout's corps, which is to be the rearguard.
Departure has been fixed for this evening at 10 p.m. An order to burn
everything we find along the road,'

reaches Césare de Laugier. On the plain beyond Malojaroslavetz Pierre
Auvray's 23rd Dragoons are doing outpost duty when an order comes for
'every soldier to light a fire'. 'At nightfall', the anonymous captain of the
16th Chasseurs goes on,

'each of us had just found some spot where we could get a little rest,
when our attention was re-awakened by a brilliant light produced by
a tall pyramid of fire. Seemingly hovering in the air, it lit up the plain
at a distance. Surprised, we watched this singular spectacle and were
losing ourselves in speculations as to what it might be, when a violent
detonation at a great distance reached us and increased our disquietude. We were told this pyramid of fire, which went on burning
through a good part of the night, was the spire of a church tower we'd
seen far off during the day and which, like the explosion we'd just
heard, was a signal for our army. At midnight, the order being given
in a low voice, each of us silently got ready to leave. Great numbers of
fires were lit to impress the enemy. At various times during the night
loud explosions were heard in the distance. At midnight, sadness in
our souls, we mounted our horses in the deepest silence, and set off,
the left leading. Crossing the plain we saw at intervals in the distance
scattered soldiers who were busy keeping fires burning, and who fell

230

back on us as our rearguard passed them. In this way we marched for two or three hours, always by the light of the pyramid of fire, as far as the Luja bridge, thrown over the fairly broad river that was mirroring it. Finally distance and heights covered with forests hid it from our view.'

'At midnight,' Auvray's dragoons too retire across the Luja: 'Any guns lacking teams were thrown into the river.'

What was this 'signal' or 'pyramid of fire'? No one else mentions it. But that the scene was lit up far and wide is certain:

'Hardly had the first troops of our rearguard marched than a mass of flames rose from a village they'd just left. The fire spread in a few instants, and I was afraid the clarity it was spreading might wake up the Russians and cause them to discover our movement, for the village lay on the line of our advanced posts. But the enemy himself was in full retreat, and we left last without being interfered with.'

Last of all to cross that bridge are two of Griois' guns, supported by some troops of cavalry and voltigeur companies. In this way, he concludes,

'towards midnight the two armies turned their backs on each other, marching in opposite directions, each being as anxious as the other that its movement shouldn't be disturbed! It even happened that the roundshot I'd been sending to the enemy with no other idea than to fool him had chanced to fall in a defile he was having to pass through and thrown a kind of disorder into the crowd pressing together there, as I read in Ségur's History of the Grand Army.'

And indeed Ségur's rhetoric, for once, isn't exaggerated when he exclaims:

'My companions! Do you remember it, this sinister field, where the conquest of the world came to a halt, where twenty years of victories were undone, where our good luck began to crumble away?'

Has his own near-capture affected Napoleon's judgement? Or even his nerve? Certainly he too has had a shock; for late that evening, in strictest confidence, he sends for Dr Yvan. Asks him to make him up a phial of quick-acting poison he can wear 'in a little leather bag round his neck', to be taken if he should be captured.[18]

NOTES

Chapter 1. 'Fire! Fire!'

1. In 1815, after Waterloo, Griois would run to the Louvre to have a last glimpse of its 'trophies' – art treasures pillaged from all over Europe, notably Italy, the ones that had so delighted William Hazlitt's heart and eye during the Peace of Amiens in 1802. His memoirs were written in 1827–31. Grouchy's 3rd 'Reserve' Cavalry Corps, only 6,800 strong at the outset of the campaign but by now, like the rest of Murat's cavalry, reduced to scarcely half its effectives, should have been commanded by Kellermann, if that veteran had not been ill. It consisted of a division of dragoons (7th, 23rd, 28th and 30th Dragoons) under Lahoussaye – whom many officers regarded as a fraud – the brigades of Seron and Thiry, a division of light cavalry, the brigades of Seron and Thiry, under Chastel (6th, 8th and 25th Chasseurs and 6th Hussars). Its cuirassier division, commanded by the 'not very intelligent' 45-year-old Doumerc, was serving with Oudinot's II Corps at Polotsk and had never joined the main body, but would do so, memorably, at the Berezina.

2. Readers of *1812, the March on Moscow* (hereinafter referred to as *The March*) will recall that it was Count Balashoff, the Tsar's police minister, who had been sent to negotiate with Napoleon at Vilna in June/July. See *The March*, p. 78 et seq.

3. Erostratos was the ancient Greek incendiary who burned down the temple of Diana in order to achieve immortal fame.

4. For Napoleon's headquarters arrangements, see p. 93.

5. This letter is dated 16 September. Evidently he had written one either on the 14th or 15th, but if so it has disappeared. If this letter was really written on 16 September it is strange that he makes no mention in it of the fire.

6. In *The March* I incorrectly translated Gourgaud's rank as 'First Ordnance Officer'. As critics have pointed out, 'Officier d'Ordonnance' has nothing to do with ordnance (artillery), but should perhaps be translated as First Orderly Officer. I was led astray by the circumstance of Gourgaud's having come from the artillery.

7. Police Superintendent Voronenko would afterwards report officially to the Moscow Administration: 'On 14 September at 5 a.m., Count Rostopchin ordered me to go to the Wine Arcade and the Custom House ... and in the event of a sudden entry by enemy troops, to destroy everything by fire, which order I carried out in various places as far as it was possible in sight of the enemy until 10 p.m.' The previous afternoon a depressed Barclay de Tolly, now commanding the 1st West Army under Kutusov, had been unhappily watching his troops march out of Moscow, when he had noticed the city's fire engines being dragged away by the fire brigade. Rostopchin happening to be nearby, he had asked him why this was being done. To which Rostopchin replied enigmatically: 'I've my good reasons.'

8. For some samples of Murat's fancy uniforms, see *The March*, pp. 125, 128, 178, 189.

9. Roos places the explosion and the great outbreak of the fire late in the evening of 14 September, i.e., the day of the army's arrival. Like some other eye-witnesses who do the same, his memory is almost certainly telescoping the events of the two evenings. The balance of the evidence seems to indicate that Rostopchin's rocket went up at about 9 p.m. on 15 September.

10. Caulaincourt had been Napoleon's ambassador at St Petersburg for four years. See *The March*, p. 16.

11. For the nepotism by which Planat de la Faye, a mere lieutenant in the Artillery

Train, had come to be Lariboisière's 'man of letters', see *The March*, p. 44.

12. This according to Colonel *Serran* of the Engineers, who had just arrived from Spain 'having done a thousand leagues from Vittoria to Moscow' – *Histoire de ma Vie*.

13. Tsar Alexander had always disliked Rostopchin, who had secretly regarded him as party to the assassination of his father Paul I. Afterwards he would detest him. The 'modern Erostratos', however, would remain enigmatic and self-contradictory about his key role in the destruction of Moscow. He would end his days in Paris, where his daughter married *Philippe de Ségur*, the campaign's second historian after Labaume.

Chapter 2. Napoleon Leaves the Kremlin

1. This isn't strictly true. Nor would Napoleon, no matter how adeptly he always feigned total impassivity at moments of crisis, have made such a claim. He was also secretly very much afraid of being poisoned. Justifiably, in the closely researched and reasoned view of the Swedish researcher Sven Forshuvud. In 1814, *en route* for Elba, the Austrian commissioner saw him fall into a panic and, for lack of his own cook, refuse to eat with him and his colleagues.

2. In his melodramatic but rhetorical account it seems that the Assistant Prefect of the Palace, *Philippe de Ségur*, afterwards gave especially free rein less to his memory than to his 'creative imagination'. He says that Napoleon 'after several *tâtonnements* [gropings about] left the Kremlin over some rocks, by a postern overlooking the Moscova'. This is directly challenged, like so much of his history, by Gourgaud, who says that Napoleon left by a main gate.

3. See *The March*, pp. 96, 97.

4. We must always remember that Labaume's account, the first to appear in print, came out in 1814, while Napoleon was on Elba. How much of its moralizing was a condition for passing the Bourbon censor? Not that his indignation is necessarily insincere. The book would afterwards go into many editions, both French and English, and was only slowly supplanted by Ségur's powerful if often inaccurate masterpiece, published in 1824.

5. See *The March*, pp. 105, 106.

6. See *The March*, pp. 123, 124, 125.

7. See *The March*, p. 32.

Chapter 3. The Fair of Moscow

1. See *The March*, Index.

2. From Rostopchin's official report to the Russian government after the departure of the French.

3. The Tsar's brother, who of course had had nothing at all to do with it.

4. The biography of Charles-Louis Schulmeister, Napoleon's arch-spy, makes fascinating reading. See Alexandre Elmer, *L'Agent Secret de Napoléon*, Fr. trans., Paris, 1932.

5. See The March, p. 162.

6. Yakovlev had an illegitimate son. In his memoirs the future great socialist Alexander Herzen would afterwards describe how his forever tergiversating father had got left behind in Moscow when everyone else had left. The account by Herzen's nurse can be read in Daria Oliver, *The Burning of Moscow*, London, 1966, p. 106, from which I have taken some of these details.

7. For other examples of this, see *The March*, pp. 26, 79.

8. I have summarised my account of the Yakovlev interviews and his mission from Olivier's imaginatively written book. Not being able to read the original documents,

I am not sure how far the details are authentic.

9. The veteran – but ferocious – Russian general Suvarov had invaded Italy and retrieved all Bonaparte's conquests there before being driven out of Switzerland by Masséna in 1799.

10. The same day (19 September) as Yakovlev took Napoleon's letter, a Piedmontese officer in the Russian service, a Colonel Michaud, reached Alexander with the appalling news that Moscow had been reduced to ashes. Alexander, shaken, told him (so he will later relate): 'Colonel Michaud, don't forget what I say to you here. Perhaps a day will come when we shall enjoy recalling it: "Napoleon or I; he or I". Now we can no longer both reign. I've come to know him. He'll not deceive me any longer.'

11. See *The March*, pp. 19, 328.

12. In *The March* I erroneously called Kergorre a Fleming. In fact he was born at Nantes.

13. Unbeknown to Caulaincourt, Napoleon, while planning the campaign in Paris, had had a huge issue of forged rouble notes of every denomination secretly printed, with the express purpose of devaluing the Russian currency.

14. The collaborators would in fact be very leniently treated after the war.

15. Chastel's light cavalry division of 3rd Cavalry Corps had followed up the cuirassiers' assault and for a while held the captured redoubt under massive Russian artillery fire. Every single one of its officers had been killed or wounded or lost his horse, and many men had been out of action for a considerable time to come. Henckens is utterly critical of cavalry having been used to carry the Great Redoubt. Henckens would never know whether it had been Napoleon's or Murat's idea. 'For a commander it's glorious to carry out heroic actions with a minimum of losses; but whoever ordered the cavalry to carry out this extraordinary attack when the enemy hadn't yet begun to waver made an unpardonable error.' Unknown to him, they had. On the eve of the battle Colonel Ledard had told Henckens that he had a clear premonition it would be his last evening, and had asked him to bury him 'as deeply as possible with my decorations, my sabre and all,' having first taken out his pocket book from his left-hand pocket with his portrait of his wife, 'and when you get back to France give it all to my wife with my adieux. He said all this with admirable composure and after asking me "have you understood?", said, "Let's talk about something else."' – Henckens had served in Italy and Hungary and had been wounded by a bayonet in the stomach at Wagram, but recovered entirely.

16. 'It was the last thing', Griois adds, 'they abandoned during the retreat. Several times I saw this kind of ingot fall from the packs of unfortunates succumbing *en route*, their weight having doubtless hastened their death by increasing their fatigue.'

17. 'Most of the gold cash', he adds, 'I spent for myself and my company and some officers during the retreat. One of these gold coins would save the life of General Gros at the Polish frontier.'

18. Ney's Württembergers, however, had six padres, three Catholic and three Protestant. So did Oudinot's Swiss regiments, the Polish Vistula Legion, and other Polish units. In fact Allied units usually had them.

Chapter 4. Murat's Disconsolate Advance Guard

1. The 41-year-old Marthod would die in captivity on 5 October, presumably from his wounds.

2. See *The March*, pp. 90, 239.

3. For once I am breaking my rule of as far as possible relating events in chronological order. For Le Roy's marauding expedition see Chapter 6, Note 2.

4. See *The March*, pp. 104, 168.

5. Or possibly another, two days later; Griois isn't quite clear.

6. Even in 1813 Kutusov would maintain that the total destruction of Napoleon was undesirable, as it would only serve British interests. He saw the campaign from a purely Russian point of view. The covert power struggle between Britain and Russia would continue right up to the Crimean War.

7. 'A good cavalry officer,' Napoleon would say afterwards of Bessières on St Helena, 'but a bit cold. He had too little of what Murat had too much of,' namely dash and audacity. See also, p. 58.

8. Dumonceau gives an extensive account of his regiment's movements, too long to be quoted here.

9. In his valuable documentary work *Napoleon's Invasion of Russia* (Presidio Press, Novado, CA), George F. Nafziger prints a map of what he calls 'the Battle of Czernicznia or Trautino', and dates it to 6 October – when, as we shall see, there was already an unofficial truce and Murat was talking to the Russian outposts. Presumably this refers to the head-on collision between the Russian army and Murat's advance guard of 4 October. By the Battle of Tarutino is usually meant the battle at Winkovo of 18 October. See Chapter 10, Notes.

Chapter 5. Settling in for the Winter?

1. Although many Poles, particularly of the officer class, had volunteered for service with the French armies in Italy in 1796, Kosciuszko, the hero of the 1794/5 uprising, who had vainly tried to modernise the country, had never trusted Napoleon, rightly as it would turn out. In 1812 he was living in retirement at Fontainebleau.

2. In 1610 the Poles had occupied the Kremlin for a while and they laid siege to

it again in 1617. This was before the establishment of the Romanov dynasty, but the wars had ended with Smolensk becoming Polish. The Latin words mean 'May someone arise from our bones to avenge us'.

3. In June 1812 Prince Dominique Radziwill had offered the Polish Diet a whole regiment of cavalry to be raised at his own expense 'on the sole condition of commanding it himself'. After the Tsar had ordered him back to Vilna, on Napoleon's arrival there he had assumed command of the regiment and lavishly provided the French with much-needed supplies. Later he was transferred to the command of the Polish Guard Lancers. He was to die in battle in 1813.

4. The guns would still be there when he visited Moscow many years later.

5. Here, as elsewhere, Bourgogne's vivid account should be read *in toto*.

6. See *The March*, Chapter 1.

7. See *The March*, p. 30.

8. See *The March*, p. 142 et seq. After his initiative and efficiency at the Molihew battle in July, Davout had been so pleased with Le Roy's behaviour that he had attached him to his staff. Evidently Le Roy is now back with his regiment.

9. Marshal *Macdonald*, commanding the mostly Prussian X Corps, sent in late June to invest Riga, represented the Grand Army's extreme left wing.

10. See *The March*, Index.

11. On 22 July Wellington had routed Marmont at Salamanca and on 11 August he had re-entered Madrid. This meant that on 25 August Soult had had to abandon the siege of Cadiz.

Chapter 6. Marauding Parties

1. Surgeon Heinrich von Roos says that Cossack lances (which he calls pikes)

rarely caused wounds that were dangerous or penetrating. 'For that they would have to be caused with unusual force and flung [*sic*] by a horseman at a gallop.' But they were also a cutting weapon, 'penetrating cavities, damaging important organs, severing blood vessels and often causing a mortal wound.' At night, they had the careless frontiersmen's habit of sticking their lances point down into the ground, which dulled them. Several Frenchmen noted this. Although they used lances skilfully, they caused many minor wounds.

2. For once, against my usual principle in this documentary, I'm backtracking chronologically. Le Roy had led his marauding party before the 85th had been ordered out on the Kaluga road with the rest of Friedrichs' division.

Chapter 7. Lovely Autumn Weather

1. As explained in *The March*, the word 'dysentery' was used indiscriminately to cover all types of diarrhoea.

2. The regiment's new colonel, however, would fail to forward Dutheillet's promotion to its depot at Strasburg, 'with the result that later, the army's baggage having been captured by the Russians and the notifications of these nominations being intercepted by the partisans, I wasn't inscribed as lieutenant at the War Ministry, and could only obtain that grade at another review by the Emperor, at Magdeburg in 1813. Thus, in returning to the Strasburg depot, I lost all the fruits of this campaign.'

3. For the structure and functioning of the General Imperial Headquarters Staff, see Elting, *Swords Around a Throne*, p. 83 et seq. which is more accurate than my own account in *The March*. For Lejeune's adventurous career and artistic achievements, etc., see *The March*, Index. Napoleon's moods and reactions on parade were always unpredictable. The day in Prussia when he had chatted with Major Boulart, a subaltern had taken advantage of his sunny mood to request a post in the civilian administration for a relative. This, thought Boulart, was going it a bit strong. But the request had been granted. Gouty old Colonel Nougarède of the 23rd Chasseurs had not been so fortunate and had come in for a nasty shock. At the Tuileries the Emperor had told Marbot that he 'loved' the old man, who had been with him in Egypt, but now could no longer mount a horse and had to use a carriage – 'a sad way of commanding a light cavalry regiment on campaign'. As soon as a post became available, he had told Marbot, he would promote Nougarède general of gendarmerie; after which Marbot could take over the regiment. So far so good. But at Insterburg Nougarède, failing to notice Napoleon's tetchy humour, had made so bold as to ask a favour for a relative who hadn't served the required time. Whereupon Napoleon had 'flown into a most violent rage, ordered the military police to eject the officer in question from the Army and galloped off, leaving him stunned,' and Marbot to serve until 15 November as acting colonel.

4. See also Brandt's account, *The March*, pp. 214, 215, and Marbot's memoirs.

5. At St Helena Napoleon would say, having evidently forgotten certain contretemps: 'I had no worries about my communications. In reality I had only 80 leagues of communications. In 40 days not a single *estafette* was taken from me. I lost more in France.' For further fascinating details of the courier service see *Memoirs of Caulaincourt*, vol. 1, p. 278, ed. Jean Hanoteau, Cassell, London, 1935.

6. See *The March*, pp. 28, 29, 30.

7. See *The March*, p. 100.

8. Since, as Aristotle points out, 'everything has the defects of its qualities' and this applies as much to character as anything else, no one is so well qualified to 'see through' us as a percipient enemy. Pradt was a prelate of the *ancien régime*. In March 1814, on the eve of Napoleon's first abdication, he would write a book about his experiences at Warsaw. Published in

September 1815, after Waterloo, it would run into at least six editions. Hudson Lowe and the ex-emperor would both read it at St Helena, and the exasperated Lowe would comment that 'after making himself an imaginary Poland, Buonaparte is making himself an imaginary St Helena'. Pradt sees in Napoleon nothing but a quasi-psychopathic adventurer, a megalomaniac, more and more carried away by his own imagination and less and less capable of seeing anything inconvenient to it:

'The Emperor is all system, all illusion, as one can't help being when one is all imagination. He Ossianizes [romanticizes public] affairs. It's enough to have seen him leaf through a book to gain an idea of how much he can acquire from it. The pages fly between his fingers. His eyes run down each page. And at the end of very little time, the hapless piece of writing is almost always rejected with a sign of scorn and generally disdainful formulae: "There's nothing but stupidities in this book; the man's an ideologist, a constitutionalist, a Jansenist." This last epithet is the *maximum* of insults. His head is always in the clouds, always carrying his flight toward the Empyrean, from this elevated point he pretends to skim the earth with an eagle's eye and, when he deigns to tread on it [to do so], with giant strides. With Napoleon it's agitation, extreme agitation, that is the basis of existence. He lives in the bosom of hurricanes as others do in the bosom of peace. Nebuchadnezzar the Superb must have been a model of humility beside a man impregnated with such a dose of self-love.'

That Napoleon was in highest degree what today is called a narcissistic personality is beyond question. Pradt seems to have been one too, although infinitely less intelligent. The sensible administrator Count Beugnot, who was in the 1814 provisional government, a Bonapartist but not a fanatical one – he too went over to the Bourbons – tells a funny first-hand story of how he and his colleagues played a practical joke on Pradt which, if true, shows that that prelate had little sense of political realities.

After his dismissal at Warsaw in December, Pradt will hear that Napoleon, fixing responsibility for the Russian catastrophe on him, had said of him 'One man less, and I'd have been master of the world.' 'Who was that man?' he goes on sarcastically, 'who, sharing in a way the power of the Divinity could have said to this torrent *Non ibis amplius*? [Thou shalt go no further]. This man was myself. Looked at like this, I'd saved the world. But far be it from me to arrogate any such [achievement] to myself!'

An acute observation on what she regarded as Napoleon's weakest point is to be found in the memoirs of Mme de Motteville: 'The closer one came to the Emperor's person the more disagreeable life became. It was always better to have to deal with his intellect than his character. What he feared most in the world was anyone in his proximity simply exercising or bringing him [*qu'on apportât*] the faculty of judgement.'

9. See *The March*, pp. 23, 40, 81.

10. See *The March*, Index.

11. On 11 June Schwarzenberg had written to Metternich: 'We are still very angry with the French. No one wants to get used to fighting alongside them. However, out of *esprit de corps* we are loath to expose ourselves to [a charge of] dishonouring the uniform.' John Elting has a high opinion of Schwarzenberg; and considers his Austrians' management of the campaign 'a better job in 1812 than either before or after'.

12. Between 1807 and 1814 the little principality of Neuchâtel, formerly with its parliament's assent belonging to the King of Prussia but arbitrarily given by Napoleon to Berthier, telling him he would be able to get twice as much income out of it as the King of Prussia had done, contributed about 2,250 men to its yellow-coated battalion. There was no conscription, as elsewhere; but the swift ruin of the principality's economy after Oudinot had occupied it in March 1806 with seven battalions of French infantry, 100 gunners and 250 horses in the depths of winter, caused many young men to accept the recruiting sergeant's offer of 180 francs,

and there was pressure on each village to provide a certain number of recruits. Almost none ever saw their native land again. For the detailed history of the Neuchâtel Battalion, see *A. Guye*'s painstaking study, to which I also owe the following statistics on Smolensk before the fire, which he obtained from the late Soviet Government.

13. Before the disaster Smolensk had had 12,599 inhabitants: 505 merchants, 2,015 workmen, 249 officials, 248 coachmen and carters, three monasteries, 21 stone and five timber churches (orthodox, Catholic and Protestant), sixteen 2-storey official buildings, 54 stone dwelling houses, 30 factories, 2,400 timber yards, two glove factories, four furriers, 27 butchers, 60 stone shops and 230 timber ones and twelve asylums. All this had been ruined.

14. Mme Burcet, who would afterwards falsely claim to have been the troupe's director, had long been mistress of the Duke of Brunswick, mortally wounded at Auerstadt in 1806, and later, also according to Dedem, an intimate of Prince Henry of Prussia (in whose hussar regiment Lieutenant Vossler is currently serving). She had known all the top people in Moscow and been familiar with what had been schemed against Napoleon.

15. 'The trouble with Napoleon', Caulaincourt thought, 'was that he never for a moment ceased playing the great emperor.'

16. '*Un chevalier qui volait au combat*
Par ces adieux consolait son arme:
Au champ d'honneur,
    l'amour guide mes pas,
Arme mon bras, ne ceaine rien pour ma vie.
Bientôt vainqueur, je viendrai vers toi.
Et j'obtiendrai le prix de ma vaillance
Mon coeur sera le gage de ta foi
Et mon amour celui de ta constance.'

Chapter 8. A Lethal Truce

1. For the cavalry's dawn routine, see *The March*, pp. 123–4.

2. Tschŭdi's Spaniards, though at first strongly inclined to desert (see *The March*, p. 107), had fought valiantly at Borodino (pp. 267, 329).

3. Since her banishment there, among other things for refusing even to mention French conquests in Germany in her book on German culture, few of her friends had dared visit her. Her daughter's tutor had even been forcibly dismissed for unpatriotically preferring the original Greek tragedies to those of Racine and Corneille. See *The March*, pp. 357, 363, 368. Her no doubt exaggerated picture of Napoleonic Europe as a prison house is confirmed by what an eye-witness to the execution of Malet and his fellow-conspirators writes of working-class life in Paris at that time: 'Everyone kept his mouth shut; one did not dare speak, for fear of being compromised. As long as the Great Empire lasted I always heard people talking in low voices, even in the family, about political events. Any individual who spoke aloud, without being afraid, was assumed to be a spy.'

The father of Germaine de Staël's daughter Albertine was none other than Narbonne, now Napoleon's ADC, for whom in the early stages of the Republic, when her salon had still been immensely influential, she had obtained the post of Minister of War. Rocca, a wounded and retired officer, also one of her party, was her second husband and father of her son.

Her book on Germany, published in London in 1813, would set its seal on its war of liberation. But when the tide went against France and Napoleon she would experience nothing but horror: 'I hate the man, but I blame events which make me wish him success.' His final overthrow shook her to the core of her being.

4. See *The March*, p. 201.

5. 'All the other versions', writes Brandt, 'are incorrect. I can vouch for this because a long while afterwards I saw this bit of writing again in the house of a former officer of my regiment, Malinski, who had carried it off and preserved it.' Caulaincourt's version of the text of Rostopchin's notice, presumably based on what was reported to Napoleon or on what was printed in the

Paris papers, is more extensive: 'For eight years I have been embellishing this country [house] and have been living happily in it in the bosom of my family. The inhabitants of this property, to the number of seventeen-hundred and twenty, are leaving it at your approach and I, I am setting fire to my house so that it shall not be soiled by your presence. Frenchmen, I have abandoned my two Moscow houses, with furniture worth half a million roubles; here you will only find ashes.' Caulaincourt doesn't usually embellish his texts; and in the light of Brandt's sober statement and claim afterwards to have seen the preserved original, one wonders where the more extensive version has come from?

6. Evidently gossip had it that Rostopchin claimed to be descended from Genghis Khan.

7. One hysteroid person usually sees through another. For Gourgaud's hysterical behaviour in 1815 and on St Helena, see Frédéric Masson and Sten Forshuvud's accounts. Also *The March*, p. 360. This does not mean of course that Gourgaud was not an excellent staff officer, a pertinent critic of Ségur's romanticized text, or, apparently, a better mathematician than Napoleon, to whom, he says, he – on St Helena – vainly tried to explain the duodecimal system. That Rostopchin was the very type of a hysteric is beyond question.

8. See *The March*, pp. 105–6, 168. In 1813 Sébastiani would cap his achievements by losing his entire corps' artillery.

9. Griois had first been recommended by King Joseph for his services in Calabria, then, by Grouchy, commander of 3rd Cavalry Corps, after Borodino. His nomination dates from 11 October 1812.

10. Luckily, Griois adds, it wasn't so. 'And it was better for him to spend a forced stay in Russia than this fateful retreat, which would probably have been too much for him.' Murat promised to indemnify Griois, 'at least in part'. But the disasters which followed would make it unthinkable for Griois even to remind Murat of his promise.

11. The Cossack word 'Hurrah' means 'death'. The army called their wild assaults 'hurrahs', and scornfully referred to the Cossacks as *hourassiers*, cf. cuirassiers.

12. See *The March*, pp. 168, 381.

13. There is no question but that Napoleon from the outset had had such a march in mind, perhaps on India. See *The March*, p.20. The French historian *Emile Bourgeois* has even traced in Napoleon a lurking lifelong obsession with the Orient, derived partly from his youthful readings of the classics and partly from his correct insight that much of Britain's power rested on the gold it was getting from India and using to finance the successive coalitions against him. While envisaging his Egyptian expedition in 1798 he had declared: 'This Europe of ours is a molehill. Only in the East, where six hundred million people live, is it possible to found great empires and realise great revolutions.' And seeing St Helena rise out of the sea he would say to Gourgaud: 'I'd have done better to stay in Egypt. If I'd done so I'd have been Emperor of the Orient by now.' – Pietr Geyl (*op. cit.*, pp. 241–9) outlines and criticises Bourgeois' thesis.

14. See *The March*, p. 201.

15. Scene of Charles XII of Sweden's decisive defeat. See *Peter Englund*'s admirable documentary.

16. The eminent historian Gabriel Hanotaux marks it as one of Napoleon's cardinal faults, mostly in civil government but also in military matters, that while he

'Always demands of his servants forcible and immediate execution, he generally places only moderate means at their disposal, and those in a niggardly fashion. Meanwhile he purposely mistakes their available resources, grudges them in fact, to show surprise when finally results do not come in. This, the greatest defect of all that can mar a man of action, the maladjustment between the imagination and the reality, is to ruin him.'

See Pieter Geyl, *op. cit.*, p. 414. This would seem to be a case in point.

17. See *The March*, pp. 110–11.

Chapter 9. Preparations for Departure

1. Actually two. Unlike the great body of our writers, Ségur is fatally given to exaggeration and inexactitudes. 'But M. de Ségur looks for every opportunity to make Napoleon look more like a man out of his wits than an able general,' Gourgaud would write in his *Examen critique* ... which would give rise to a duel between them and is certainly very much more objective than Ségur's romanticised and 'literary' masterpiece.

2. For Berthier's declining powers and Napoleon's paralysing influence on his subordinates' initiative generally, see *The March*, pp. 65–6. Berthier, though ageing and sick, would nevertheless be an efficient aid to Eugène in gathering the remnant of the shattered army in 1813. Allowance must of course always be made for subjective and retrospective assessments, especially in Ségur's case. There is also contrary evidence that Berthier tried to get Napoleon moving. As for Berthier's glamorous, aristocratic aides, as Edmund Horton says, 'They were acknowledged to be frequently insufferable, but arrived always where they were intended to arrive, never got lost, knew how to speak high and low, even to marshals. A message entrusted to them was always delivered,' which was not invariably the case with other ADCs, sometimes with fatal consequences, as we shall see at Witebsk.

3. Salomon, was Berthier's chief assistant. See *The March*, p. 94.

4. See *The March*, pp. 46–9.

5. 'And he was going to be punished', Ségur adds, 'when the retreat began. The loss of the army would be his salvation.'

6. At St Helena Napoleon would point out to Gourgaud that such handmills had been used by the ancient Romans and ought to be an important logistic feature of any modern army.

7. It was at Mittau in Estonia that Macdonald's mostly Prussian X Corps had been held up in its march to invest Riga. But not for long. They had occupied Mittau and come up to Riga by late July.

8. See *The March*, p. 36.

9. Excerpts from Roeder's detailed account of the Hessians' experiences should be read in Helen Roeder's book. Roeder's memoirs are among the most living and vivid of any. Since the book is obtainable in English I refrain from quoting as exhaustively as it deserves.

10. This was exactly what had happened. See *The March*, p. 240.

11. Afterwards Napoleon would say frankly at St Helena: 'I didn't believe the winter could be like that. I imagined the one we had had at Eylau.'

12. Weatherwise Napoleon would turn out to have misjudged the situation by about a week. Had the whole army got to Smolensk by 1 November the outcome might have been considerably different.

13. The statutes still apply. Oddly enough the stage-struck Gustaf III of Sweden, another 'enlightened' dictator, had done exactly the same thing for his newly founded national theatre, whose statues he modelled on the original ones of the Comédie Française, during his almost equally disastrous Finnish campaign of 1789.

14. Mlle Contat, like Mme de Staël, had been Narbonne's mistress.

15. For a picture of how they were received, see *The March*, pp. 22–3.

16. '*fer*', perhaps a misprint for '*feu*'.

17. Stendhal's diary, unfortunately for us, would be lost in the retreat; only a few flippant letters have survived.

18. As happens with our eye-witnesses now and again, Le Roy's memory seems perhaps to be confusing the events of two

separate days. For according to Schuerman/Caulaincourt it was on Wednesday 15 October that the dismounted cavalry were reviewed. This would agree with Gouttenoire's telling Le Roy that all the sick and wounded are leaving the same day for Smolensk.

19. 'It was covered in gold plate to the thickness of a sou. The architect charged with getting it down had done his business so badly that the ropes had broken and the cross was broken into several pieces as it fell on the pavings, having made several holes in the church tower. It seems it had never been able to be used without breaking all the windows and bringing the town's pregnant women to bed.'

20. No doubt the reader will have already gained the impression from *The March* that no regimental officer ever got decorated or promoted if he couldn't appear on parade. In fact, as John Elting points out, Napoleon's correspondence shows that he periodically checked up on deserving officers who were not with the Grand Army (*Swords*, op. cit., p. 600*)*.

Chapter 10. Battle at Winkovo

1. 'But I always kept my horse,' Bréaut des Marlots adds, 'and at the end of ten days I was cured.'

2. Thirty guns, according to Lejeune, who hears about it in Moscow. But Wilson, who was on the spot, says 36, whereof, Zalusky hears to his indignation, '18 not even taken by the Russians but purely and simply abandoned'.

3. The final loss of the cavalry at Winkovo, from starvation and the battle, added to all the losses during the advance on Moscow, was the last straw, and was decisive; not only to the retreat, but also in the longer term, when, together with all the other losses, lack of cavalry would prove crucial at Leipzig in 1813. Cavalry took much longer to train than infantry. See *The March*, p. 49.

4. So was Kutusov's chief-of-staff Bennigsen, who wrote to his wife: 'I can't get over it! This magnificent, brilliant day could have had incalculable consequences if only I'd been reinforced. But Kutusov had forbidden it.' No doubt wisely – for the Grand Army, its cavalry apart, was considerably restored and Kutusov wanted to avoid another head-on confrontation. His plan, as we shall see, was to see it off Russian soil, leaving its destruction to 'General Winter'. – Kutusov's motives for his Fabian tactics, romanticized by Tolstoy and approved by *Tarle*, are in fact very difficult to assess. Virtually all his contemporaries, like Bennigsen and Wilson, criticised him violently for his *fainéantism* and for not seizing opportunities for momentary advantages. Did he really realise that only time – and winter's inevitable approach – would do the job more efficiently for him than any amount of battles?

5. A report drawn up in October for Napoleon had revealed that in Moscow there were about 12,000 French and allied sick and wounded, few of whom were fit enough to stand the rigours of a journey. Captain T-J. Aubry of the 12th Chasseurs was one of the few left behind who did survive – but only after spending eight horrible months in the typhus-ridden hospital:

'We'd been 43 officers in our hall. All died one after the other and in the delirium of this disease, most singing, some in Latin, some in German, some in Italian, psalms, canticles, the Mass ... It was almost always their death-throes. Only three of us were left, among us a cuirassier officer who'd been amputated at the thigh. Mortality was in the same ratio among the rank and file, more than 1,800 dying out of the 1,850 shut up in the hospital. Finally we were moved, and the mortality ceased at once.'

Chapter 11. Taking French Leave

1. Napoleon had left the Kremlin at 7 a.m., after writing to Marie-Louise to tell her he's been thinking of asking her to come and meet him in Poland: 'We've had no cold weather at all, we haven't yet had

any experience of the rigours of the northern climate.' The Winkovo setback he had written off as 'a vanguard skirmish with Cossacks'. One must remember that all his letters to Marie-Louise, gossip being what it is, really had an eye to public consumption in Paris, therefore in Europe. Their propaganda value was important.

2. Opinions seem to differ sharply as to whether the French or their so-called allies were the worst plunderers. One of my critics writes in the margin: 'Disagree totally! Discipline in the German regiments was *always* better than in the French! The French [had] pillaged and scrounged on a professional level everywhere they went since 1796.' This is certainly true; and indeed not only since then, but since the revolutionary armies' very first campaigns. *Xavier de Vernères'* first experience of pillage, in 1792, shocked him deeply. The town of Menin having just been taken by storm from the Dutch, out of sheer curiosity he got permission to walk some 3 or 4 miles to view what was going on there:

'My first instinct was to turn back, not to be counted among those who were dishonouring the laurels they'd just won. But my curiosity got the better of me, and I stayed in this desolate town, most of whose inhabitants had fled. Soon I repented of yielding to this impulse when, upon seeing the commander-in-chief [Houchard] and terror-stricken at this apparition, I thought he'd have me arrested as one of the authors of this pillage. But I was quickly reassured and, let me say, indignant, when I saw him, with no sign of discontent, watching the excesses being committed under his eyes, by his indifference even seeming to encourage them. Delivered from this fear, I did none the less hasten to leave behind me a town whose disorder I didn't view with the same apathy as General Houchard.'

But again young Xavier's curiosity had got the better of him. Entering a grocer's shop he went into the house at its rear:

'There I saw a mob of soldiers smashing the furniture to remove their contents and linen. Immediately I quit this painful scene of pillage, admittedly not without yielding to its evil influence, for in again passing through the shop I couldn't resist a strong temptation to take something myself; and seeing a stove-in barrel full of Corinthian raisins I complaisantly plunged my hand into it to fill my pockets; then, encouraged by this first attempt, I provided myself with pens and further appropriated two clay pipes to the value of two centimes apiece, to teach myself to smoke.'

Everywhere, for the next fifteen years, it was to be the same story. Xavier Vernères' filched clay pipes and raisins could stand for the ruin and pillage of Europe. Anyone who still has a sentimental or merely colourful view of the Napoleonic wars should read Jean Morvan's *Le Soldat Impérial, 1800-1814, 2 vols., Paris,* 1904. If the British and German troops could sometimes be restrained from committing rapine and pillage it was merely by fear of the lash. When France was invaded two years later the French would be horrified at Prussian and Russian retribution. 'One notable phenomenon,' Volunteer Janke of Breslau – who would notice how the ubiquitous scenes of pillage 'knocks all the gaiety out of me' – observes 'is the fact that the Prussians enter houses from the front, whereas the Russians always go in from the back, thus proclaiming their thievish character.'

3. Chambray's book, the first 'serious' history of the campaign, came out in 1825, a year after Ségur's, and he seems to have gone to some trouble over facts and figures, but to have taken his figures here from Labaume, whose book had come out in 1814, while Napoleon was on Elba. Wilson estimated the retreating Moscow army at 'about 90,000 effectives mostly infantry, 12,000 men under arms in artillery, gendarmerie, staff, equipages and commissariat, and more than 20,000 non-combatants sick and wounded ... altogether about 140,000 individuals.' Recent historians give the total effectives leaving Moscow as about 108,000, plus several thousand Russian prisoners and civilians, and 569 guns.

4. E. Blaze, in his *La Vie Militaire sous l'Empire,* relates how at the outset of a campaign the infantry regularly went through the ritual of throwing away their knee-breeches 'which constricted even the stoutest marcher'. Next day these

would be picked up by the commercial suppliers, and stored away until after the campaign was over. Whereupon they would be sold back to the colonels who had already paid for them perhaps twice over! But for the Guard to throw them away must have been unusual. At any moment they could be called upon to wear them on some *journée* – e.g., at Borodino, or marching into Moscow. Presumably the Guard, being among other things 'parade troops', did not – they might be needed for triumphal entries into conquered cities. On the other hand they did *not* normally march in their bearskins, which were carried from the waist belt in oilcloth bags or, more usually, in a ticking bag on top of the pack.

5. 'These objects seem to have escaped the general ruin and I still keep them as relics,' Bourgogne adds at the time of writing.

6. Henckens was certainly not the only member of the army to be extremely bitter about the privileged status of the Old Guard in 1812. 'Its only role was to *impose on* the enemy'. And in fact its 1st and 2nd Grenadiers and 1st and 2nd Chasseurs would be virtually unique among the army's regiments in not losing a single officer killed and only five wounded. On the march any Guard unit took precedence over any Line unit. Elzéar Blaze tells a funny story, no doubt endemic in the Napoleonic armies, of how,

'A wagon belonging to the Old Guard, harnessed up to four mules, tries to cross my regiment's path, and the men, crossing under the noses of these poor beasts, took a malicious pleasure in preventing them from getting on, because they belonged to the Imperial Guard. One of them called out in a mocking voice: "Come on, soldiers of the Line, give way to the Mules of the Guard." "Bah!" replied another, "They're donkeys." "I tell you they're mules." "And I that they're donkeys." "Very well, but even if they're donkeys, what of it? Don't you know that in the Guard donkeys have the rank of mules?" – Each man in the Guard rated one rank higher than he would in the Line.'

7. Caulaincourt says that both the privileged young gentlemen got safely home to Paris. Abandoning Napoleon in 1814 like many of the aristocratic party, Mailly-Nesle would become ADC to the Duc de Berry – who in 1814 had taken his foster-brother Gourgaud under his protection – and in August 1815 be made a peer of France. Such behaviour would be characteristic of virtually all the aristocratic officers Napoleon had promoted and favoured.

8. For reasons known only to himself but probably quite simply out of fear of Napoleon's counter-action, Kutusov had never whole-heartedly approved of the so-called Battle of Tarutino, at which he hadn't even been present in person, and to Bennigsen's fury had refused point-blank to send in reserves thereby risking the entire Russian army with its thousands of raw recruits, who so far hadn't been in a battle and of whom Murat's exasperated troops might have made mincemeat. After it was over Kutusov had again withdrawn his army into the entrenched Tarutino camp.

9. Mathieu Dumas was in fact 49. 'In Paris,' Kergorre observes, 'with every medical art to help him, this sickness would have been the end of him. In the retreat, having no other room or other bed but his carriage, or other remedy but a little wine and broth, nor other doctor than Desgenettes, he arrived at Vilna cured.'

10. See *The March*, p. 100.

11. Le Roy would remember it as happening 'just after 2 a.m.'

12. Gourgaud regards Vaudoncourt as a particularly reliable historian and eye-witness. Many other first-hand accounts agree. The prisoners were treated atrociously. See also *The March*, p. 377, note 3.

Chapter 12. 'Where our Conquest of the World Ended'

1. See also *The March*, p.119. Many years later at Munich Planat would see Eugène,

who 'in 1812 had been as thin as a pin', and find him 'big and fat, full-faced with a high colour, his eyes shining and to all appearance in excellent health'. But with the years, from being the firm and enterprising man of 1812, he had become 'apathetic and circumspect. Except in a *tête-à-tête* one could only get an insignificant word out of him. The fall of the imperial regime and the humiliation he had been obliged to submit to in his children's interests had broken down his spirit and seemed to have taken all the bounce out of him.' He had become dependent on his wife, the Bavarian princess whom Napoleon had married him off to, and on the good graces of Tsar Alexander, against a promise never to get mixed up in political intrigues 'and I shall keep my promise'. He also told Planat he would have liked to have been a sailor, and that he was sure he would have succeeded in that career. A private person in the Europe of the Great Reaction, he would marry off his daughter Josephine, named after her grandmother the Empress Josephine, to Bernadotte's son Oscar, so that in due course she became Queen of Sweden.

2. Doumerc's cuirassier division, which had been split off at the campaign's outset, was serving in II Corps.

3. 'It was this two-hour delay that changed the face of affairs,' Dedem goes on, 'and decided the fate of the army and the peace. If he'd carried out his orders punctually he'd have seized the position without firing a shot.' Actually, Delzons and Eugène seem to have been loath to send in a full division at night on the far side of a tricky river crossing. The thought that Delzons' leniency decided the fate of Europe is certainly dramatic, but must be written off as coming within the teasing category of great matters hanging on tiny threads.

4. David Chandler says that they didn't. But Césare de Laugier, who's at pains to defend the Italians' military honour on this as on every other occasion, says that they did. On the other hand the Italian Guard had not reached Malojaroslavetz,

so neither can he have known at first hand.

5. Césare de Laugier, who can only have heard about, not witnessed Delzons' death, gives a slightly different version, according to which 'a discharge of grapeshot throws him down. His brother, who was also his ADC, tries to run to his aid and falls into his elder brother's arms, stricken down by a second gunshot.'

6. No more than any others of Junot's Westphalians was *Wilhelm Heinemann* at Malojaroslavetz – he was with his fellow-prisoners being driven like harassed cattle to Archangel – See *The March*, pp. 275, 377. Heinemann scorns as 'madness' the notion – advanced by both Wilson and Césare de Laugier – 'of deriving the ranker's courage from any independent self-confidence or from feelings of national honour. And should anyone have such higher ideas, or at least wish to boast about it [the fact is], the mass goes into battle animated by a kind of despair which nevertheless not uncommonly does wonders of bravery.'

7. In 1815 Wilson would save Lavalette's life by helping him to escape from prison in Paris after he, like Ney, had been condemned to the firing squad for his role in the Hundred Days. Labédoyère was executed.

8. Like Zalusky, the glory-seeking Césare de Laugier wrote his memoir to stress the exploits of their respective armies, which until then (in the opinion of Italians and Poles) had been under-estimated by French historians, notably Thiers. The naïve military enthusiasm of at least some Italian units, repeatedly described by Laugier, should not, I think, be written off as romantic hindsight. See also *The March*, pp. 126, 152. IV Corps' performance at Malo-jaroslavetz shows what remarkable *esprit de corps* the Army of Italy still had.

9. For similar scenes of Italian cordiality, see *The March*, pp. 126, 183.

10. I'm taking Laugier's account of the battle, partly because it's the only more or

less complete and coherent one from the French side, and partly because it would seem to render the Italians' greatest exploit of the campaign as they would afterwards remember it.

11. According to Denniée's *Itinerary* he had left 'the first bivouac' after Borowsk at 11.30, and only at 1 p.m. 'arrives on the plateau which fringes the valley of the Luja, goes on to Gorodnia, goes forward half a league in the direction of Malojaroslavetz, and gets there as the combat between Prince Eugène and Docturov is ending.' Denniée is usually correct on such matters, being himself at headquarters as Inspector of Reviews.

12. Séruzier will afterwards remember, almost certainly incorrectly, I Corps as arriving on the scene at 'about 10 a.m.'

Chapter 13. 'Enough, Gentlemen. I Shall Decide.'

1. To judge by what would afterwards occur at Smorgoni, Napoleon may have used Bessières as his stool-pigeon to make a suggestion he wished to avoid making himself. This would accord with his way of keeping up a façade of infallibility, necessary to the whole imperial regime.

2. In *The March* I inadvertently promoted Auvray to captain's rank in the 21st Dragoons. In fact he was a sous-lieutenant of the 23rd Regiment.

3. In fact the escort had been doubled after the Cossacks' attempt on IHQ on the morning after Borodino.

4. Analyzing the causes of the near-fatal episode that was to follow, Caulaincourt explains (as Castellane had done at Vilna in July) how 'by day or night the Emperor would mount his horse without warning; he even took pleasure in going out unexpectedly and putting everyone at fault'.

5. Lignières says that it was a horse grenadier who ran Lecoulteux through. 'But God preserved him for us, he's still

alive.' Zalusky too says that he had never heard of the Guard Dragoons forming part of the imperial escort. But according to John Elting all four Guard cavalry regiments did so ordinarily in rotation.

6. All this has happened so suddenly and quickly and in such a bad light that different eye-witnesses would afterwards have different memories of it. Lignières, for instance, entirely disapproves of both Ségur's and Rapp's accounts:

When I saw how far away the Cossacks were, I began crossing the plain to rejoin the regiment. I passed through an artillery park. Some of the horses had been killed, others carried off. The soldiers of the Train and other combatants had been killed. A *cantinière* was dead as result of ... She was in a horrible state.'

7. Zalusky dismisses Gourgaud's statement that the 3rd Troop of the Dragoons of the Guard had been in the advance guard commanded by Lieutenant Joachim Hempel:

'That's as may be. I wasn't there. But I've never seen a troop of dragoons figure in the advance guard marching ahead of the Emperor.'

8. And ends: 'And we weren't attacked until the evening, and then by some Cossacks who stabbed 15 or 20 wounded men with lances. There, Madame,' concludes the future novelist and Napoleon-worshipper, with a Stendhalian flourish:

'is the best episode of our journey. It was proper that I should render you an account of it. Although I always remain hopeful, during the night I did what I believe everyone else did: I drew up the balance-sheet of my life and reproached myself bitterly for not having had the sense to tell you just how devoted to you I am.'

9. Once again we must remember that Labaume's book was published in 1814 during the first Bourbon restoration, and heavily slanted against Napoleon – perhaps had to be, to pass the censorship; but is not necessarily insincere for that. His

Relation circonstanciée would be republished in numerous editions, both French and English, during the next thirty years.

10. Zalusky says Kobylanski 'afterwards carried off by the French grenadiers, happily reached Poland'.

11. That is, from Kaluga via Yelnia, the route Kutusov would in fact take, tracking the retreating army. Clausewitz, who was serving with the Russian army, regards the notion of marching through the Ukraine with the Russians at their heels, making it impossible really to exploit the countryside, as utterly impracticable. Naturally the pros and cons of Napoleon's fateful decision have been endlessly discussed by historians. As *Tarle* explains, Clausewitz 'was the first military writer to explode the widespread opinion that' the decision to retreat via Mojaisk 'was a blunder. 'Where could Napoleon have found provisions for his army, if not in the stores he had prepared in advance? What good was an "untapped region" to an army which had no time to lose and was constantly forced to bivouac in large masses? His entire army would have been starving within a week. A retreating army in enemy territory needs, as a rule, a previously prepared route. By "prepared route" we understand a route secured by garrisons along which stores required by the army have been organised.'

12. Afterwards (according to Gourgaud) Napoleon was several times heard to regret aloud having taken others' advice instead of relying on himself alone.

13. Later, at Mantua, Labaume would hear Wilson say that Eugène, with 20,000 men, had stood up to nine Russian divisions of 10,000 men each.

14. Quoted in Bertin, *Etudes sur Napoléon*, pp. 161–2.

15. It was the Polish Guard Lancers, led by Auguste de Caulaincourt (hero of Borodino), who in an 'impossible' feat of arms had forced the Somosierra Pass in the teeth of an entire Spanish army and opened up the road to Madrid.

16. Chlapowski, of the Polish Guard Lancers, had a very low opinion of their Dutch colleagues' ability to defend themselves. Certainly the two regiments forming Colbert's brigade were of very different calibre. Though exposed to the same dangers and vicissitudes, none of the Poles' officers would be killed although six were wounded, while the Dutch regiment lost ten killed and four wounded. Chlapowski was unusually chauvinistic, even for a Pole, but these Poles were picked veterans and this war was the first campaign for most of the Dutch.

17. It would be the contents of this phial that Napoleon, according to Caulaincourt, would swallow after his first abdication, at Fontainebleau in April 1814; but by then 'the poison had lost its force' and merely made him vomit.

BIBLIOGRAPHY

This bibliography is supplementary to that given in *1812: The March on Moscow*, (Greenhill Books, London, and Stackpole Books, Mechanicsburg, Pa., 1993). For the sake of convenience I have reiterated all authors whose memoirs are here important.

Anthouard, Charles-Nicolas. 'Notes et documents du Général Anthouard', published by F. Masson in *Carnet de la Sabretache*, 1906, pp. 286–307, 337–54, 386–409, 452–69

Aubry, Capitaine Thomas-Joseph. *Souvenirs du 12ème de Chasseurs, 1799–1815*. Paris, 1889

Auvray, Pierre. 'Souvenirs militaires de Pierre Auvray, sous-lieutenant au 23 régiment de dragons (1897-1815)', *Carnet de la Sabretache*, 1919

Bausset, Joseph, Baron de. *Mémoires anecdotiques sur l'intérieur du Palais et de quelques événements de l'Empire, de 1805-1814*. Baudoin, Paris, 1827–9

Beauchamp, A. de B-Ch. *Histoire de la destruction de Moscou, en 1812 et des événements qui ont précédé, accompagné et suivi ce désastre* (trans. from German), Paris, 1822

Beaulieu, Drujon de. *Souvenirs d'un militaire pendant quelques années du règne de Napoléon Bonaparte*, vol. I, Paris, 1831

Begos, Louis. *Souvenirs des campagnes du lieutenant-général Louis Begos, ancien capitaine adjutant-major au 2ème régiment suisse au service de la France*. A. Delafontaine, Lausanne,1859

Belliard, Augustin-Daniel. *Mémoires du comte Belliard, lieutenant-général, pair de France, écrits par lui-même, recueillis et mis en ordre par M. Vinet, l'un de ses aides-de-camp*. Paris, 1842

Bertin, Georges. *La Campagne de 1812 d'après des témoins oculaires*. Flammarion, Paris, 1895

Bertrand, Vincent. *Mémoires du capitaine Vincent Bertrand, recueillis et publiés par le colonel Chaland de la Guillanche*. Siraudeau, Angers, 1909

Beugnot, Jean-Claude, comte. *Mémoires du comte Beugnot*. Paris, 1866, Librairie Hachette, Paris, 1959

Beulay, Honoré. *Mémoires d'un grenadier de la Grande Armée (18 avril 1808 – 18 octobre 1815), Préface du commandant Driant*. Champion, Paris, 1907

Biot, Hubert-François. *Souvenirs anecdotiques et militaires du Colonel Biot, aide-de-camp du Général Pajol, avec une introduction et des notes par le comte Fleury*. Vivien, Paris, 1901

Blaze, Elzéar, *La Vie Militaire sous le Premier Empire, ou Moeurs de Garnison, du*

Bivouac et de la Caserne. Paris, 1837. Translated as *Life in Napoleon's Army: The Memoirs of Captain Elzéar Blaze,* with commentary by Lieutenant-General Charles Napier, and introduction by Philip J. Haythornthwaite (Greenhill Books, London, 1995); and newly translated as *Military Life under the First Empire* by John R. Elting (The Emperor's Press, Chicago, Illinois, 1995)

Bonnan, C-A. *Mémoire sur la Russie 1812.* nd

Bonnet, Guillaume. 'Journal du capitaine Bonnet du 18ème ligne', in *Carnet de la Sabretache,* 1912, pp. 641–72

Boulart, Jean-François. *Mémoires militaires du Général Baron Boulart sur les guerres de la République et l'Empire.* Librairie Illustrée, Paris, 1892

Bourgoing, Baron Paul-Charles-Amable de. *Souvenirs d'histoire contemporaine. Episodes militaires et politiques.* Paris, 1864

– *Souvenirs militaires du baron de Bourgoing (1791–1815), publiés par le baron Pierre de Bourgoing.* Plon-Nourrit, Paris, 1897

Brandt, Heinrich von. *Souvenirs d'un officier polonais. Scènes de ma vie militaire en Espagne et en Russie (1808–1812),* ed. Baron Ernouf, Charpentier, Paris, 1877

Bréaut des Marlots, Jean. *Lettre d'un capitaine de cuirassiers sur la campagne de Russie, publiée par Leher.* Paris, chez tous les librairies, 1885

Bussy, Marc. in *Soldats suisses au service de la France.* Geneva, 1909

Calosso, Jean. *Mémoires d'un vieux soldat.* Gianini, Turin, 1857

Castellane, Victor-Elisabeth Boniface, comte de. *Journal du maréchal de Castellane (1804–1862),* 5 vols., Plon-Nourrit, Paris, 1895–7

Caulaincourt, Armand de. *Mémoires du Général de Caulaincourt, duc de Vicence, Grand Ecuyer de l'Empereur.* Introduction and notes by Jean Hanoteau. 3 vols., Plon-Nourrit, Paris, 1933. English trans. vol. 1 *Memoirs of General de Caulaincourt.* Cassell, London, 1935; vol. 2 *With Napoleon in Russia.* Morrow, New York, 1935; vol. 3 *No Peace with Napoleon.* Morrow, New York, and Cassell, London, 1936

Chambray, marquis de. *Histoire de l'Expédition de Russie.* Paris, 1825

Chandler, David. *The Campaigns of Napoleon.* Macmillan, New York, 1966, and Weidenfeld, London, 1966

– *Dictionary of the Napoleonic Wars.* Macmillan, New York, 1979, and Arms & Armour Press, London, 1979; Simon and Schuster, New York, and Greenhill Books, London, 1993

– *The Illustrated Napoleon.* Henry Holt, New York, and Greenhill Books, London, 1990

– *On the Napoleonic Wars.* Greenhill Books, London, and Stackpole, Mechanicsburg, Pa., 1994

Chevalier, Jean-Michel. *Souvenirs des guerres napoléoniennes, publiés d'après le manuscrit original par Jean Mistler et Hélène Michaud.* Paris, 1970

Chuquet, Arthur. *1812, La guerre de Russie, Notes et Documents*. 3 vols., Paris, 1912

Clemenso, H. 'Souvenirs d'un officier valaisan' in *Annales Valaisannes*, 1957, Ch. 5, pp. 12–110

Coignet, Capitaine Jean-Roch. *Cahiers*. Hachette, Paris, 1883, English trans. *The Notebooks of Captain Coignet*. Davies, London, 1928, reprinted Greenhill Books, London, 1986

Curely, Jean-Nicholas. *Le général Curely. Itinéraire d'un chevalier léger de la Grande Armée (1793–1815) publié d'après un manuscrit authentique par le général Thoumas*. Paris, 1887

Dedem van der Gelder (see Gelder)

Denniée, P. P. *Itinéraire de l'Empereur Napoléon*. Paris, 1842

Dumas, Mathieu. *Souvenirs du lieutenant-général comte Mathieu Dumas de 1770 à 1836, publiés par son fils*. 3 vols., Paris, 1839

Dumonceau, François. *Mémoires du général comte François Dumonceau, publiés d'après le manuscrit original par Jean Puraye*. 3 vols. Brépols, Brussels, 1958–63

Dupuy, Victor. *Souvenirs militaires, 1794–1816*. Calman-Lévy, Paris, 1892

Dutheillet de la Mothe, Aubin. *Mémoires du lieutenant-colonel Aubin Dutheillet de la Mothe*. Brussels, 1899

Duverger, B.T. *Mes Aventures dans la Campagne de Russie*. Paris, nd

Elting, John R. *Swords Around a Throne*. London, 1989

Englund, Peter. *Poltava*. London, 1994

Everts, Henri-Pierre (1777–1851). 'Campagne et captivité en Russie, extraits des mémoires inédits du général-major H. P. Everts, traduits par M. E. Jordens' in *Carnet de la Sabretache*, 1901, pp. 620–38, 686–702, Paris, 1900

Faber du Faur, G. de. *La campagne de Russie (1812), d'après le journal illustré d'un témoin oculaire*. Texte explicatif, par F. de Kausler, Introduction par A. Dayot, Flammarion, Paris, 1895

Fain, Baron Agathon-Jean-François. *Manuscrit de Mil-Huit Cent Douze, contenant le précis des événements de cette année, pour servir à l'histoire de l'Empereur Napoléon; par le baron Fain, son secrétaire-archiviste à cette époque*. 2 vols. Paris, 1827

– *Mémoires du Baron Fain, premier secrétaire du cabinet de l'Empereur, publiés par ses arrière-petits-fils*. Plon-Nourrit, Paris, 1908.

Fezensac, M. le duc de. *Souvenirs militaires de 1804 à 1814*. Domaine, Paris, 1863

– *A Journal of the Russian Campaign of 1812*. London, 1852; Trotman, Cambridge, 1988

Franchi. *Récit de Franchi, sous-officier dans la compagnie d'élite des 8ème Chasseurs à Cheval, Loisirs d'un soldat*. Etienne et Beauvoir, Le Mans, 1861

François, Charles. *Journal du Capitaine François (dit le Dromadaire d'Egypte), 1793–1830.* 2 vols., Carrington, Paris, 1903–4

Freytag, Jean-David. *Mémoires du général Freytag, ancien commandant de Sinnamary et de Conamama dans la Guyane française, accompagnés de notes historiques, topographiques et critiques par M.C. de B.* Nepveu, Paris, 1824

Fusil, Louise. *Souvenirs d'une Femme sur la retraite de Russie.* 2 vols., Dumont, Paris, 1841

Gelder, Baron A-B-G van der. *Mémoires publiés d'après le manuscrit original par Jean Puraye.* 3 vols., Brussels, 1958–63

Geyl, Pieter. *Napoleon, For and Against.* Jonathan Cape, London, 1949, 1964, 1968

Gourgaud, Gaspard. *Napoleon and the Grande Armée in Russia.* A critical examination of Count Philippe de Ségur's writings. Anthony Finlay, Philadelphia, 1825

Griois, Charles Pierre Lubin. *Mémoires du général Griois, 1792–1822.* 2 vols., Plon-Nourrit, Paris, 1909

Grunwald, Constantin de. 'L'Incendie de Moscou, mystère de la campagne de Russie' in *Miroir de l'Histoire* 68 (1955), pp. 287–95

– *La Campagne de Russie.* A collection of excerpts from the participants' memoirs, etc. Julliard, Paris, 1963

Guye, A. *Le Bataillon de Neuchâtel, dit les Canaris, au service de Napoléon à la braconnière.* Neuchâtel, 1964

Henckens, Lieutenant J. L. *Mémoires se rapportant à son service militaire au 6ème Régiment de Chasseurs à cheval français de février 1803 à août 1816. Publiés par son fils E. F. C. Henckens.* Nijhoff, The Hague, 1910.

Herzen, A. *Erinnerungen von Alexander Herzen, aus dem russischen übertragen, herausgegeben und eingeleitet von Dr. Otto Buck.* 2 vols., Wiegandt und Grieben, Berlin, 1907

Holzhausen Paul. *Die Deutschen in Russland, 1812. Leben under Leiden auf der Moskauer Herrfahrt.* Morawe und Scheffeldt Verlag, Berlin, 1912

– *Ein Verwandter Goethes in russischer Feldzuge, 1812.* Berlin, 1912

Jacquemot, Porphyre. 'Carnet de route d'un officier d'artillerie (1812–1813)', in *Souvenirs et Mémoires,* pp. 97–121, 1899

James, J. T. *Journal of a Tour through Russia.* London, 1813

Kalckreuth, von. 'Erinnerungen' in *Zeitschrift für Kunst, Wissenschaft und Geschichte des Krieges,* V, 1835

Labaume, Eugène. *Relation circonstanciée de la campagne de Russie.* Paris, 1814 and successive augmented editions. A new translation by T. Dunlas Pillans, with an introduction by W.T. Stead, appeared as *The Crime of 1812 and its Retribution.* Andrew Melrose, London, 1912

Langeron, A.-L. Andrault comte de. *Mémoires de Langeron, général d'infanterie dans l'armée russe. Campagnes de 1812, 1813, 1814. Publiés d'après le manuscrit original pour la Société d'histoire contemporaine par L.-G. F. Picard.* Paris, 1902

Larrey, Baron Dominique-Jean. *Mémoires de chirurgie militaire et campagnes.* J. Smith, Paris, 1812–17

Lassus-Marcilly, F.N. 'Notes sur la campagne de Russie', in *Carnet de la Sabretache,* 1914, pp. 86–92

Legler, Thomas. *Beresina.* Bern, 1942

Lejeune, Louis-François. *Mémoires du général Lejeune, publiés par M. Germain Bapst.* 2 vols., Paris, 1895–6

Lemoine (-Montigny), E. *Souvenirs anecdotiques d'un officier de la Grande Armée.* Firmin-Didot, Paris, 1833

Le Roy, C. F. M. *Souvenirs de Leroy, major d'infanterie, vétéran des armées de la République et de l'Empire.* Dijon, 1908

Lignières, Marie-Henry, comte de. *Souvenirs de la Grande Armée et de la Vieille Garde Impériale.* Pierre-Roget, Paris, 1933

Lorencez, Guillaume Latrille de. *Souvenirs militaires du général comte de Lorencez, publiés par le baron Pierre de Bourgoing.* Paris, 1902

Macdonald, Marshal J.-E.-J.-A. *Souvenirs du maréchal Macdonald duc de Tarente.* Introduction par Camille Rousset. Paris, 1892

Mailly(-Nesle), A.-A.-A., comte de. *Mon journal pendant la campagne de Russie écrit de mémoire après mon retour à Paris.* Paris, 1841

Majou, L. J. L. 'Journal du commandant Majou', in *Revue des Etudes Historiques,* 1899, pp. 178–202

Méneval, Baron Claude-François de. *Mémoires pour servir à l'histoire de Napoléon I depuis 1802 jusqu' à 1815.* Paris, 1894; English trans., London, 1894

Merme, J. M. *Histoire Militaire.* Paris, 1852

Molé, Mathieu, comte, marquis de Noailles. *Le comte Molé (1781–1855). Sa vie, ses mémoires.* 6 vols., Champion, Paris, 1922

– *Souvenirs d'un témoin de la Révolution et de l'Empire (1791–1803). Pages inédites, retrouvées en 1939, publiées et présentées par la marquise de Noailles.* Le Milieu du Monde, Geneva, 1943

Muraldt, Albrecht von. *Beresina.* Bern, 1942

Nafziger, George. Napoleon's Invasion of Russia. Presidio Press, Novato, Ca., 1988

Ney, Maréchal Michel, prince de la Moskova, duc d'Elchingen. *Mémoires du Maréchal Ney. Publiés par sa Famille.* Fournes, Paris, 1833; English trans., Bull and Churton, London, 1833; Carey, Pa, 1834

Nottat, N. 'Souvenirs de la campagne de Russie', in *Revue du Train,* 1953, pp. 35–41

Paixhans, General Henri-Joseph de. *Retraite de Moscou, Notes écrites au Quartier-Général de l'Empereur.* Metz, 1868

Pastoret, Amédée-David, marquis de. 'De Witebsk à la Bérézina' in *Revue de Paris*, April 1902, pp. 465–98

Pils, François. *Journal de marche du Grenadier Pils (1804–1814), recueilli et annoté par M. Raoul de Cisternes. Illustrations d'après des dessins originaux de PILS*. Offendorff, Paris, 1895

Pion des Loches, Antoine-Augustin. *Mes Campagnes (1792–1815). Notes et correspondance du colonel d'artillerie Pion des Loches, mises en ordre et publiées par Maurice Chipon et Léonce Pingaud*. Paris, 1889

Planat de la Faye, Nicolas Louis. *Vie de Planat de la Faye, aide-de-camp des généraux Lariboisière et Drouot, officier d'ordonnance de Napoléon 1ᵉʳ. Souvenirs, Lettres, dictés et annotés par sa veuve*. Offendorff, Paris, 1895

Pouget, François-René (known as Baron Cailloux). *Souvenirs de guerre du général baron Pouget, publiés par Mme de Boisdeffre*. Paris, 1895

Poutier, R. *Souvenirs du chirurgien Poutier sur la campagne de Russie*. Brive, 1967

Pradt, D.-G. Dufour de. *Histoire de l'Ambassade dans le Grand Duché de Varsovie en 1812*. Paris, 1815

Prétet, Ch-J. 'Relation de la campagne de Russie', in *Revue Bourguignonne*, pp. 419–51

Puybusque, L.-G. de. *Souvenirs d'un invalide pendant le dernier demi-siècle*. 2 vols., Paris, 1840

Rapp, Jean. *Mémoires écrits par lui-même et publiés par sa famille*. Bossange, Paris, 1823; English trans., Henry Colburn, 1823; Trotman, Cambridge, 1985

Réguinot. *Le Sergeant Isolé*. Paris, 1831

Renoult, A. J. *Souvenirs d'un docteur*. Paris, 1862

Rigau, Dieudonné. *Souvenirs des Guerres de l'Empire, avec reflexions, etc.* Paris, 1845

Rocca, A. J. M. de. *In the Peninsula with a French Hussar*. Greenhill Books, London, 1990; Presidio Press, Novato, Ca., USA

Roeder, Helen. *The Ordeal of Captain Roeder, from the Diary of an Officer of the First Battalion of Hessian Lifeguards during the Moscow Campaign of 1812–13*. Trans. and ed. from the original manuscript. Methuen, London, 1960.

Roguet, François. *Mémoires militaires du lieutenant-général comte Roguet, colonel en second des grenadiers à pied de la Vieille Garde*. Dumaine, Paris, 1862–5

Roos, Heinrich von. *Avec Napoléon en Russie. Souvenirs de la campagne de 1812, traduits par le lieutenant-colonel Buat*. Introduction et notes par P. Holzhausen. Chapelot, Paris, 1913

– *Souvenirs d'un médecin de la Grande Armée, traduits d'après l'édition originale de 1832 par Mme Lamotte*. Perrin, Paris, 1913. (These two books have been translated from the original *Ein Jahr aus meinem Leben oder Reise von den westlichen Ufern der Donau an die Nara, südlich von Moskva, und zurück an die Beresina, mit der grossen Armee Napoleons, im Jahre 1812*. St. Petersburg, 1832)

Roustam Raza. *Souvenirs de Roustam, mameluk de Napoléon*. Introduction et notes de Paul Cottin, préface de Frédéric Masson. Paris, 1821

Saint-Chamans, A.-A.-R. *Mémoires du général comte de Saint-Chamans, ancien aide-de-camp du Maréchal Soult, 1802–1832*. Paris, 1896

Sayve, A. de. *Souvenirs de Pologne et scènes militaires du campagne de Russie 1812*. Paris, 1833

Schuerman, A. *Itinéraire de l'Empereur Napoléon 1ᵉʳ*. Paris, 1911

Schumacher, Gaspard. *Souvenirs*. Paris, nd

Séruzier, T.-J.-J, Baron. *Mémoires militaires du baron Séruzier, colonel d'artillerie légère, mis en ordre et rédigés par son ami M. Le Mière de Corvey*. Paris, 1823

Soltyk, comte Roman. *Napoléon en 1812. Mémoires historiques et militaires sur la campagne de Russie*. Bertrand, Paris,1836

Staël, Germaine de. *Mémoires de dix années d'exil*. Paris, 1848; English trans., London, 1814.

Stendhal (Henri Beyle). *Journal de Stendhal (1801–1814), publié par Casimir Stryienski et François de Nion*. Paris, 1888, Gollancz, 1955

– *Vie de Henri Brulard, nouvelle édition établie et commentée par Henri Martineau*. Le Divan, Paris, 1955

Stiegler, Gaston. *Le Maréchal Oudinot, duc de Reggio, d'après les souvenirs inédits de la Maréchale*. 2nd edn., Plon, Paris, 1894; English trans, Henry, London, 1896

Suckow, Karl von. *Aus meinem Soldatenleben*. Stuttgart, 1862; French trans. *D'Iéna à Moscou, fragments de ma vie*. Paris, 1902

Surugué, l'Abbé Andrien. *Lettre sur l'Incendie de Moscou en 1812*. Paris, 1821, and *Un Témoin de la campagne de Russie, par Léon Mirot*. Paris, 1914

Tarle, E. *Napoleon's Invasion of Russia, 1812*. Moscow, 1938; London and New York, 1942

Tascher, Maurice de. *Notes de campagne (1806–1813)*. Châteauroux, 1938

Tchitchakov (Tchitchakoff), P.V. *Relation du passage de la Bérésina*. Paris, 1814

– *Mémoires*. Berlin, 1855

Teste, François-Antoine. 'Souvenirs du général baron Teste', in *Carnet de la Sabretache*, 1906, 1907, 1911, 1912

Thirion, (de Metz), Auguste. *Souvenirs militaires, 1807–1818*. Paris, 1892

Trafcon, J. *Carnet de campagne*. Paris, 1914

Turno, Boris. 'Les Mémoires du général Turno, par A. Skalkowski', in *Revue des Etudes Napoléoniennes*, vol. II, pp. 99–116, 129–45. Paris, 1931

Van Vlijmen, B. R. F. *Vers la Bérésina*. Paris, nd

Vaudoncourt, F.-G. de. *Mémoires pour servir à la guerre entre la France et la Russie en 1812, par un officier de l'état-major français*. 2 vols., Deboffe, London, 1815

– Quinze années d'un proscrit. 4 vols., Paris, 1835

Victor, Claude Perrin, Maréchal, duc de Bellune. *Mémoires.* vols., V and VI, Paris, 1847

Villiers, C. G. L. de. *Douze ans de campagnes.* Paris, nd

Villemain, Abel François. *Souvenirs contemporains d'histoire et de littérature.* 2 vols., Paris, 1854

Vionnet, Lieutenant-Général Louis-Joseph, vicomte de Marignoné. *Campagnes de Russie et de Saxe, 1812–1813.*

– *Souvenirs d'un ex-commandant des Grenadiers de la Vieille Garde, avec une préface de Rodolf Vagnair.* Paris, 1899

Walter, Jakob. *The Diary of a Napoleonic Foot Soldier,* ed. Marc Raeff, Windrush Press, Gloucestershire, and Doubleday, New York, 1991

Warchot, R. *Capitaine au 8ème chevauxlegers polonais. Notice biographique sur le général-major Edouard de Mercx de Corbais.* Namur, 1855

Ysarn, François-Joseph d': *Rélation du sejour des Français à Moscou et de l'incendie de cette ville en 1812, par un habitant de Moscou annoté et publié par A. Gadaruel.* Brussels, 1871

Zalusky, Joseph-Henri. 'Souvenirs du général comte Zalusky. Les chevau-légers de la garde dans la campagne de 1812', in *Carnet de la Sabretache,* 1897, pp. 485–95, 521–33, 601–15

A work I would particularly recommend to all students of the period is Jean Tulard's admirable *Bibliographie critique des mémoires sur le Consulat et l'Empire.* Librairie Droz, Geneva and Paris, 1971. This, although confined to memoirs written in or translated into French, is exhaustive and useful for evaluation.

INDEX

PAUL BRITTEN AUSTIN

1812: The March on Moscow

1812: Napoleon in Moscow

1812: Retreat from Moscow

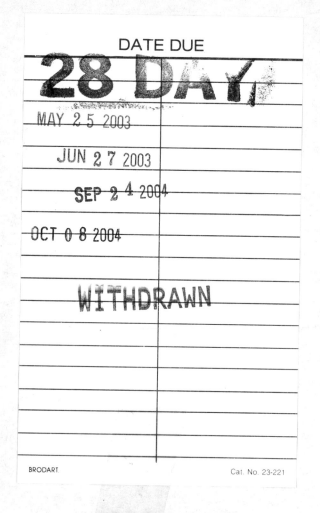